D0906154

# THE AGE OF
# TOTAL WAR,
## 1860–1945

# THE AGE OF

# TOTAL WAR,
## 1860–1945

*Jeremy Black*

Studies in Military History and International Affairs

PRAEGER SECURITY INTERNATIONAL
Westport, Connecticut • London

**Library of Congress Cataloging-in-Publication Data**

Black, Jeremy.
   The age of total war, 1860–1945 / Jeremy Black.
       p.   cm.—(Studies in military history and international affairs, 1537–4432)
       Includes bibliographical references and index.
       ISBN 0–275–98710–8 (alk. paper)
       1. Military art and science—History—19th century.   2. Military art and
   science—History—20th century.   3. Military history, Modern—19th century.
   4. Military history, Modern—20th century.   I. Title.   II. Series.
       U41.B582   2006
       355'.0330034—dc22          2005032302

British Library Cataloguing in Publication Data is available.

Library of Congress Catalog Card Number: 2005032302
ISBN: 0–275–98710–8
ISSN: 1537–4432

First published in 2006

Praeger Security International, 88 Post Road West, Westport, CT 06881
An imprint of Greenwood Publishing Group, Inc.
www.praeger.com

Printed in the United States of America

*For*
*Dominic and Nancy Casserley*

# Contents

# Abbreviations

AWM     Canberra, Australian War Memorial

NAA     Canberra, National Archives of Australia

RUSI     *Journal of the Royal United Services Institute*

# Preface

It is a pleasure and a challenge to be asked to write this book—a pleasure because I find this a fascinating period in military history, and a challenge because of the difficulty posed by writing about it within the allocated span of words. Heather Staines has proved to be a rewarding editor to write for, with a fine grasp of historical processes. I have benefited greatly from the opportunities to consider aspects of this subject provided by invitations to lecture in 2005 at the Universities of California, San Francisco, Chicago, Copenhagen, Hawaii, and Odense; at Adelphi, Auburn, Drexel, Hawaii Pacific, Mary Washington, and Roger Williams universities; for the Virginia Historical Society and the Departments of Continuing Education of the University of Oxford and Virginia University; on the deck of the USS *Missouri* in Pearl Harbor; and for the International Chapter of the Young Presidents' Organization (YPO). I am grateful to Simon Barton, Ian Beckett, John Lamphear, Stephen Manning, Anthony Saunders, and Gary Sheffield for discussing the subject with me, and to Peter Hoffenberg, Mike Neiberg, and Dennis Showalter for commenting on an earlier draft. I am delighted to dedicate this book to Dominic and Nancy Casserley. Their company on the YPO trip was much appreciated, and it is a pleasure to record three decades of friendship with Dominic.

# CHAPTER 1
# Introduction

Much ink has been spilled about the concept of total war, "one of the central defining concepts of the modern age,"[1] and about its logical counterpart, limited war. The scholarship is generally excellent. In line, however, with the all-too-typical practice among historians of arguing that what they work on is particularly important, there is a tendency among scholars to discern total war, as well as key developments in military history, in their own period of study. This is often linked to a teleological analysis in military history—a sense that it moves in a clear direction, with developments from one period to another, and particular characteristics in each. This approach is an aspect of modernization theory. In the case of military history, indeed, the nineteenth-century sense of progress is repeated, albeit with the caveat that the decision to treat it as progress is a generally reluctant one. Such a teleological approach is especially associated not only with the general focus on the military history of leading Western powers, but also with the notion that in the late nineteenth century and early twentieth century, they created a system of warfare characterized by total war.[2] As totality is in the eye of the beholder, total war has been variously defined (the definitions being seen as far from incompatible), especially in terms of the intensity of struggle, the range (geographical and/or chronological) of conflict, the nature of the goals, and the extent to which civil society was involved in war, not only as victims but also because of an unprecedented mobilization of the resources of societies in order to permit a pursuit of war that was, at once, more intense and more extensive than hitherto. No consensus definition exists.

The definition in terms of unprecedented mobilization is related to the idea that total war was a cause of, or at least a contribution to, significant change. As advanced by Arthur Marwick, a cultural, not a military, historian, this led to a description of total war in terms of greater destructiveness and disruption, a fundamental challenge to the socio-political order, greater popular participation due to the mobilization of national resources, and a major impact on value systems.[3] This approach, however, omits crucial issues of political purpose and military means, and also does not focus on the question of whether a definition that might be appropriate for one or two of the categories—leaders, ordinary military, and civilians—might not be appropriate for the other or others. Additional questions include the relationship between military or non-military change and total war, with the additional specific problem of whether the notion of incremental improvement in warmaking is incompatible with, in the sense of insufficient for, total war.

Furthermore, if total war is seen as a development, then the nature of the key tipping point chronologically, and/or the crucial multiplier in terms of content, becomes significant. There is the issue of whether tipping points in military development occurred before, during, or after wars, and also whether they were the cause or consequence of impasse during a conflict—in this case, particularly World War I (1914–18), but also the American Civil War (1861–65). There is also the question whether the crucial multiplier arises from goals, doctrine, resources, technology, or social context, and, if so, how far they are free-floating variables, how far cumulative in impact (and, if so, in what order of importance), and how far synergetically dependent on the developing existence of total war itself. Phrased differently, how far, in the context of an industrial system and a bellicose socio-political system, is the very existence of a multiplier constitutive of total war, rather than causing it as a separate state?

As with most historical terms, descriptions, and theories—for example, the overused one of "military revolution"—there is a measure of ready applicability in the concept of total war, but its use can also be contested in both specifics and in more general terms. In terms of geographical range of conflict, for example, the extent of some earlier wars between Western powers raises the question of how best to treat this as a criterion. Philip IV of Spain (r. 1621–65, also ruler of Portugal until 1640) and the Dutch fought from 1621 to 1648 in Europe, the West Indies, Brazil, West Africa, the Indian Ocean, and Southeast Asia. Between 1754 and 1815, Britain and France fought in Europe, North America, the West Indies, West Africa, India, and the Indian Ocean in 1754–63, 1778–83, 1793–1802, 1803–14, and 1815. In 1762, Britain anticipated the American success in 1898 of capturing Havana and Manila from Spain, clearly showing that the technologies of steamships and telegraphic communications, both seen as important in teleological accounts of warfare that link capability to modernization, were not in fact necessary in order to wage a war in both hemispheres. Aside from this issue of geographical range, it is also worth considering, when discussing the definition and quality of totality, the extent to which this should be judged in terms of the parameters of what was possible in any given chronological period. In short, aside from cultural relativism in terms of the definition of total war, it is also necessary to add the chronological dimension of detailed discussion for particular cultures. This relates to the possibility that total war is a continuous phenomenon across time, the forms of which change in particular environments.

The same point can also be seen with issues of intensity, mobilization of available resources, and indeed brutality toward civilians, a topic discussed for prehistoric society by Lawrence Keeley.[4] In aggregate terms, these indices were greater in the period covered by this book than ever before, but that is not the sole possible criteria. If total war represents the "absolute war" discussed by the Prussian officer and military theorist Clausewitz (1780–1831), in terms of the end of the restraints arising from the "friction" of combat and issues of policy, then this is not the condition or product of some theory of modernization, nor restricted to any particular period. Furthermore, totality does not become a permanent state. The United States fought what some commentators have seen as a total war in 1861–65, but a limited (if global) one in 1898. Clausewitz admitted that "war and its forms result from ideas, emotions, and conditions prevailing at the time," before claiming that "Theory . . . has the duty to give priority to the absolute form of war and to make that form a general point of reference."[5] In practice, the total destruction of cities, and the slaughter and enslavement of whole peoples were, albeit on a smaller scale, features of antiquity more than the modern age, while conflict in Rwanda in 1994 suggests that modern technology is still not necessary for such slaughter.

Indeed, the demographic impact of war on the societies of antiquity, which were far less populous than those of the modern world, was probably far greater than its impact on societies in the last two centuries, although disease may well have had an even greater impact on them. The bubonic plague of the fourteenth century probably killed more people in Eurasia than the conflicts of the period, while the outbreak of Spanish influenza after World War I killed more than died in the war. Conflict encourages the spread of disease, particularly as a result of the movement of troops and the disruption of social systems, but is also dwarfed by it.[6]

As far as the last two centuries are concerned, the fate of the British army and accompanying civilians retreating from Kabul in the winter of 1841–42—all, bar one killed by the Afghans—is a contrast to the general fate of defeated forces in the age of total war: There was a willingness to take prisoners, as with the German surrender to the Soviets at Stalingrad in 1942, even if some countries mistreated them. In both world wars, the conventions about the treatment of prisoners operated—for example, between the Western Allies and Germany/Italy in World War II[7]—alongside serious refusals to abide by such practices.

If fighting to the death was proclaimed as the choice by German and Japanese leaders in 1944–45, and given physical form in Japanese kamikaze attacks, the reality was that both powers in fact surrendered with significant forces extant. The vocabulary of total war thus proved misleading. There were also criteria of possible totality that were not reached on any scale in the period covered by this book, for example, large-scale mobilization of women for combat, or eating prisoners. Winston Churchill subsequently wrote of World War I, "Torture and Cannibalism were the only two expedients that the civilized, scientific Christian societies had been able to deny themselves,"[8] but these exceptions were aspects of the physical contact between combatants that had become less important in Western conflict.

Furthermore, fighting "with an exceptional tenacity, brutality and 'moral energy,'"[9] let alone to the death, was no monopoly of this period, nor of those societies seen as advanced, whether defined in terms of modern industry or mass politics. Indeed, the relationship between the "totality" of deliberately accepting being killed, and the state of society is far from clear. Cultural norms seem most important, and these are difficult to comprehend in theories of modernization based largely on the Western experience. Rather than focusing on the kamikaze attacks, which did not involve the leadership of Japan nor more than a fraction of their military, it is instructive to turn to Bali in 1906. At Den Pasar and later at Pamescutan, the two raja families ritually purified themselves for death and fought their final battle (*puputan*): Armed only with daggers and lances, they were all slaughtered as they advanced in the face of Dutch firepower, killing their own wounded as they did so. On Sumatra in 1907, the Dewa Agung of Klungkung staged his own *puputan* when the Dutch attacked. Insofar as the concept of total war is helpful, this attitude and practice correspond to it better than much that is discussed in Western Europe and the United States. In November 1946, the *puputan* was echoed at Marga on Bali, when the nationalist I Gusti Ngurah Rai and ninety-four guerrillas fought to the death against far greater Dutch forces.

In addition, when considering the period covered by this book, it was not always the "advanced" societies that experienced greater mobilization. Conflict among "tribal" peoples, instead, embodied the essence of total war. In precolonial Africa, societies such as the Ateker, the Maasai, and the Zulu committed all possible economic and human resources to the waging of warfare, although these resources tended to be small by the standards of the industrialized West. The Zulus, whom Britain fought in 1879, expected all men aged above fifteen to fight, a commitment that extended into their sixties. This enabled them to field substantial numbers. During World War I, in comparison with more industrial societies, New Zealand, with its relatively pastoral economy, mobilized a particularly high percentage of its men for service.

Mobilization was not the sole criterion. Furthermore, in terms of waging war against enemy communities in their entirety, including brutality toward civilians and prisoners, non-Western societies in this period could practice a very grim policy. In Africa, the elderly, women, and children were caught up in long cycles of raiding war every bit as much as fighting men. It is also possible in considering anti-societal warfare, to point to other societies that matched, or even exceeded, the situation in 1860–1945, even if not in scale. Within Europe, the slaughter and enslavement of civilians had been seen, for example, in the Greek War of Independence against Turkish rule in the 1820s.

The Western vocabulary of total war dated from World War I, with the French minister Georges Clemenceau pressing for "la guerre intégrale" when he took office in 1917, and the German general Erich Ludendorff using the term in his post-war memoirs and eventually writing a book on *Der Totale Krieg* (1935).[10] As such, the notion was a response to particular lessons drawn from the Great War, as World War I was called, a struggle that became the definition of, and thus template for, total war. The notion of total war was also an aspect of a cultural and intellectual milieu in which traumatic violence of a non-providential kind was seen as inevitable; indeed, widely believed to be necessary. The key role of such beliefs readily extended to the creation of the concept of total war.[11]

However, the goal of apocalyptic violence, and the means to that end of violence, scarcely had to wait for the mobilization of industrial society, a system that in fact represented constraints at the same time as it produced resources. Indeed, the apparently (although often only to outsiders) anarchic violence of acephelous societies was not really possible for industrial society, which instead prepared for the deliberate destruction of planned killing. That the latter in fact also existed in acephelous societies required anthropological insights that have not generally been allied to modern military analysis and history. Instead readily apparent and large-scale, hierarchy, order, and control were integral to the industrial notion of total war, and to those societies seen as advanced, although their manifestations were different.

This issue is an aspect of the relationship between social structures and military organization discussed by the Scottish economist Adam Smith in his *An Inquiry into the Nature and Causes of the Wealth of Nations* (1776). The notion of stages in social development, the "stadial" approach, was widely held among progressive European eighteenth-century thinkers seeking to define a sphere for human progress that was not dependent on Divine Providence, being also seen, for example, in Adam Ferguson's *History of Civil Society* (1767). Smith differentiated nations of hunters (such as Native Africans) and shepherds (such as Tartars and Arabs), among whom every man is a warrior, alongside nations of husbandmen (agricultural workers, such as the ancient Greeks and early Romans), among whom every man may fight, from more advanced societies, in which the proportion of fighting men was smaller. This approach has interesting consequences for the notion of total war. Smith indeed defined the "nations of shepherds" as heavily militarized societies that risked destruction if unsuccessful in war:

When such a nation goes to war, the warriors will not trust their herds and flocks to the feeble defences of their old men, their women and children; and their old men, their women and children, will not be left behind without defence and without subsistence. The whole nation, besides, being accustomed to a wandering life, even in time of peace, easily takes the field in time of war. Whether it marches as an army, or moves about as a company of herdsmen, the way of life is nearly the same . . . Among the Tartars, even the women have been frequently known to engage in battle. If they conquer, whatever belongs to the hostile tribe is the recompense of the victory. But if they are vanquished, all is lost, and not only their herds and flocks, but their women and children, become the booty of the conqueror. Even the greater part of those who survive the action are obliged to submit to him for the sake of immediate subsistence . . . Nothing can be more dreadful than a Tartar invasion has frequently been in Asia.[12]

An absence of restraint, therefore, was not seen as the product of ideologies, still less of modern ideologies, but as the consequence of social structure. As Smith noted, the participation ratio in conflict in an industrial society was necessarily lower, with pay serving as a form of contract to bind together workers and soldiers. This was linked to "improvement" in the art of war, which brought its own form of division of labor and specialization. Industrialization both enables and obliges societies to mobilize fewer men so that the military can have the weaponry it requires. Smith saw the invention and use of firearms as particularly important because they replaced strength by skill, but discipline was considered even more significant in ensuring combat effectiveness. In combination, they were force multipliers, enabling "opulent and civilized" nations to overcome "poor and barbarous" counterparts.[13]

Smith's claim that the rate of participation in combat was not the same as effectiveness in conflict, was linked to his argument that this was an aspect of what was termed "stadial" progress. The notion that military force depended on social differentiation ensured that there was a fundamental continuity between the age of Smith and subsequent periods. Even, or, indeed, especially, in the age of "total war" discussed in this book, when obligations to military service were very widespread for men in the combatant powers (although not in World War I, for example, in India, or until the close, Ireland), there was a process of specialization that excluded those engaged in the war economy from combat. This was particularly marked in the United States in World War II: In "the 90-division gamble," the army was kept relatively small (although the air force and navy absorbed large numbers) and economic growth that involved large numbers of workers indeed brought much prosperity on the "Home Front."

This was an aspect of the degree to which World War II was a limited war for the Americans. It certainly emerges as such in comparison, for example, to the Chinese, Soviets, and Japanese, undeniably suggesting that in order to compete, powers economically weaker than the United States had to engage in a more total war experience, at least insofar as greater mobilization was concerned; although Japan and especially China and the Soviet Union were more exposed to attack than the United States. As another sign of limited war, partisan politics continued in the United States, with a contested presidential election in 1944 (four-year elections are required by the U.S. Constitution), in contrast to the absence of a general election in Britain during either world war until after Germany was defeated. Yet, from another perspective, such a conclusion about the United States also indicates the drawback of adopting a single criterion for total war. To argue that, in World War II, the United States fought a modern war, and not total war, risks making both overly clear-cut, and also underrating the variety of experience that the war entailed. Such an argument also runs the danger of underplaying the American commitment and contribution to Allied victory.

Mobilization, in part, was an attitude of mind, and, as such, an aspect of socio-political attitudes. A sense of being under threat was important, and, from this perspective, total war overlapped with paranoia, and can, indeed, be seen as a particular formulation of it. In the case of the United States in World War II, the internment of Japanese Americans can be seen as a symbolic act of totality in a society fighting what was, as far as its home base was concerned, an essentially limited war, but it also reflected anxiety about their loyalty combined with fear of Japanese capability. Paranoia itself was far from constant, and, in fact, can be located in terms of particular social circumstances. Thus, modern societies, in the shape of industrial economies, depended on reliable workforces, and sensitivity about the latter was increased by the trade unionism of the late nineteenth century, the left-wing activism of the early twentieth, and the challenge of Soviet power, particularly from the late 1940s. Paranoia played a role, but, at the same time, the need to maintain the effectiveness of the industrial economy ensured that it had to be policed as well as regulated. In February 1941, when Australia was at war with Germany, and the latter allied to the Soviet Union, the Australian War Cabinet was concerned about Communist subversion, specifically "the continued state of industrial unrest in the community."[14]

The "stadial" approach raises the question of whether social, economic, and indeed military, developments in the nineteenth and twentieth centuries, subsequent to those considered by Adam Smith and his contemporaries, were less significant than those they discussed. If, for example, David Hume was correct to claim that "the invention of gunpowder changed the whole art of war,"[15] then it is pertinent to ask whether the changes of the period 1860–1945 were as, or more, significant, and, if so, which, and why. In this, and other respects, the relationship between circumstances, changes, and effectiveness is complex and often far from clear. For example, the transformation in supplies, so that they became overwhelmingly factory-produced, and then had to be transported to the front, increased military capability, for example, in terms of petrol-borne mobility, but also ensured that logistics became a more serious constraint.[16]

The social context is key in definitions of total war that seek to do more than focus on means of fighting, but it is difficult to offer an account of this context that makes particular sense of the period 1860–1945. If, for example, "the idea of total war implies the breakdown of the distinction between organized combat and the societies, economies, and political systems that support it,"[17] then that is also true of many societies. Industrial warfare may be seen to provide the answer, but it is clear from World War II that this entailed different consequences in particular states: ideological objectives and political practices were clearly not dependent on the industrial background of society.

Moreover, there is the issue that total war for one participant might be limited war for another, as with the Vietnam War for the United States, but also with the transoceanic imperial wars of 1860–1945. This also includes, to a degree, America's participation in World War I, which she entered only in 1917. More generally, total war for one participant, but limited war for another, could be a function not only of political goals and the type and degree of socio-economic mobilization, but also of the strength of the participants; however, this strength was of varied type. There is a tendency to focus on technology gaps in explaining the possibility "for an advanced, sophisticated state of conducting total war without having to wage war totally."[18] Indeed, relatively small, professional regular forces played a crucial role in establishing and sustaining transoceanic imperial positions, and this remained the case after World War I. In many respects, this represented a commitment to limited war that was taken up by post-1918 protagonists of mechanized warfare, both in the air and on land. In practice, as far as imperial wars were concerned, qualitative difference was not the only cause and definition of relative strength. Manpower could also be a key factor in Western strength, and one in which local support could be very important.

The notion of total war for only one participant is an instance not only of the conceptual difficulty of definition, but also of the extent to which individual terms do not offer a range of qualification and variation necessary to describe the different characteristics at issue. Furthermore, like "absolute" in the case of the discussion of absolutism, the term "total" carries with it connotations that are not always help-ful. For example, within the context of a perceptive discussion of whether the Boer War of 1899–1902 (the Second Boer War; the first was in 1881) fits into "the emergence of totality," the following de-scription of British policy is unclear:

whatever the unwillingness to confront the possibility of actual hostilities in the summer and autumn of 1899, the risk of conflict was never one entirely ruled out. Moreover, there was an over-riding totality of aim in terms of achieving the supremacy in southern Africa deemed essential...for the consolidation of British imperial unity and power, the frustration of the efforts of European rivals to infiltrate the region, and the safeguarding of the route to India.[19]

"Totality of aim" is a problematic term. One major problem arises from the conceptual difficulties caused by the conflation, in much discussion, of modern war with total war, Churchill indeed declaring in 1943 that "modern war is total." In practice, there was no necessary relationship between them. In part, this conflation rested on a failure to consider the ends at stake, a key issue in total war, and instead a focus on the means employed, which is, in practice, a definition of the degree of modernity.[20] Modern, however, understood as contemporary or recent (in whatever way the latter is defined), covers a wide variety of means of warmaking, as indeed of goals. From this perspective, in-dustrial might be a more useful term than modern. Industrial, in turn, has to be relativized, not so much in terms of the technologi-cal, manufacturing, and organizational capacity of the societies in question, as that would make, say, ancient Roman warfare industrial, but rather by considering this capacity within the context of the pos-sibilities created by the nineteenth-century Industrial Revolution.

In this book, the working criteria adopted is that the age of total war is used to describe a particular period of military history, 1860–1945, without assuming that it necessarily matches the descriptions, or ful-fills the implicit assumptions frequently entailed by the use of the term total. In that, total war is little different from many other analytical terms such as absolutism,[21] or revolution, military or otherwise; albeit with the important caveat that, unlike many concepts, total war was one used at the time. At the same time, the concept and term total war were not employed until after the experience of World War I, although by World War II, they had become commonplace, being used, for example, by Churchill in his address to the joint Houses of Congress on May 19, 1943 (quoted above). This caveat aside, there is no doubt that 1860–1945 was a period in which war, the prospect of war, and the consequences of it, were all crucially important for human history, and also a period that bulks large in the study of military history. The human, ideological, and economic resources provided by population growth, nationalism, economic development, globalization, and imperial strength provided the wherewithal for large-scale conflict.[22] It is necessary to put the definitions offered for total war into this wider context.

# CHAPTER 2

# Overawing the World, 1860–1914

The study of war in the period covered by this book generally focuses on conflict between Western powers, with the addition of Japan from the Russo-Japanese War of 1904–1905. These indeed were the conflicts that most engaged these powers, and these states dominated the world economy, but it is also necessary to consider another narrative of world history and warfare, provided by the attempts of these powers to control much of the Earth. As far as standard indices of totality are concerned, the resulting conflicts lacked the scale of those between the major states, but they were very important in terms of impact. The year 1860, in which Anglo-French forces briefly occupied Beijing, was part of a tipping point in terms of Western relations with South and East Asia, the area in which the bulk of the world's population lived. The subsequent Chinese capitulation was followed by a treaty that led to the opening of China to trade and missionaries, and the expansion of the British colony of Hong Kong to include the Kowloon Peninsula. Hankou and Tientsin swiftly became "treaty ports," where the British presence included concessionary areas. Other key dates, within a decade either way of 1860, included the intimidation of Japan into opening its harbors by the U.S. Navy in 1853–54; the British defeat of Persia in 1857, and suppression of the Indian Mutiny in 1857–59; and the Russian gain of Tashkent (1865) and Samarkand (1868). This was also a key period in terms of Western relations with Africa and Oceania, as well as of the consolidation of U.S. control over much of North America.

During the following half century, much of the world was brought under Western control, including peoples noted for their martial fervor, such as the Apaches, Sioux, Asantes, and Zulus. Most of the world was divided up between the Western powers. Some states that remained independent did so because they inflicted serious checks on Western forces, as with Afghanistan and the British and Ethiopia and the Italians. Others did so because they were protected as buffer zones between competing Western powers, as with Siam (Thailand) between Britain and France, Persia (Iran) between Britain and Russia, and Manchuria (the key economic zone in China) between Japan and Russia.

The situation was a marked contrast to the beginning of the nineteenth century, which raises the question about changes in the effectiveness of Western armed forces. The extent to which non-military elements played a major role in Western expansion is also important. This was partly a matter of the general organizational development of the Western world, seen not only with innovations in communications technology, such as the telegraph, but also with the creation of systems that made their effective use possible, predictable, and normative. By 1900, more than 170,000 miles of ocean cables were in use, and in 1901, wireless messages were received across the Atlantic.[1] The gathering of information was also important, as it increased the chances of successful operations and helped overcome the problems posed by distance and unfamiliarity. Information ranged from physical geography, such as sounding coastal waters or establishing climatic conditions, to the assessment of social and political situations. The categorization and analysis of the information was frequently flawed, but it helped fill a void. A similar process characterized other expansionist states, such as Japan, which gathered data on China.[2]

Information, for example, played a major role in directing the process of railway building, which helped speed the movement of troops, making garrisons appear part of a mutually-supporting system, and also integrated conquests with metropoles, and, in doing so, replicated the impact of steamship lines and harbors. By 1906, a rail system in Russian Central Asia had been created, serving strategic and economic interests.[3] In conflict, railway lines could serve as axes of movement, as when the Russians advanced against the Chinese in Manchuria in 1900.

Forts also served to anchor Western advances and to provide safety both to European traders and to natives willing to trade with Europeans, although the individual function of forts differed, and also changed.[4] Forts were important defensive bases and force multipliers in the Russian steppes, the American West, and in Africa. Forts such as Archambault were also used as the bases for advances, in this case, for the French campaign in Chad in 1899. On the northwest frontier of India, British forts were the focus of attacks, for instance, in Chitral in 1895, and by Pathans in 1897; for example, Forts Gulistan and Lockhart and their relief was the crucial aspect of British campaigning, such as in 1897, when a relief column ended the siege of the fort at Shabkadr. In the Sino-French War of 1884–85, the French succeeded, in March 1885, in relieving the besieged garrison at Tuyen-Qang, northwest of Hanoi. Similarly, in confronting risings, the Germans had to be able to defend positions, such as Mahenge in East Africa in 1905. The relief of the foreign legations at Beijing was the crucial episode in the China campaign of 1900. A comparable totemic significance was associated with the British failure to relieve General Gordon in Khartoum in 1885. Positions that could repel attack—such as Makale, where the Italian garrison held off the Ethiopians for six weeks in the winter of 1895–96—could nevertheless be starved into surrender if there was no relief.

At the level of the individual soldier, the situation was less happy, and this led to high casualty rates from disease. This was a serious problem due to the difficulties of operating in the tropics, and death rates from disease remained higher than combat fatalities, for example, between 1894 and 1902, with the French in Madagascar, the Americans in Cuba and the Philippines, and the British in the Boer War. Typhus hit German forces in Southwest Africa in 1904. Yet, death rates were lower than in the early-nineteenth century, and it therefore proved possible to deploy substantial Western forces. Furthermore, major efforts were made to improve facilities. In the case of the United States, a Department of Military Hygiene was established at West Point and all cadets had to take the course. Other reforms included the establishment of a medical officer reserve and a permanent female nurse corps. These changes reflected the practice of seeking rational analysis as a basis for policy formation. In the American case, the Dodge Commission played the crucial role.[5] At the same time, difficulties persisted. Thomas Blamey, the Australian commander in New Guinea, wrote from there in 1942, "The wastage in tropical warfare in undeveloped areas is immense. For example, at least one-third of our force at Milne Bay is already infected with malaria."[6]

Weaponry was also important. The improved firepower of artillery increased the effectiveness of relatively light pieces. Their lightness ensured that they could be moved rapidly in difficult terrain and climate conditions. Artillery, for example, was used by the French against a much larger force under Samory Touré at Kéniéra in Guinea in West Africa in February 1882, while in southern Africa, artillery and Maxim (machine) guns helped a British camp to defeat Matabele attackers at the Shangani River in October 1893. In September 1912, cannon and machine guns helped a French square repel a Moroccan attack at Sidi Ben Othman, with more than two thousand Moroccans killed, before the French pressed on to occupy nearby Marakesh. Artillery was often a key force multiplier, as it overcame the defensive advantage provided by prepared positions. In July 1889, resistance in East Africa to German control by the Arab leader Abushiri ibn Salim was overcome when his main base at Pangani was bombarded and captured. In West Africa in 1898, it took French artillery two weeks to destroy the walls of Sikasso, which had resisted a lengthy year-long siege by Samory Touré in 1887–88. A focus on the use of firepower should not lead to a neglect of the extent to which Western forces also closed with opponents. Bayonet charges were frequently used, for example, by the Italians against Turkish and Arab attackers at Two Palms in Libya in March 1912.

In part, however, the focus on Western military effectiveness distracts attention from an issue that is frequently overlooked if a military approach to imperialism is taken, but one that is nevertheless important when considering all empires. This is the issue of the extent to which the role of the outside, apparently conquering, power has to be understood in terms of the power-plays of local interests, especially allies, so that the conqueror is used and, indeed, becomes effective only insofar as it takes part in such relationships. This reciprocal, patron-client, relationship[7] was critical to British control of India, while in southern Africa, Britain benefited from native opposition to the Zulus, whose expansion, like that of the Asantes and of Samory Touré in West Africa, had left much discontent. In 1887–88, King Tieba of Kénédougou sought French aid when attacked by Samory Touré in modern Mali. The French also had some success with non-military efforts at pacification and assimilation, particularly in Senegal, Madagascar, and Morocco.

The problems of pacifying large areas of often-difficult terrain ensured that co-operation was important. Thus, in Burma, where King Thebaw was defeated in the Third Anglo-Burmese War in 1885 and then surrendered, opposition continued, with a widespread rebellion in 1886–90. In confronting the situation there, the British benefited from the use of Indian military resources and also from some local support. Border treaties with Siam, France, and China helped consolidate claims to the frontier zones of Burma, although it was necessary to subjugate the tribal groups of the peripheries, including the Shan and Wa states, and the Kachins, Kerens, and Chins. Difficulties in pacification could also lead to a harshness that can be seen as an aspect of total war. For example, aside from refusing to take prisoners and killing the wounded—both seen in British operations against the Zulus[8]—there was also the use of destruction, such as the burning down of the Asante capital Kumasi in 1874, and the devastation of Maori villages in New Zealand, in order to end resistance via humiliation and a statement of power.

Such methods, as well as the ability to win local support, can be seen as particularly important if the distinction between battle and war is grasped. The range of factors that led to Western victory in battle—including, as the nineteenth century drew toward its close, more deadly weapons, such as machine guns[9] and effective cannon—did not necessarily ensure success in war or pacification. Instead, relatively small Western forces sought in their own apparent interest to direct states and peoples, which often meant claiming formal sovereignty, but found that the means available for doing so were limited. As a consequence, they took part in local power-plays, particularly recruiting local military support, which was used with considerable success by all imperial powers.[10] For example, the British force sent against Kano in what became northern Nigeria in 1902 was essentially one of White officers and eight hundred African troops. They benefited from artillery support, which destroyed the gates, permitting the capture of the city. The year before, in Somaliland, the British force that repelled the army of Mullah Sayyid Muhammed, when it attacked its camp at Samala, was largely composed of Somalis. This was not only a case of transoceanic expansion. In the Americas, expanding states made use of native allies. This was particularly the case in the United States and Argentina, although, due to the co-operation of some tribes with the Confederates, the U.S. Army did this less often after 1865. In 1872 in Argentina, the force that defeated the Indian (native) leader Juan Calfucurá at San Carlos—the key engagement in the Indian raids—included not only government troops, but also Indian allies under Cipriano Catriel.

Native military support continued to be the pattern for Western imperialism in the twentieth century, whether on the offensive or on the defensive. In December 1934, an Italian force, composed largely of Somali irregulars, played the key role in a border clash at Walwal, which was used by the Italian dictator Benito Mussolini to justify the conquest of Ethiopia in 1935–36. In this conquest, the Italians benefited not only from Eritrean auxiliaries, but also from native allies such as the Oromo, whom they armed. After World War II, on the defensive against Communist Vietnamese advances, the French, and later the Americans, used hill tribes in Southeast Asia.

An emphasis on the role of local power-plays risks demilitarizing military history, but this perspective is important: battle was an enabler of war, and war of the extension of control, but neither exhausts the subject, nor provides a sufficient explanation of success. At the same time, the role of politics has to be placed in a military context. For example, Japan benefited in its conflict with China in 1894–95 because it was more united, not least in contrast with the acute divisions between the Manchu rulers of China and their Chinese subjects, but, at the same time, despite these divisions in China, this was a war that had to be waged. In this, the Japanese benefited from a better understanding of recent developments in warfare, for example, in the use of their warships, and also in major improvements in their military over the previous decade, but also from limiting their goals. The sustained large-scale conquest of China that was pursued from 1937, with dire consequences for Japanese warmaking, was not prefigured in the 1890s, not least because, although then there was a bold plan for a pincer attack on Beijing, the Japanese also had more restrained alternative plans.[11] As with most conflicts between non-Western powers, those between China and Japan, both in 1894–95 and in 1931–45, were generally ignored by contemporary Western commentators, although from 1941, once at war with Japan, the United States used Chinese bases and co-operated with Chinese forces.[12]

Military historians understandably tend to focus on a "battle" approach to Western expansion, concentrating, for instance, on clashes—such as Islandhwana and Rorke's Drift in the Anglo-Zulu war of 1879, and Tell-el-Kebir in the conflict between Britain and Egypt in 1882. However, by omission, this underrates other approaches to Western expansion. Furthermore, much of the writing on these battles is very separate from that on the conflicts within the West during this period. In part, this reflects the dominance of Prussia (its king, Wilhelm I, became emperor of Germany in 1871) in the discussion of military developments, and Prussia/Germany indeed played a key role in European conflict from 1864 to 1945. On the world scale, however, it was less important, particularly in Asia, and, in fact, was a late entrant to the competition for colonies. Prussia's major rival in the 1860s, Austria, did not enter at all into this competition, instead directing its expansionism within Europe, particularly into the Balkans. This was an aspect of the extent to which imperialism was directed at nearby territories. This was true outside Europe, in particular, of Russian expansion in the Caucasus and Central Asia, and also of French and Italian expansion in North Africa, although colonies were also established at a distance from current possessions. Logistical reach was not a variable that depended on physical proximity.

Treating inter-Western conflicts separately from imperial expansion at the expense of non-Westerners is less convincing where there were significant overlaps in personnel, as with France, much of whose army fought in Algeria as well as in Europe, or, on a smaller scale, the United States, as veterans of the Civil War subsequently played a major role in campaigns against the Native Americans. The impact of imperial expansion could also be significant for Western militaries, encouraging them to develop a range of capabilities that were often different to those required for conflict within the West. Indeed, the two types of requisite resources could be in competition with one another. In Europe, there were powerful pressures from within the armies encouraging a focus on capability for conflict with other European powers.

Rather than treating advances at the expense of non-Westerners as secondary in the military history of the period, it is valuable to note their scope and impact. The latter was most acute for those who were conquered, as societies and states were disrupted, if not transformed. This was particularly severe in countries that had no recent experience of foreign rule, such as Burma, annexed by Britain in 1886, and New Zealand. The Anglo-Maori wars there reflected the range of Western military commitment. A memorial in the churchyard at Russell, New Zealand, to four British naval sailors killed there in 1845 included:

> Go stranger track the Deep,
> Free, free the white sails spread,
> Wave may not foam, nor wild wind beat,
> Where rests not England's dead.

The pace of expansion increased from the 1860s, in part because Britain, the Western power with the largest empire, had been involved in conflict in the 1850s, first with another European power (the Crimean War with Russia in 1854–56), and then with a large-scale rising in its most important colony, India (1857–59). Victory in the latter left Britain the dominant power in South Asia. In subsequent years, a series of opponents were defeated by the British in campaigns that were a testimony to the range of Western power, and to the extent to which it was driven and organized by government, rather than partially by private enterprise and autonomous organizations, as it had been before. In the quarter century from 1860, there were British victories at the expense of New Zealand Maoris and the Asantes and Zulus of Africa, as well as the forces of Burma, Ethiopia, and Egypt. In 1868, the ability to send a force from India, with instructions from London, to fight in Ethiopia, was permitted by the use of technology-telegraph and steamship, and, as such, was modern war. These successes were echoed, albeit on a smaller scale, by other Western forces.

The French were particularly active in Africa, but also in Southeast Asia and Oceania, although they were not invariably successful. In the Sino-French War of 1884–85, the French found it difficult to prevail on land. An offensive from Tonkin (northern Vietnam) was successful in February 1885, but a vigorous Chinese counter-attack led the French to accept peace. In Africa, they displayed the capacity to operate deep into the interior that was necessary if the European powers were to move beyond the littoral power projection that had characterized their activities prior to the nineteenth century. Rabih az-Zubayr, the "Black Sultan," who led resistance in distant Chad, suffered as a result. In October 1899, he was seriously defeated at Kouno, to the southeast of Lake Chad, and on April 22, 1900, was defeated and killed at Kousséri, to the south of the lake, after his room for maneuver had been limited by converging French forces from Algeria, Congo, and Niger. The ability to mount such operations was an important display of capability. Converging columns were also used by the French against the town of Khenifra in 1913, as part of the attempt to end resistance by the Zaia of central Morocco, but, in this campaign, the French encountered the problem of fixing their opponent: the Zaia resisted the advance before successfully escaping.

More generally, column advances proved the means most suitable, both operationally and tactically, for imperial forces in a variety of terrains, whereas conventional methods were inappropriate. The French demonstrated this at Settat in 1908, when they attacked, but failed to prevent the Moroccans from escaping. The relatively close-packed nature of column formations contrasted with increased interest in looser formations on the Western battlefield, but this reflected a different ratio between firepower and shock on the part of non-Western opponents. Column advances continued to be used after World War I, for example, by the British fighting the Iraqi insurgency in 1920, and the French overcoming the Druze rising in Syria in 1925. They were of value both in advancing on enemy centers, and in seeking to relieve besieged garrisons, such as Samawah in Iraq in October 1920. However, columns risked ambush, as a German one was at Lugalo in East Africa by the Hehe tribe in 1891, with the loss of most of the three-hundred-strong force, and another by the Herero at Owikokorero in Southwest Africa in April 1904. Columns, therefore, needed to be capable of all-round defense; they benefited from support by light artillery or machine guns. This helped German columns at Owikokorero and Onganjira when ambushed by the Herero in March and April 1904, respectively. The impact of firepower, however, was affected by vegetation and subsequently, in April, the latter column was forced to retreat after being ambushed at Oviumbo.

Aside from columns, it was also useful in some terrains, such as southern Africa, to have mounted infantry, who provided both mobility and firepower.[13] Both columns and mounted forces were useful in attacking the supply bases of opponents, which compensated for the frequent difficulty in bringing them to battle. This policy led to assaults on villages and camps, as in 1874, when Colonel Ranald Mackenzie and the American 4th Cavalry attacked the Kiowa base in Palo Duro Canyon, capturing supplies and horses and making it difficult for the Native Americans to continue the Red River War. Similarly, he destroyed Apache villages near San Remolino in 1873, and destroyed Dull Knife's camp at Crazy Woman Creek in 1876. Many American campaigns were conducted in the winter in order to reduce the Native Americans' mobility.

In the late nineteenth century, the Russians also greatly expanded their empire. They were able to display effectiveness against both Turkey and China. In 1858, the Russians advanced to the Amur and, in 1860, to the Sea of Japan, ensuring that Vladivostok became a Russian port. The Russians also established themselves on Sakhalin and in the Kurile Islands, while Manchuria became a Russian sphere of influence in 1896, and Mongolia another one in 1899. This brought Russian influence close to Beijing. The Russian force that invaded Manchuria in 1900 stormed Tsitsihar. The Russians also advanced their position in Central Asia, overrunning the khanate of Bukhara in 1868, defeating the khanate of Khiva in 1873, overrunning that of Khokand in 1876, after a victory at Makhram, and conquering Merv in 1884.

The Germans established themselves in West, Southwest, and East Africa, as well as in New Guinea and the western Pacific. They encountered considerable opposition, much of which was guerrilla in character—for example, by the Nama in Southwest Africa (Namibia) in 1893–94. Relatively weak powers, such as the Netherlands, Portugal, Belgium, and Argentina, also took part in the expansion. The ability of the latter was more suggestive of a major change in military capability than that of major powers, such as Britain, France, Russia, and Germany. Having been unable to dominate the interior of Angola and Mozambique, the Portuguese made major gains in both in the 1890s, while the Dutch overran much of modern Indonesia in the 1900s, and Belgium seized what became Congo.

The ability of these relatively minor powers to make these gains was, in part, a product of the extent to which there was no conflict between the Western powers over imperial expansion prior to the struggle between America and Spain (1898); although, in one respect, the conflicts between Britain and the Boers in 1881 and 1899–1902 were struggles over expansion in southern Africa. The Spanish-American War was contained in terms of its range and intensity. The American Civil War is sometimes held to have led to an American Way of War, emphasizing a strategy of annihilation,[14] but that scarcely described 1898. Furthermore, although there were tensions and war panics—for example, between Britain and Russia over Turkey in 1877–78, Britain and France in 1898 over Sudan, and Germany and France in 1905–1906 and 1911 over Morocco—disagreements were settled short of conflict. The war scare of 1877–78, a response to Russian advances at the expense of the Turks, nevertheless, indicated the flexibility of imperial military systems and the ability to move forces considerable distances. British forces in the Mediterranean were reinforced, with Indian units swiftly sent to Malta via the Suez Canal (opened in 1869), and a British fleet was sent to Constantinople through the Dardanelles in February 1878. In turn, the Russians planned commerce raiding in the Atlantic and Indian Oceans, and attacks on the ports of the British Empire, such as Sydney.[15] In 1885, when a Russian invasion of India seemed a prospect, due to the Penjdeh Crisis over the Afghan border, the British placed the navy on full alert and considered plans for attacks, including a bombardment of Kronstadt, Russia's Baltic naval base, and amphibious operations against Batum on the Black Sea and Vladivostok, the latter to be preceded by the establishment of a base in Korea.

As a consequence of the avoidance of wars between the Western powers prior to 1898, there was no need, as a pre-condition for power projection, to have the naval capability to guard sea-lanes. Further-more, the normative character of imperial expansion, the sheer range of opportunity, and the willingness to accept notions such as equiva-lent gains or to share in open access, the latter the key to policy toward China, enabled the major powers to cope not only with the aspirations of each other, but also with both new entrants (Germany, Italy, Japan, United States) and minor powers (Portugal, Dutch). The arrangements that were made between the Western states made scant reference to local sensitivities. In 1871, when the Dutch sold their forts on the Gold Coast of West Africa to Britain, the views of the king of Asante, Kofi Kakari, who saw them as trading bases under Asante sovereignty, were neglected, helping lead to war in 1873. Similarly, Britain and Russia settled their long-standing competition in Asia, agreeing, for example, on spheres of interest in Persia (Iran) in 1907.

Across the world, what were seen as frontiers and spheres of control were defined to the benefit of Western powers. This was seen, for in-stance, in the Pacific. Concerned about the spread of Western interests and impressed by foreign military models, particularly as a result of his tour around the world in 1881, King Kalākaua of Hawaii built up the military on foreign models, the tiny army or King's Guard being modeled on the Prussian army. He also bought new arms, including two Gatling guns and Austrian field artillery. A warship, the *Ka'im-cloa*, a sometime guano trader, was commissioned and fitted out. Intended as a training vessel for the fledgling Hawaiian navy, this was equipped with four brass cannon and two Gatling guns. The captain was British and the standing regulations for the British navy were adopted for its Hawaiian counterpart, which was designed to give effect to the plan for a Pacific confederation of Hawaii, Samoa, Tonga, and the Cook Islands, intended to prevent Western annexa-tions; to that end, the ship was sent to Samoa in 1887. Germany saw this as interference in her plans, and shadowed the ship, but, faced by serious indiscipline among the crew, the Hawaiian vessel was re-called and mothballed.[16] Land frontiers were also defined in Western interests. In 1909, the Malay sultanates of Kedah, Kelantan, Ter-engganu, and Perlis were transferred from Siamese (Thai) to British protection. The absence of conflict over empire between the Western states, certainly prior to 1898, is a powerful limit to any description of the period in terms of total war. The experience for those who suffered imperial conquest may well have been total, but the situation was very different not only from the perspective of imperial metropoles, but also in terms of their competition.

This was also seen in the Americas. Instability in Mexico and its repudiation of international debts led Britain, France, and Spain to intervene in order to secure repayment, and their troops landed at its main port, Vera Cruz, in the winter of 1861–62. The Mexicans did not change their policy, but the British and Spaniards evacuated their troops in 1862. In contrast, the French increased their role, eventually trying unsuccessfully to establish a client government, but American pressure encouraged them to abandon their effort in 1866, rather than to risk a new war. Similarly, also after the American Civil War, the Americans chose not to use their military strength for expansionist ends, other than against Native Americans, and Anglo-American differences were settled by the Treaty of Washington of 1871. This enabled the British to reduce their garrisons in Canada. American diplomatic support for Venezuela, in her 1895–96 dispute with Britain over the border of British Guiana, was also contained, while subsequent tensions over the Canadian-American frontier were settled by the British being more conciliatory than the Canadians would have preferred. In 1902–1903, American intervention led Britain, Germany, and Italy to end their blockade of Venezuela in pursuit of unpaid debts. In 1908, the British Committee of Imperial Defence and the Foreign Office concluded that the possibility of war with the United States was remote.

Future opponents were also able to settle colonial issues. In 1898, the grave Portuguese financial crisis led to a secret Anglo-German treaty allocating Angola and Mozambique, the major Portuguese colonies in Africa, in the event that Portugal wished to sell them, which in fact she was not to do. In 1906–14, Britain and Turkey successfully settled differences over Turkey's frontiers with Egypt and Persia (Iran), and over spheres of influence in Arabia. Having fought Spain in 1898, the Americans did not feel the need to use their newly-expanded fleet to fight another Western power again until 1917. In 1907–1909, when the sixteen battleships of the American Great White Fleet sailed round the world, it did so only as a show of power. The ability to handle differences short of conflict was an aspect of the action-reaction cycle of Western imperialism. The Berlin Congress of 1884–85 that delimited future colonies in Africa, and the notion of effective occupation helped settle what might otherwise have been serious problems. The achievement, however, should not be exaggerated because there were still a series of crises.

A learning cycle can more clearly be seen in the case of fighting methods. Far from simply seeking to impose the patterns of Western warfare elsewhere, armies responded to different environments and showed more flexibility in doing so than is often appreciated. This flexibility entailed learning how to respond to particular challenges. For example, in the Zulu war, the British developed more effective entrenched positions from which they were able to use their firepower with greater impact. Whereas at Isandlwana, where they were defeated in 1879, the British had had two cannon; at Ulundi, where they were victorious later that year, they deployed twelve cannon, as well as Gatling machine guns. The range of British commitments, and their relative importance for a state not engaged in conflict in Europe, ensured that the British proved particularly adept at adapting to the varied environments and changing patterns of irregular opposition.[17] Their practice and doctrine of colonial warfare developed, not least in encouraging an understanding of counter-insurgency. This was seen in particular in Charles Callwell's *Small Wars: Their Principles and Practise*, which went through three editions in 1896, 1899, and 1906, and which drew on a significant literature on the subject.[18] The age of "total war" thus produced the key text on "small wars."

Yet, a small war to the imperial power was generally very different to the people or state that experienced the process. Alongside the emphasis on an interaction with the power-plays of local interests given above, has to come the realization that conquest often entailed the goal of total victory in the shape of a surrender that, however conditional, led to a change in sovereignty. The changes that the latter brought helped lead to rebellions, and a series of them challenged formal, or informal, imperial control. Anglo-Egyptian dominance of Sudan was challenged by the rising of Muhammad Ahmad-Mahdi, the Mahdi, from 1881, and was only reimposed in 1898–99. Most challenges were more short-lived, the Boxer Rising in China in 1900 against foreign influence being a good instance. This rising, like the Mahdist opposition in Sudan, and that of the Pathans on the northwest frontier of India, and the Ghost Dance movement among American Natives, indicated the role of religion in mobilizing resistance to Western influence, expansion, or control. In New Zealand, the Maori use of religion included Christianity. The Mahdists and the Pathans were inspired by Islam, as was resistance to the Americans in Mindinao on the Philippines. This was an aspect of the quest for spiritual ways to offset material inferiority.

Within Western colonies, there were a series of challenges, including the Islamic rising in Fergana against the Russians in 1898, the Herero rebellion in German Southwest Africa in 1904–1905, the Nama rebellions there in 1890 and 1905–1909, the Maji-Maji rebellion in German East Africa in 1905, an anti-French revolt in Madagascar in 1898–1904, and an anti-British Zulu revolt in Natal in 1906. The ability of Western powers to suppress risings was not the same as controlling discontent, but the military set the parameters within which processes of integration, assimilation, and exploitation could be attempted. These processes all occurred in a world that appeared increasingly under imperial control, because of a fresh series of gains by Western powers in the last years of the nineteenth century and the early years of the new century. These were particularly extensive in Africa, where the French gained control over most of Morocco,[19] and the Italians established themselves in coastal Libya; and in Southeast Asia, where the Dutch seized most of the East Indies. All of these were bitterly contested, and in some areas, there were repeated defeats before success was finally achieved. This was true, for example, of the Spanish defeats at Annual (1921), and Tizzi Azza (1922) in the section of northern Morocco claimed by Spain. Elsewhere, resistance was less bitter, for example, in Madagascar; the French conquest of the island in 1895 involved battles such as Tsarasoatra, but the prime problems facing the French were those of logistics and disease.

At the same time, the variety of goals, types, and means of war-making, and therefore the different trajectories of development, can be seen, even at the height of Western power. There were also non-Western states that both consolidated their authority and expanded through conflict. These included China, Thailand, Ethiopia, and Afghanistan. As with Western powers, forts and garrisons consolidated their position, as with the Chinese in frontier regions and the Turks. The Turkish garrison of Medina held out against the Arab Revolt from June 1916 to January 1919. These non-Western states also witnessed large-scale internal conflict, as Japan had with the War of the Meiji Restoration in 1868, and the Satsuma Rebellion in 1877, and China with a series of failed rebellions in the nineteenth century and, more successfully, with the overthrow of Manchu imperial rule in 1911. For example, the death of Amir Dost Muhammad of Afghanistan in 1863 was followed by a succession war between his sons. The severe defeat of his heir, Sher Ali, at Sheikhabad in 1865, was followed by his deposition, and two of his brothers were declared joint rulers. This, however, did not end the warfare in Afghanistan. Ayub Khan, having been defeated by the British in 1880, when he sought to overthrow his cousin, Abdur Rahman, one of the grandsons of Dost Muhammad and the British choice as amir of Afghanistan, made a fresh attempt the following year once the British had withdrawn. Ayub Khan besieged

Kandahar, the leading position in the south, only to be beaten outside the walls by his cousin, a type of conflict long past in most of the world. Ayub Khan then fled to Persia. While the type of fighting was generally different to that within the West, there could still be parallels, for example, between the dispute over the succession to the Spanish throne that led to the Carlist Wars, and the struggles in Zululand in 1883–84 when King Cetshwayo, restored by the British, was attacked by opponents, being defeated at Msebe and Ondini in 1883.

Across much of the world, Western expansion ensured that if non-Western states sought also to expand, they increasingly faced the problem of confronting Western powers. A Mahdist force that invaded Egypt was destroyed by a British-commanded Egyptian army at Toski in August 1889. Such confrontation, however, was not always the case, at least directly, as shown by the conflict between Ethiopia and the Mahdists of Sudan, and by Chinese pressure on Tibet in 1909–10. Earlier, this had also been true of Egyptian expansion southward. For example, in 1872, Egyptian forces under Samuel Baker moved south into modern Uganda, fighting the Bunyoro. An attack by the latter was defeated at Masindi, but Baker had to retreat in the face of continued opposition. Success in battle had not brought the necessary verdict.

Subsequently, Egyptian forces became part of a lengthy Anglo-Egyptian struggle with the Mahdists of Sudan. The course of the conflict indicated the difficulty of moving into the interior successfully. In 1883, a force advancing from the port of Trinkitat to relieve nearby Tokar was routed, and another advance in 1891, this time intended to capture Tokar, was only successful after a hard-fought battle. These battles, as well as others such as at Hashin and Tofrek, tend to be ignored as a result of the focus on the decisive victory of the British at Omdurman in 1898, but that presents a misleading guide to the difficulties of the task and the major effort involved.

One consequence of the consolidation and expansion of governmental authority was that the role for enterprising individuals operating outside the ambit of the state was more limited than it had been earlier in the century. Indeed, increased control by central government was a feature of totality. A key turning point had occurred in Rivas in Nicaragua in May 1857, when the American adventurer William Walker was defeated. In 1860, he attempted a comeback, seizing Trujillo in Honduras, but he won no backing. The U.S. Navy had actively thwarted Walker's activities in 1857, and in 1860, a British warship turned him over to the Hondurans, who executed him. Filibustering was now only acceptable at the behest of the state.[20]

# CHAPTER 3

# Developments within the West, 1860–71

Contemporary attention was dominated in the United States by the American Civil War (1861–65), and in Europe by the Wars of German Unification in 1864 (Prussia versus Denmark), 1866 (Prussia versus Austria), and 1870–71 (Prussia versus France), and, to a lesser extent, the Wars of Italian Unification, particularly the conquest of much of southern Italy on behalf of the new state in 1860. The American Civil War was the longest of these conflicts, and the inability of the more populous and prosperous Union to knock out the Confederacy in 1861–62, followed by the related Confederate ability to mount powerful attacks in the East, led to a lengthy struggle in which there was a major mobilization of resources. Combined with organizational advances, particularly the transport and control potential offered by railway, steamship, and telegraphs to enhance the delivery, support, and predictability of the use of force, this has led to suggestions that the war saw the origins of modern and/or total warfare.[1] Indeed, it has been argued that a realization of the need for such a transforming effort was central to the Union's ability to overcome serious limitations and eventually win victory.[2] Capacity and capability, industrial and organizational, were certainly important to the Union's ability in 1864–65 to mount campaigns on all fronts, which prevented the Confederates from moving their troops, in response, between fronts.

Modernity, like totality, however, not only does not define the other, but is also a difficult concept. The term modernity needs to be employed with far greater care than when it was seen to describe the allegedly total warfare of the two world wars. Even if attention is directed solely to the world wars, they each encompassed a range of very different conflicts. These differences were prefigured by the contrasts between the conflicts of the 1860s and early 1870s in the United States and Europe, let alone those further afield. In part, these contrasts reflected a marked difference in goals. The American Civil War took far longer than the individual wars of German and Italian Unification, as well as America's war with Mexico in 1846–48, which in no way foreshadowed the totality of the Civil War. The goals of the latter were more extensive, one possible definition of "total" war. In the Wars of German Unification, Prussia aimed to defeat, not to destroy, Denmark, Austria, and France. In contrast, the Union forces had no such limited option: their goal was that the Confederacy cease to exist as an independent state. Another contrast was seen with Prussia's war of 1866, which is mistakenly seen, in general, only in terms of war with Austria. In fact, the war also embraced Austria's German allies. However, although Hanover, Hesse-Cassel, and Nassau (but not Bavaria) were annexed after they were defeated, these operations, unlike those of the Union forces in the Civil War, were against opponents who lacked strategic depth and who could be speedily defeated.

The goal of destroying the Confederacy entailed a magnitude of task that helps explain the idealism and tenacity of the volunteer forces on both sides, the length of the conflict, and thus the need to mobilize resources. This was taken further when slave emancipation also became a Union goal, one that made a compromise peace even less likely, and thus a limited war an implausible goal. By this point, however, Ulysses S. Grant had already given an "unconditional surrender" ultimatum in Tennessee to a rapturous Union reception. The recruitment of all-black regiments for the Union army in the second half of the war, numbering more than 120,000 men, was both a major operational help to the Union and also a symbol of what to the Confederacy was indeed a total war. Black troops were given combat roles, the action at Fort Wagner in July 1863 proving a key watershed, and could be the majority of a force. The force under John Newton that landed south of Tallahassee and advanced into Florida, before being defeated at Natural Bridge on March 6, 1865, was mostly black. The symbolic power of black troops was shown in February 1865, when the forces that occupied Charleston, where the first shots of the war had been fired, included black troops recruited from former Carolina slaves.[3] Racial tension also led to atrocities before and during the war.[4]

Idealism on both sides drew much on a strong sense of religious mission that helped empower the soldiers, and encourage them to prefer war for victory to negotiations. In the 1864 presidential election, 78 percent of the Union soldiers who voted did so for Abraham Lincoln, the more bellicose of the two candidates. Determination was not in short supply on either side. Alongside the non-negotiable character of Union versus disunion, came that of freedom versus slavery. Indeed, in July 1864, Jefferson Davis, the president of the Confederacy, responded to the terms offered in Lincoln's amnesty proclamation of December 1863 by declaring, "We are fighting for Independence—and that, or extermination, we will have . . . You may emancipate every Negro in the Confederacy, but we will be free. We will govern ourselves . . . if we have to see every Southern plantation sacked, and every Southern city in flames."[5]

The Union's task was made more difficult because—in contrast to the situation facing the Piedmontese in Italy in 1860, and the Prussians in 1866 and 1870—it was the Union's more poorly-commanded army that had to mount the strategic offensive. Command skills indeed proved important to all the wars of the period. In part, this was a matter of directing mass, although this was scarcely a novelty. Indeed, compared to the coordination issues of strategic and operational command in the Napoleonic Wars, most obviously in the campaigns of 1805 and 1812–15, it is difficult in 1860–71 to see any quantum change, despite the opportunities offered by new technologies.

The availability and impact of railroads and rifles offer comparisons between the wars of 1860–71, but it is problematic to seek comparison largely in terms of chronological simultaneity, rather than looking for non-simultaneous comparisons. The Napoleonic Wars indeed offer a more apt comparison to the American Civil War than the Wars of German Unification, both because of the scale of operations in the Napoleonic Wars and the American Civil War, and because of the absence, in both, of any war of the frontiers equivalent to that which Prussia waged with Austria in 1866. In 1814–15, the allies sought the overthrow of Napoleon, just as the Union sought to conquer the Confederacy, and in 1812–15, the scale of operations was from Moscow to the Portuguese frontier. This was unique in European history until the twentieth-century world wars. Even had Prussia fought all its opponents in 1864–71 simultaneously, as it studiously avoided doing, there would have been no equivalent to this scale.

The problems of mass and range on the strategic level were largely addressed by independent operations. In the French Revolutionary and Napoleonic Wars, this also reflected political realities, not only rivalries between the generals of Revolutionary France in the 1790s, but also the distinct forces and contrasting goals of France's rivals. In turn, Napoleon's ability to provide a degree of strategic direction and operational coordination gave France a major advantage over its opponents in the 1800s, although much also rested on grasping the initiative and attacking opponents sequentially. The last was also clearly an advantage for Prussia in 1864–71, but the mechanics of command had also been enhanced since 1815, to a degree that enabled the Prussian high command, under Helmuth von Moltke the Elder, to control the tempo of operations reasonably effectively. Telegraph and railway did not solve all problems, and were of very limited value on the battlefield, but they were considerably better than what had been available before. Yet, this capability cannot be divorced from the political context. More modest goals on the part of Prussia than those of Napoleon were also very important.

In the American Civil War, strategic coordination was limited, but the physical scale of operations was more akin to Napoleon's Europe than Moltke's sphere of operations in an individual war. Furthermore, there were important institutional limitations. Despite Lincoln's efforts, civilian government did not provide the necessary direction or coordination for either Union or Confederacy, but, in addition, there was no effective general staff for either: the War Board created by the Union in 1862 was short-lived. As a result, army-navy co-operation was generally, although not invariably, poor on both sides, while generals fought in particular regions with only episodic strategic oversight or operational co-operation. Furthermore, they had had no experience of directing the size of forces they were expected to command: corps-level organization was unprecedented in America. Indeed, alongside the flaws of the Union generals, their Confederate colleagues were not nearly as brilliant as their post-war collective reputation. This was abundantly clear with Joseph Johnston, Beauregard, Bragg, and Pemberton, while the reputations of Stonewall Jackson and Albert Sidney Johnston were enhanced and preserved by their early deaths. The Napoleonic legacy in the American Civil War was seen more in tactical and operational, than in strategic, respects: the impact of the prevalent interpretation of the Napoleonic Wars encouraged an operational emphasis on interior lines and defeating opponents in detail; while there was a tactical stress on turning the opponent's flank and on the ethos of gallant advances on enemy positions.

As with conflict throughout the period covered by this book, it can be argued that these ideas and ethos failed to take note of successive improvements in firepower technology, and the destructive capability this endowed on the defensive. Yet, as an instance of the danger of coming to a simple conclusion, it is also pertinent to suggest that, as later with World War I, most generals were aware of this strength, but could see no other way to achieve their goals. Attacking reflected more than cultural factors and cleaving to outdated notions. It also appeared the way to fix opponents, to force engagements, and to win ground, each of which was an important objective. This focus on the offensive has been seen as made disastrous by the increased use of rifled muskets by defending forces,[6] but it has also been argued that the potential of the weaponry was not grasped during the Civil War, in part as a result of inexperience.[7] Indeed, bayonet charges remained important.[8]

If attacking thus brought together strategic, operational, and tactical perspectives, the emphasis on the offensive also posed serious problems in coordination. Training of staff officers gave the Prussian army a coherence its opponents lacked; and the Americans conformed more to the French system of muddling through.[9] Lacking peacetime conscription, the Americans relied heavily on untrained citizen-soldiers, even at senior levels. As basic competence was low, this was a serious problem. The absence of effective command structures meant that mediocrities were not tested adequately before being entrusted with independent command, nor removed sufficiently rapidly thereafter. Histories of particular armies were frequently an account of squandered opportunities.[10]

Prussian staff officers, in contrast, were given an assured place in a coordinated command system, and the system of joint responsibility between commanders and staff officers provided not only a necessary coherence, but also a means to ensure the high level of forward planning that was valuable in order to maintain the effectiveness of offensive operations. Prussian operational art provided generally informed responsiveness under pressure, and therefore an ability to achieve victory despite all the fog and friction of war. It was also central to a self-conscious intellectual professionalization of war. In contrast, although the Confederate general James Longstreet organized an effective staff, and then used it sensibly to take over particular tasks, the Union and Confederate forces were more dependent on individual ability and initiative.[11] This was the long-established practice of command, but one more suited to the battlefield that could be scanned by one pair of eyes than to more complex campaigning.

Both sides in the Civil War took longer than the Prussians to appreciate the value of organizing artillery at corps level, so that it could be massed in more than an ad hoc fashion, and to develop effective systems for accumulating, assessing, and using intelligence, which was an important adjunct to staff work. Yet, progress was made. Grant, for example, revitalized the Bureau of Military Information.[12] The systematization of intelligence was (and is) an aspect of change that properly deserves to be described as modernization. Information was not always pursued in such a fashion, but when it was, as by the Blockade Board founded by the Union's Navy Department in 1861, it could be very effective.

The Union and Confederacy, moreover, faced command tasks that the Prussians did not encounter. The most significant were the creation of new military systems in the context of an unpredictable civil war, but there was also the issue of preparing for, and waging, naval and amphibious warfare. This involved a range of environments, from rivers and inshore waters to deep-sea operations, as well as responding to the possibilities of new technology, particularly the ironclad warship, but also mines and submarines, in tactical, operational, and strategic realms. The Union was superior in resources for shipbuilding and at sea, and therefore able to mount both a blockade and amphibious operations.[13] Each reflected and contributed to an enhanced capability compared to America's earlier wars, but it is also useful to note the contrasts between capability and execution. In part, this reflected the long-term problem in amphibious warfare of translating the force projection it offered into a capacity for mobility, and retaining the initiative for troops once landed. The contrast between capability and execution could also be seen with supply systems. Alongside the emphasis on the role of the railway, it is instructive to note the continued importance of wagons, which, in turn, ensured a major need for forage and for the shodding of horses.[14]

Command skills notwithstanding, the destructive impact of weaponry was also evident in the Wars of German Unification. In the Franco-Prussian War, German breech-loading, steel-tubed Krupp's artillery was the key battle-winning tool, although, as ever, it was the use made of technology that was crucial. Departing from the Napoleonic tradition of gun lines laying down frontal fire, the Germans operated in artillery masses: mobile batteries formed by enterprising officers, which converged on key points, annihilated them with cross fires, and then moved on. The effective use of artillery as an integral part of tactical and operational planning, and execution, overcame the impressive defensive role of the French infantry. The latter, indeed, inflicted heavy casualties on German attacking formations. As a result of the French chassepot rifle, German losses were thirteen times higher than they had been at the hands of the Austrians in 1866. The chassepot's rounds had a tendency to tumble through the body, smashing bones, tearing tissue, and blowing exit holes four times bigger than the entire wound: German casualties mentioned the "razor pain" of the French bullet. As a consequence of these casualties, Wilhelm I did not initially accept that Gravelotte was a German victory, although it had, in fact, severed France from its principal army.

Despite the experience of costly and unsuccessful infantry attacks in both the American Civil War and the Franco-Prussian War, there was a general view that the moral force of attacking infantry would prevail on the battlefield. Indeed, the Russians in 1877–78 sought to emulate the Germans, launching frontal attacks on fortified positions, only to lose heavily to Turkish riflemen, particularly at Plevna, which instead fell finally to siege.[15]

If these lessons about the impact of attacking infantry scarcely suggested much of a contrast with the Napoleonic Wars, there were also intimations of a different type of war, each of which has been seen as anticipating elements of what has been termed total warfare. Aside from the resource-mobilization and military-organizational elements already mentioned, three repay consideration: first, at the tactical and operational levels, the signs of trench warfare seen in the American Civil War; second, in the same conflict, the willingness to target civilian property in order to weaken opponents; and, third, in the American Civil War,[16] and in the last stage of the Franco-Prussian War, signs of insurrectionary and counter-insurrectionary warfare.

Trench warfare did not originate in Virginia in 1864–65. For example, the Anglo-French force that besieged Sevastopol (Russia's leading naval base on the Black Sea) during the Crimean War in 1855, had to face a kind of trench warfare that was different to earlier sieges. The defending Russian army was strongly entrenched outside the town, making able use of earth defenses, and supported by more than one thousand cannon. In part in order to help overcome them, the Allies fired 1,350,000 rounds of artillery ammunition during the siege. The scale of operations suggests a clear difference of order to major sieges a century earlier, for example, the French siege of the major Dutch fortress of Bergen-op-Zoom in 1747. By way, however, of illustrating the more general difficulty of making comparisons, the killing of wounded British prisoners by the Russians in the Crimean War might, instead, seem to anticipate the savageries of fighting between German and Soviet forces on the Eastern Front ninety years later, but to a British cavalryman, the frame of reference was rather that of conflict with non-Westerners. He wrote of the Russians, "They are perfect savages."[17]

Although the scale was impressive, nevertheless, the trenches near Sevastopol were more an aspect of a traditional siege than the development of field entrenchments seen in Virginia in 1864. The latter were enhanced by barbed wire, originally devised to pen cattle. Its first recorded battlefield appearance was at Drewry's Bluff in May 1864. The entrenchments—for example, at the lengthy battle of Spotsylvania in 1864—were designed to offer troops protection in response to the weight of fire, and looked toward those in World War I, although the more fluid nature of operations ensured that they were less developed than in that conflict. If defensive firepower, the trenches, and the more limited role of cavalry in 1864–65, all suggested anticipations, there were also important differences. It was not necessary to resist lengthy bombardments by heavy guns firing plunging shots, as in World War I; nor, indeed, was there reinforced concrete with which to protect positions. Trenches in Civil War battlefields were shallower than on the Western Front in World War I, and were designed to protect against non-plunging shot, although deep trenches were dug during the drawn-out siege of Petersburg. The great difference was that, in America, there was no equivalent to the Channel and Switzerland to anchor the trenches at each end, as there was to be on the Western Front, and, as a result, there was no stalemate and the trenches could be outflanked, as Grant did with Robert E. Lee in 1865.

In addition, as a sign of total war, the willingness to seize and, even more, destroy civilian property was very marked during the American Civil War, although initially there was an emphasis on a conciliatory approach, which, it was believed, would win over support, not least on the model of the Union slave states, especially Maryland, whose support for the Union was very important in moving the area of combat south. Whereas George B. McClellan, the Union general in chief in 1862, had opposed attacks on private property, which to him included slavery, Ulysses S. Grant, however, pressed such attacks from the spring of 1862, in order to hit Confederate supplies and, thus, warmaking. Moreover, Union confidence that the war could be ended swiftly evaporated, and this led to political support for rigor. John Pope, commander of the Union's Army of Virginia in 1862, destroyed a large amount of property, in accordance with a hardening of the Union strategy from July 1862, as Lincoln told his cabinet that he would issue an Emancipation Proclamation and also signed the Second Confiscation Act. This was declaring war on the culture, ideology, and economy of an entire people. Such harshness was not novel, and had been employed in counter-insurgency warfare in Europe earlier in the century—for example, by Napoleonic forces in Calabria and Spain—but the Americans were certainly not used to it, although they were willing to apply such techniques against Native Americans, while Confederate cavalry had also targeted Union private property. Advances into hostile territory led to treatment of civilians that aroused outrage, and to clashes with them and other irregulars that in turn led to an escalation into what has been termed "hard war."

Ruthlessness also served operational ends, enabling Union generals, such as Grant round Vicksburg in 1863, to live off the land. Furthermore, the destruction of transport infrastructure, which badly hit civil society, was also intended to limit the Confederate ability to respond militarily to Union moves.

Operational goals, however, were not the main purpose of devastation. Marching from Atlanta to the Atlantic in late 1864, William T. Sherman set out to destroy the will of Confederate civilians by making "Georgia howl." Private property was devastated, and the infrastructure crippled. The *Confederate Union* of December 6, 1864, offered an apocalyptic comparison, "if an army of Devils, just let loose from the bottomless pit, were to invade the country they could not be much worse than Sherman's army."[18] The ability to spread devastation unhindered across the Southern hinterland helped destroy Confederate civilian faith in the war, hamstrung the strategic reserve, defense in depth and economic resources provided by the size of the Confederacy, and made the limitations and penalties likely to accrue from the outbreak of guerrilla warfare apparent. Similarly, the Great Valley of Virginia was devastated by Philip Sheridan in 1864, in order to deny its resources to the Confederacy, while, turning north toward the rear of the Confederate forces in Virginia, Sherman extended his ravages to South Carolina in early 1865.[19] Union strategy hit both Confederate resources and the Confederate will to fight. The latter collapsed in 1865, with the fall of the capital, Richmond, such that it was not necessary for the Union forces to destroy their badly-battered opponents in order to win the war. Although the term "total war" was not employed in this period, much of the application of the concept rests on the practice of Grant, Sherman, and Sheridan. Furthermore, this is held to have been of lasting impact, not least with the application of the methods of Sherman and Sheridan (rather than those of Grant at Petersburg and Cold Harbor) subsequently against the Native Americans.[20]

The devastation of civil society was also seen in the Franco-Prussian War, particularly with the German bombardment and 133-day siege of Paris. For the French, this was a trauma akin to that of the sack of Rome in 1527 for the Italian Renaissance. Although Paris had been captured by Napoleon's enemies in 1814, and occupied anew in 1815, there had not been devastation similar to that in 1870. The latter was captured by newspaper writers, illustrators, and painters, for example, in the devastation depicted by the painter Camille Corot in his "Le rêve: Paris incendié par les Prussiens,"[21] although the suppression of the Paris Commune in 1871 by the forces of the French Third Republic also caused great damage. War was even more devastating in Latin America. The Paraguayan War or War of the Triple Alliance (1864–70) had a disastrous (although controversial) consequence for the demographics of defeated Paraguay, whose forces included young boys,[22] but also serious consequences for its rivals.[23]

Yet, the deficiencies of victory had also become apparent in the latter stages of the Franco-Prussian War. After successes in the decisive battles fought near the frontier in 1870, the Germans encountered difficulties as they advanced further into France, not least of which were supply problems and opposition from a hostile population. Each reflected the extent to which the Germans were not prepared for, and did not want, a "total" war; but their response to the latter was to be seen as a significant stage in the development of "total war."[24] The resources for a conquest of France were simply not present, and this was not an option the government or Moltke sought. Instead, they wanted a swift and popular conflict, with relatively low casualties. The rate at which resources were used up militated against a long-run struggle, a factor that was to force a much higher rate of economic mobilization during the two world wars when it became clear that the conflicts would not be short. Costs also encouraged demands for reparations, and the armistice announced on January 28, 1871, stipulated that France was to pay 200 million francs.

Prefiguring the two world wars, the Germans in 1870–71 also experienced a degree of political uncertainty not seen in the American Civil War. Whereas the defeated Danish and Austrian governments had been in a position to negotiate terms, the Germans were now obliged to fight on because the defeated Napoleon III was replaced in 1870 by the Third Republic under a Government of National Defense that was determined not to surrender territory as the price of peace, and that was able to appeal to the tradition of republican enthusiasm, reviving the idea of revolutionary war associated with the 1790s. Although enthusiasm was severely limited in some areas, the numbers of troops the French were able to raise were formidable. In January 1871, 84,000 National Guardsmen assembled for the unsuccessful attempt to recapture Versailles.

In the event, the new French armies were outfought, and the insurgent tactics of the *francs-tireurs* (French deserters or civilians who fought back) also did not seriously inconvenience the Germans. Nevertheless, the Germans responded harshly, treating the *francs-tireurs* as criminals, not soldiers. Summary executions helped dampen opposition, but they were also part of a pattern of German brutality that included the taking of hostages, the shooting of suspects (as well as of those actually captured in arms), the mutilation of prisoners, and the destruction of towns and villages, such as Châteaudun. In part, this reflected German frustration at the difficulty of protecting increasingly lengthy supply routes, as well as the problems posed by hostile citizen volunteers who did not wear uniforms and were impossible to identify once they had discarded their rifles. In response, the Germans adopted a social typology that prefigured those of the following century, treating every "blue smock," the customary clothes of the French worker, as a potential guerrilla.[25]

In practice, guerrilla warfare only played a minor role in the conflict. German casualties as a result of this warfare were fewer than one thousand, compared, for example, to the 297 German soldiers who died from smallpox and the approximately 180,000 German civilians who died from the same disease as a result of infection from French prisoners in nearby prisoner-of-war camps. However, the idea of such violence threatened not only to introduce a level of "friction" and uncertainty that the Germans did not want operationally, but also to usher in a chaos that they could not accept psychologically. The use by regulars of violence against civilians suspected of opposition, in order to ensure that the regulars had a monopoly of force, was not new, but it entered a deadlier cycle when it was seen by the Germans as necessary and became an automatic response.

As yet, however, the notion of popular warfare was not pushed hard. Despite the Partisan Ranger Act of 1861, the Confederate political and military leadership proved largely unwilling to encourage the guerrilla warfare that, while particularly important in Appalachia and in the Missouri-Kansas region, was not so in crucial war zones. Furthermore, some of what, describing the American Civil War, is now termed guerrilla warfare (with the misleading implication that it was not waged by regulars) can better be described as irregular warfare by regulars, particularly engaged in raiding activities. The Union forces were able to counter these methods, both by defensive means (blockhouses, patrols) and by action designed to provide the exemplary threat of retribution and/or to find and engage those directly involved.[26]

Nevertheless, the Franco-Prussian War had made apparent the difficulty of ending a war. Military planning could not control the political environment. This lesson was driven home in both world wars, as the deficiencies of apparently impressive plans, and hitherto victorious forces, were exposed by the German and Japanese inability to understand the wider context. In particular, they did not appreciate that victory depends on persuading the other side to accept a given equation of military capability that it may, otherwise, be able, and willing, first to reject and, then, to thwart.

Another instance of the difficulty of closing a conflict occurred in Mexico, where French intervention from 1861–62 in the civil war between Liberals and Conservatives—in order to establish a client state under Napoleon III's candidate, the Austrian Archduke Maximilian—was unsuccessful. Advances led to the fall of positions, as when the French successfully besieged Puebla in 1863, or when they captured Oaxaca in February 1865, having built roads in order to bring up their siege guns; but the French then found it difficult to consolidate control. Guerrilla conflict played a much bigger role in Mexico than in the American Civil War or the German Wars of Unification. It helped compensate the Liberals for failures in battle, as at San Luis Potosí in 1863. However, conventional warfare was also significant in Mexico in eventually defeating the Franco-Austrian forces and their Conservative Mexican allies. For example, in 1866, the Republicans under Porfirio Diaz besieged an Imperial force at Oaxaca, repulsed an Austrian relief column at La Carbonera, and then received the surrender of Oaxaca. The following year, the Liberals were victorious. Puebla, Queretara, and Mexico City were successfully besieged, while Imperial-Mexican forces were defeated in battle, as at San Lorenzo. The execution of prisoners, including Maximilian, helped underline victory. Such executions were a frequent consequence of battles, whichever side won. They were designed to intimidate in a situation in which it was difficult for either side to prevail. In part, this difficulty arose because neither side could deploy the necessary resources. Furthermore, a lack of political cohesion helped ensure that there was no center of gravity, control over which dictated lasting victory.

In contrast, a verdict was delivered in 1860, in the Ecuadorian civil war between the rivals Guillermo Franco and the Conservative Gabriel García, based in the rival centers of Guayaquil and Quito, when Juan José Flores, a former president commanding the Conservative army, won a decisive victory at Bodegas. Flores then advanced on Guayaquil, Franco went into exile, and Moreno was president until 1865.

As a reminder of the variety of European conflict in this period, it is instructive to note the unsuccessful Polish attempt to gain independence from Russian rule in 1863. Furthermore, the struggle for Italian unification involved not only the regular forces of the Piedmontese state, but also the irregulars organized by Giuseppe Garibaldi. The latter were successful in overthrowing Bourbon rule in Sicily and Naples in 1860, defeating Bourbon forces at Calatafimi, Palermo, and Milazzo in Sicily, but Garibaldi was less successful in 1867, when he tried to end the temporal power of the papacy in central Italy. Although papal troops were defeated at Monterotondo, French regulars smashed Garibaldi's men at Mentana near Rome. Garibaldi's role in furthering Italian unification was not invariably successful, but underlined the different forms that successful forces could take. As in other conflicts, the role of morale was important. At Milazzo, the Bourbon army lost fewer men, but fell back.

Discussion of nineteenth-century warfare focuses on land conflict, while consideration of total war concentrates on the same subject with the addition, for the twentieth century, of strategic bombing, naval blockade, and submarine warfare. There is a tendency to neglect discussion of naval capability and warfare in general discussions of warfare for the period after the Napoleonic Wars ended in 1815 until the Russo-Japanese War of 1904–1905. This owes something to the limited nature of such conflict in 1860–1903, but underrates the extent to which the capability for total warfare was further advanced at sea than on land. This was certainly the case in terms of creating the means to destroy opposing naval forces, and therefore to win a command of the sea that could be employed to strategic effect, the thesis of the American naval strategist Alfred Thayer Mahan's *The Influence of Sea Power upon History, 1660–1783* (1890) and of British admiral Philip Colomb's *Naval Warfare: Its Ruling Principles and Practice Historically Treated* (1891). There was a parallel between the benefits supposed to stem from command of the sea and those that were being allegedly gained from the scrambles for empire.

The pace of technological advance at sea was considerable. Completed in 1861, HMS *Warrior* was a revolutionary ship design, the first large sea-going iron-hulled warship. There were also major advances in steam technology, with results in terms of fuel efficiency, speed, range, and reliability. In the 1860s, high-pressure boilers were combined with the compound engine, and in 1874, the triple-expansion marine engine was introduced, although it was not used in warships until the 1880s. This engine was followed by the water tube boiler. By 1885, only distant-service ships still required sail, an equivalent of the use of cavalry in imperial warfare. The pace of change was very high, a key aspect of modern military capability. This was true not only of propulsion, but also of armament and armor. The practice of locating heavy guns in an armored casement began with the British *Research* in 1864. Two all-steel cruisers were completed for the British navy in 1879.

Technological possibilities were translated into practice through investment—Britain, in the 1880s, spending on its navy close to the combined figure of the next two high-spending powers, France and Russia. Thus, at sea, as on land, the innovations and events of the 1860s created the potential for major developments in capability. Perceived need, thereafter, was the crucial factor. Britain had won the ironclad-building race with France in 1858–61, which was confirmed by France's defeat by Prussia in 1870–71, as it led France to focus on strengthening its army for a future war with Germany. As a result, Britain enjoyed a global lead, prefiguring that of the United States from the 1940s. This offered Britain a world-wide capability that was more potent than she had enjoyed in the age of sail. To those on the receiving end, this was formidable.

# CHAPTER 4
# Uneasy Peace and Small Wars, 1872–1913

All periods of peace are inter-war, and each can be seen in terms of digesting the lessons of one conflict and anticipating (or not) the likely nature of another. The latter is the dominant theme in the analysis of the military history of this period. This reflects a sense of World War I as particularly horrific and also as uniquely unanticipated in many of its features. This is an approach that encourages the attempt to search for explanations in terms of failure. Accompanying this is the extent to which, thanks to their general staffs, their large peacetime forces, and their industrial strength, the Great Powers were able to plan and prepare for conflict to a novel extent. This guides attention, and also provides an obvious link to the previous point. The conflicts of the period 1872–1913 can be absorbed to this model by asking whether contemporaries appreciated the lessons they offered for the development of warfare. The entire period thus becomes an object account of how lessons were not learned.

While containing much of value, this approach is incomplete. As an analysis, it suffers from a serious degree of teleology. Not only was it unclear that a major war would break out, despite the changes in the international system in 1848–71,[1] but it was also uncertain which powers would be involved and in what configuration, while the likely course and nature of any such conflict was very ambiguous. As far as the powers were concerned, the role of Britain and, even more, Turkey, Italy, and the United States, in any major European war, remained uncertain until the 1910s, and the last three remained neutral at the outset of World War I, with Italy joining Britain and France in 1915, and departing from its pre-war alignment with Germany and Austria. Earlier, in the 1870s, it was unclear that the key alignments would necessarily be, as they were immediately preceding World War I, Austria-Germany versus Russia-France.

Possible alliance permutations affected strategy and, more generally, the relationship between goals, force structures, and strategic choices. Rather than necessarily seeing pre-1914 military processes (both planning and practice) as flawed, it is worth considering the degree to which the political direction bears the responsibility for eventual failure.[2] This was partly a matter of the understandably unfixed nature of parameters and goals. In addition, there was a widespread unwillingness to consider the nature of alternatives in the event of failure. This was due partially to an emphasis on willpower, and the related reluctance to countenance the possibility of failure.

Considering the period in light of the anticipation of World War I risks drawing only a limited range of lessons from the developments and conflicts of the period. The general emphasis on certain conflicts leads to a tendency to neglect others, particularly those of 1872–97, for example, the Russo-Turkish War of 1877–78, and the War of the Pacific (1879–83) involving Bolivia, Chile, and Peru. This is part of a more general problem of studying conflicts in bands, with a rhythm such that the first band in each pair is generally neglected. For instance, far more attention is devoted to the Seven Years' War (1756–63) or, as it is sometimes called, French and Indian War (1754–63) than to those of the Polish (1733–35) and Austrian (1740–48) Successions, and to the Napoleonic War (1803–15) than to the French Revolutionary Wars (1792–1802). Moreover, the wars of 1816–53, not least the successes of the French in Spain, the Austrians in Italy, and the Russians in Poland and Hungary, tend to be neglected in favor of a focus on the conflicts of 1854–71. The chronology is not precisely the same in the New World, but there are also conflicts that are neglected. For example, the Central American conflict at the start of the 1850s, in which the president of Guatemala, José Rafael Carrera, defeated an attempt by El Salvador and Honduras to aid his Liberal opponent, and then forced Conservative governments on El Salvador and Honduras, is generally neglected. More generally, there is a lack of attention to conflict in Latin America between the wars of independence of the 1810s and 1820s, and the Paraguayan War of 1864–70.

Neglect of the period 1872–97 reflects a relative lack of interest in Latin America and Eastern Europe, while the Chinese success in overcoming Yakub Bey of Khokand, which culminated in May 1877, with the capture of his capital at Turfan and his suicide, is almost entirely overlooked. In part, this neglect of the period was because full-scale wars did not occur. Like the United States after the Civil War, Brazil after the War of the Triple Alliance did not use its large army in order to pursue territorial expansion through war with its neighbors, despite frontier disputes with Argentina and others. There was also no sustained large-scale conflict between Russia and Turkey.

The Russo-Turkish War of 1877–78 and the War of the Pacific of 1879–83 were both instructive. Topical flavor is lent to this crisis by the role of Balkan atrocities in the background to the first. Such atrocities were far from new, but the press attention to the brutal nature of the Turkish crushing of the Bulgarian rising in 1876 was novel, and helped to discredit the Turks with European public opinion. The extent to which the rebels themselves massacred many Muslims was ignored, while the numbers of Bulgarians killed were considerably exaggerated. Russian Pan-Slavism led to the dispatch of many volunteers to help the Serbs when they declared war on the Turks in 1876, only for the Serbs to be defeated.

Russia proved a more formidable foe, although the Russo-Turkish War underlined the tactical problems with frontal attacks, particularly when poorly coordinated. The war also demonstrated the operational disadvantages arising from essentially untrained commanders appointed through patronage, in this case, the relatives of Tsar Alexander II. This system undermined efforts at military reform.[3] At the same time, having crossed the Danube at Svistov in June 1877, rapidly bombarded the garrison at Nicopolis into capitulation the following month, and finally, after unsuccessful attacks, starved Plevna into surrender in December 1877, the Russians encircled another Turkish army at the Shipka pass the following month, and then pressed on to take Plovdiv and Adrianople, and to threaten Constantinople. The harshness of winter brought no end to the fighting. On the other side of the Black Sea, the Russians also tried storm tactics, failing at the major fortified city of Erzurum, but succeeding at Kars, both in November 1877. The Austrians were more successful the following year, bombarding and storming Turkish-held Sarajevo in order to establish a protectorate over Bosnia-Herzegovina.

The War of the Pacific indicated the need for frontal assaults and storming, for example, by the Chileans of the port of Arica in 1880, in part because, in what was a conflict of rapid advances, there was no time to bring up heavy artillery in order to attack fortified positions.

The war also indicated the ready resort to devastation as a strategic means. In 1880, the Chileans used their naval strength to attack the Peruvian coast in order to inflict material damage and underline a sense of vulnerability, rather as Sherman had done. Railways and ports were destroyed or damaged, and private property seized. The previous year, having gained a dominant naval position as a result of victory off Punta Angamos, the Chileans landed at Pisagua, captured Dolores, defeated a Peruvian force, and then captured Iquique.[4]

Both wars, nevertheless, showed that it was possible to keep conflict limited, as did the wars of 1898–1913. The War of the Pacific did not attract international intervention, while, in the Russo-Turkish War, British pressure led the Russians to moderate their aims, and the conflict did not escalate. Another neglected war, a month-long conflict between Greece and Turkey in 1897 that arose from Greek border incursions, was also contained in part because Russian intervention deterred the victorious Turks from advancing on Athens: the Turks had successfully attacked at Mati. In Crete, the fighting was characterized by both sides committing atrocities.

Aside from the practice of neglecting particular wars, there is an understandable tendency in the military history of the period to underrate developments that left scant impact in conflict, such as shifts in fortification methods. For example, casemented forts, which were vulnerable to new guns, were replaced by more widespread fortifications constructed of earth.[5] Improvements made with rifled artillery interacted with this process, which was comparable to that between stronger armaments and armor in surface shipping.

The customary emphasis is on the Spanish-American (1898), Second Boer (1899–1901), Russo-Japanese (1904–5), and First and Second Balkan (1912–13) Wars, each of which was indeed important, but, as with the wars of the 1860s, this distracts attention from the variety of conflict in the period. One important aspect of this variety was the frequency of rebellions. These tend to attract attention when, as in 1861 with the Confederacy, they led to the formation of what were in effect new regular forces, but these were atypical of civil conflict. The extensive range of the latter included separatist risings, such as (unsuccessfully) in Poland against Russian rule in 1863, in Cuba against Spanish rule,[6] and in Albania against Turkish rule in 1910–11. Civil warfare also arose from opposition to control by the center, for example, in southern Italy to the authority of the new Italian state, especially in Sicily in 1866, and, repeatedly, in Brazil and Mexico,[7] or from demands for political change in the metropole.

The insurgency in Cuba indicated both the difficulties of counter-insurgency operations for regular forces, especially for a weak power like Spain, and the nature of low-level conflict. This was a war in which raids and ambushes played a major role, and in which control over supplies was important both to the regulars and to the insurgents. Preventing opponents' access to supplies, therefore, was the goal of many operations. Thus, in December 1895, the insurgents attacked a Spanish column at Mal Tiempo, capturing two hundred rifles and replenishing supplies of ammunition. The use of machetes in this attack underlines the extent to which insurgency warfare still involved hand-to-hand conflict. In turn, the Spaniards sought to fix their opponents, so that they could use their firepower, as at Manacal earlier that month when Spanish artillery helped drive the insurgents from a defensive position. The Americans employed the same tactics in the Philippines against Filipino opposition from 1899. The Cuban rebellion against Spain ended when the Americans defeated Spain in 1898 and Cuba became independent.

The role of the military in many states in maintaining authority in the regions was a reminder of their long-term part in the consolidation of power, and, indeed, in the extent to which the enforcement of sovereignty was a slow process in many states, and one that had to be maintained as notions of rightful authority were frequently contested. In parts of Latin America, force was the key element in attempts to gain power in the metropole. Contested elections, for example, led to risings, as in Argentina in 1874. In addition, in Argentina in 1870, there were also serious problems due to rebellions in particular regions. State building involved force, but so also did the normal processes of politics, while institutional struggles, such as in Chile in 1890–91, led to civil war. Many of these conflicts have been ignored in military history texts, creating the misleading impression that the sole wars in South America during this period were the War of the Triple Alliance and the War of the Pacific.

In fact, there was also a series of lower-level conflicts. Chile, for example, was not only involved in the War of the Pacific, but was also affected by civil war in 1890–91, when the army backed the president, and the navy supported the eventually victorious Congress.[8] Low-level conflicts included international wars that have received limited attention. Border disputes were a particular point of contention, as between Ecuador and Colombia, with Ecuador defeated at Tulcán in 1862 and at Cuaspud the following year. Divisions within states related to personalities and policies, and domestic conflicts overlapped with international ones, Conservatives and Liberals both looking for support from foreign colleagues. This was particularly the case in Central America. The collapse of the United Provinces of Central America, the state that had governed Guatemala, Honduras, Nicaragua, and Costa Rica from the end of union with Mexico in 1823 until separation in 1838, had left a series of small states each close together. Their rivalries interacted with domestic conflicts. For example, in 1863, Guatemalan forces invaded El Salvador, only to be beaten at Coatepeque, after which Salvadoran forces intervened in Nicaragua in order to back a Liberal rising. Gerardo Barrios Espinosa, the president of El Salvador, was defeated at San Felipe by Tomás Martinez, the president of Nicaragua, and then faced a renewed Guatemalan invasion, backed by Nicaragua. Besieged in his capital, Barrios surrendered, and Guatemala installed a new president, Francisco Dueñas. Guatemala and Nicaragua also succeeded in ensuring that their client prevailed in Honduras.

Foreign intervention was also frequent elsewhere, as in 1864–65, when Brazilian forces aided the Colorados of Uruguay in their successful conflict with the Blancos. Rebellions affected the ability to take part in international conflict. In 1867, while at war with Paraguay, Argentina was affected by a rising in the West, but government forces were victorious at San Ignacio. The political history of state after state recorded the role of force. The Liberals defeated the Conservatives in Mexico in 1860 at Guadalajara, Calderón, and Calpulalpam. In Colombia in 1860–61, Tomás Cipriano de Mosquera, president in 1845–49, rebelled and regained his position, which he held until 1864, and then again in 1866–67. At Pavón in 1861, Bartolomé Mitre and the army of Buenos Aires defeated Santiago Derqui, president of Argentina, which paved the way for Mitre to become president until 1868. In 1870, an attempt to overthrow President Vicente Cerna of Guatemala, who had played a major role in the Central American conflict in 1863, was defeated, but he was overthrown in 1871 by the Liberals in renewed conflict, the battle of San Lucas Sacatepéquez proving crucial. One of the Liberal commanders, Miguel Garcia Granados, then became president.

Neighboring Honduras and El Salvador went to war in 1871, each concerned that the other was backing internal disaffection. The Salvadoran forces were victorious at Pasaquina, but could not gain control of Honduras. In turn, the Salvadoran rebel Santiago González, backed by Honduras, defeated the army of the Salvadoran president, Francisco Dueñas, at Santa Ana and became president, ending the war, only to attack Honduras successfully the following year: victorious at

Comayagua, he overthrew President José María Medina. In 1876, Guatemala, in turn, invaded El Salvador, winning victories at Apaneca and Pasaquina, and installing a client president. Also in 1876, former president José María Medina regained power in Honduras by winning the battle of La Esperanza, only to be speedily defeated at the San Marcos River and at El Naranja, and then fleeing. The same year, the Diaz revolt broke out in Mexico. Unwilling to accept defeat in the presidential election of 1875, Porfirio Diaz, a veteran of the Mexican-French War, seized power after a series of battles, including Icamole, San Juan Epatlán, and Tecoac.

Soon after, the Liberal government of Colombia resumed its conflict with Conservative rebels, defeating them in 1877 at La Donjuana and Manizales. The victorious general Julián Trujillo became president from 1878 to 1880. In turn, a Liberal revolt in Colombia in 1899 was defeated at Palonegro in 1900, a closing scene in a long pattern of conflict that had begun in 1839.[9] Similarly, Venezuela was involved in civil war in 1892, 1898–99, and, more seriously, in 1902–1903. President Cipriano Castro seized power by force in 1899, after a struggle over the presidency, the "Revolution of Liberal Restoration," which had begun in 1898, and culminated in his victory at Tocuyito in 1899. In 1902, he was confronted by a revolution led by General Manual Antonio Matos, who was the victor in initial clashes, only to be heavily defeated at La Victoria (1902), a major engagement, and, finally, at Ciudad Volivar (1903). Four years later, Nicaragua successfully invaded Honduras in a successful attempt to overthrow the president, defeating the Hondurans at San Marcos de Colón, Namasique, and Maraita, and capturing the capital. In Mexico, in February 1913, a military coup by General Félix Diaz against President Francisco Madero was successful when Madero was abandoned by the commander of the government forces, General Victoriano Huerta, who became president. Madero was murdered. This, in turn, led to a revolt by Francisco (Pancho) Villa and Venustiano Carranza.

Due to force-space ratios, and the difficulty of sustaining forces, much of the fighting was a matter of rapid advances and short battles. Towns were usually stormed rather than besieged. As with Latin American civil wars from the outset, the killing of prisoners was frequent, both because the facilities for holding them were limited, and in order to hit opponents' morale and to intimidate others from lending them support. In Mexico in August 1913, for example, Villa stormed San Andrés, defeating a federal force and then executing more than three hundred prisoners. Two months later, he stormed Torréon, executing the officers who were captured. The willingness of troops to resist was a key factor in the fighting. When Villa attacked Torréon again, in March-April 1914, the resistance was much fiercer, and he lost heavily before taking the town after a week's fighting. Attitudes toward civilians and prisoners in this period tend to be discussed in terms of the situation in Europe and in the United States, but the situation in Latin America is instructive as it indicates the degree to which restraints on violence were limited and the extent to which the situation did not change. Aside from the killing of military prisoners, there was also the slaughter of civilians and the destruction of property by regulars and irregulars alike, and the latter frequently overlapped with guerilla operations. In March 1882, for example, in the War of the Pacific, after Chilean troops destroyed the village of Nahiumpuqio, killing its inhabitants, they were attacked by guerillas at nearby Tongos, and the heads of the troops killed were displayed on pikes.

The scale of the Mexican Revolution, and the related conflicts it led to, was different to that of the other Latin American wars of the period,[10] but also serves as a reminder of the diversity of conflict in the 1910s, and the extent to which particular types of weapons did not lead to the same form of warfare. The Mexican Revolution was exceptional in scale, but the earlier discussion of internal conflicts in Latin America is intended to underline the problem with the conventional account of military history in this period. Far from being a meaningless list, these conflicts indicated the legacy of the Wars of Liberation in the nineteenth century and the widespread normative role of force. The Latin American wars also show the extent to which ideology, in the shape of struggles between Conservatives and Liberals, played a major role in conflict before the revolutionary warfare touched off by the Russian Revolution.

The role of militaries in suppressing demands for political change served as a reminder that their primary purpose, as the armed force of the state, lay in domestic control and security, not foreign expansionism. The French army suppressed the Paris Commune in 1871, while in 1905 Russia, troops were employed against those demanding change. The suppression of the Commune included large-scale bombardment by government forces, although the defenders also set fire to many monuments, in part to cover their retreat, but also out of desperation. Over thirty thousand Communards were possibly killed in the suppression, and it entailed the summary execution of many prisoners, particularly, but not only, by the government forces. Fear and bitterness were in ample supply.[11] This was a conflict in which the

Communards constructed about five to six hundred barricades that had to be stormed,[12] a practice of urban warfare, particularly in Paris, that had been common earlier in the century. The radicals who pressed for revolution in France and Russia were seen as a greater threat than external opponents, Germany and Japan respectively, and indeed revolution challenged the cohesion of the Russian military, leading to mutiny.[13] After suppressing the Revolution of 1905, the army was engaged against rebellious peasantry, prefiguring the situation with the Russian Civil War after World War I. More generally, concern about the outbreak of domestic opposition affected many aspects of military policy, including recruitment practices, especially in multi-ethnic states,[14] the location of garrisons, and the attempt to use conscription to inculcate loyalty. Ethnic tension could itself contribute to internal conflict.[15]

Armies could also play a prominent role in supporting or resisting coups. Army units, for example, played a key role (both in supporting rebellion and in failing to oppose it) in the successful coups that led to the "Bayonet Constitution" in Hawaii in 1887, and to the overthrow of the Brazilian and Portuguese monarchies in 1889 and 1910, respectively. In Brazil, the leader of the 1889 coup, Field Marshal Deodoro da Fonsea, became head of state of the new republic, while army officers benefited from salary increases, influential appointments, and an increase in the size of the army.[16] Force became normative in Brazil, with Deodoro resigning in 1891 in the face of a naval revolt in support of the vice president, Floriano Peixoto, an army leader who had played a key role in the 1889 coup. The authoritarianism of the latter, however, led to a fresh naval revolt in 1893, but it was unsuccessful in the face of army support for the government. Military rule, nevertheless, came to an end in Brazil after the presidential election of 1894.

In Spain, there was a long-established practice of using force in internal conflict. The Spanish army faced Carlist opponents supporting a different candidate for the throne in the Second Carlist War (1873–76), and also had to suppress the Cantonist uprising in 1873–74. The Second Carlist War was typical of many conflicts in the period in that the force-space ratio was much lower than in the Wars of German Unification. Forces were relatively small and there were no clear front lines. Instead, this was a conflict in which raiding played a major role. At the tactical level, ambushes and surprise attacks were important, for example, the surprise and routing of a government force at Lácar in February 1875. As this nearly led to the capture of King Alfonso XII, the battle might well have had strategic effect. As another example of a surprise attack that might have had a strategic political effect, the Transvaal was invaded in 1896 from British South Africa by six hundred mounted police and volunteers under Dr. Jameson who aimed to raise a rebellion by the non-Boer Europeans. They were defeated by Boer forces. The role of the military in supporting and resisting coups was demonstrated in Constantinople in 1909, when a rising by troops unhappy with the program of modernization was suppressed by the "Action Army" led by the radical Young Turks, martial law was declared, and the reactionary sultan, Abu-ul-Hamid II, was deposed.

Labor activism was also an issue, with troops frequently used to break strikes, a practice that helped increase sensitivity (by governments and radicals alike) to loyalty in the ranks. In 1900, sabotage by striking miners in South Wales led to the deployment of troops, while in 1911, a national rail strike in Britain led to the deployment of troops who killed two strikers in Liverpool. The United States also used troops to crush strikes, most notably in 1877 during a national railroad strike.

A decade before confronting the national rail strike in 1911, much of the British army had been deployed in southern Africa, fighting the Afrikaner republics of the Transvaal and the Orange Free State, which were to the north of British possessions in South Africa. In some respects, from the perspective of 2005, the war prefigured recent conflicts, particularly the Gulf War of 2003, with metropolitan society in Britain able to continue life apparently scarcely affected by a war made possible by the state's unprecedented capability in power projection, although this was challenged by radical Islamic terrorism in London in 2005. Other anticipations included debate over goals. Just as the role of oil in recent Western policy toward the Middle East is a matter of contention, so the Boer War is often seen as a classic instance of capitalist-driven empire-building, with British policy allegedly dominated by the gold and diamonds of the region, paralleling the argument that concern over nitrates played a key role in provoking the War of the Pacific (1879–83).[17]

South African gold and diamonds were indeed important, but it is necessary to be cautious before ascribing too much to the capitalists: those in business were less important than government figures, who were concerned about power and prestige rather than mercantile profits. British ministers were fearful that gold and diamond discoveries would enhance Boer power and lead the Boers to work with Britain's imperial rivals. The British made a much greater effort than they had done in 1881, when Boer victories over British forces had led them to accept the Transvaal's independence. As a result of this effort in 1899–1902, again prefiguring recent expeditionary wars, the financial burden stemming from the Boer War proved much greater than anticipated: income tax had to be doubled in Britain to pay for the war, and government borrowing rose greatly, ensuring that the Conservative government's policy of low taxation, especially low income tax, and financial retrenchment had to be abandoned.

Another anticipation of recent warfare was provided by domestic and international sensitivity to the treatment of Boer civilians, not least the policy of moving them from their farms and incarcerating them in camps, in order to prevent them from serving as a base and support for guerrilla attacks. To later critics, lacking a sense of comparative perspective, these concentration camps were an early anticipation of subsequent horrors. The detention camps were not intended as death camps, although it was certainly true that the disease that spread there proved fatal to many of the inmates.

All of these elements proved as anticipatory as the tactics that tended to excite attention. The long-range, smokeless Mauser magazine riles used by the Boers underlined the strength of defensive firepower, while the Boer use of trenches limited the impact of British field artillery. In turn, the British use of cover for the infantry, creeping barrages of continuous artillery fire, and infantry advances in rushes coordinated with the artillery, indicated the response cycle that was so important to success during the period. So also did the deployment of massive resources, not least as Britain drew on its imperial system for troops.[18]

The isolation of the war from other global confrontations prefigured recent expeditionary conflict rather than the world wars. As with their other imperial crises since the American War of Independence, the British were able to operate without hostile foreign intervention. Despite some sympathy for the Boers, Germany had agreed to leave South Africa to British interests, and fears that France would exploit the situation proved groundless. In contrast, there was a coincidence of threat in 1914, when the outbreak of World War I led to a Boer rising in South Africa, but it was small-scale, poorly led, and rapidly suppressed, unlike the opposition to the British in 1899–1902.

The need to practice counter-insurgency in the latter stages of the Boer War matched the problems the Americans were then facing in the Philippines. Swift American success against Spain in Cuba, the Philippines, and Puerto Rico in 1898 had rapidly led to the overthrow of Spanish imperial power. The newly-developed, large American fleet played a particularly important role in isolating the Spanish garrisons by destroying Spanish squadrons. Complete victory over the Spanish fleet off Santiago in Cuba on July 3 gave vital leeway in Cuba to the poorly-trained American army, much of which was outgunned by the Spaniards. The operational advantage provided by naval strength was demonstrated on July 21, when an American squadron captured Bahia de Nipe on the north coast of Cuba, destroying the Spanish warship defending the port. This provided a new sphere of operations for the American army, although the war ended before it could be exploited: the defeat of the Spanish fleet led the Spanish commander in Santiago to surrender. Naval force was also crucial in the fall of other Spanish colonies. In May 1898, the Americans bombarded San Juan, Puerto Rico, before blockading it and, in July, invading the island.

Once victorious over Spain, however, the Americans chose to demand the Philippines, even though the total American naval victory in Manila Bay on May 1 (the Spanish fleet was destroyed with only one American killed) had been followed not by an invasion by American forces (they were not initially in place, but, instead, concentrated on Cuba, a much closer target), but rather by the revival of the nationalist Filipino revolution that had broken out in 1896, only to be defeated by the better-armed and better-trained Spaniards the following year. In 1898, however, Filipino forces defeated most of the Spaniards on the major island, Luzon, and declared independence. The arrival of American forces led to inconclusive talks with the Filipinos, and to the outbreak of war in early February 1899, with fighting in Manila that was won by the Americans. That year, the Americans did well in a conventional war with the Philippine army in Luzon, capturing the revolutionary capital at Malolos in March, but from November, the Filipino forces shifted to guerrilla operations.

For the Americans, this led to grave difficulties that were seriously exacerbated by a hostile environment in which disease was a particular problem. In recent years, this counter-insurgency war, which continued to be large-scale until 1902 and significant thereafter, has attracted scholarly attention.[19] The Americans benefited greatly from the lack of geographical, ethnic, religious, and political unity in the Philippines, but, although this gravely weakened the nationalists' appeal, it also ensured that there was no central target for the Americans to defeat or conquer, which helped lead to frustration and also to encourage harsh policies toward civilians. Without suggesting any equivalence in goals or conduct, similar problems of control were also important (but

underrated) for other powers that conquered and/or occupied territory, and indeed for powers engaged in interventionist wars since
World War II.

In operational terms, the Americans found it hard to fix their
opponents; for example, on the major island of Mindanao, they found
it difficult to defeat Datu Ali, the leader of Moslem Moro resistance. When attacked at his fortress at Kudarangan in March 1904
by American forces enjoying a major advantage in artillery, he and
his force escaped under the cover of night. On other occasions, the
storming of strongholds led to the killing of numbers of opponents, as
when the Moro base near Lake Seit on the island of Jolo, held by
Panglima Hassan, was stormed in November 1903. Panglima Hassan's
base at Pangpang was captured in March 1904 by an American force
supported by artillery, and the leader was killed soon after. Datu Ali
was finally cornered and killed on the Malala River in October 1905, in
an action in which women and children were also killed. Force projection was less of a problem than controlling terrain because of the
American capacity for amphibious operations, as in March 1901, when
an American force landed at Casiguran Bay and marched overland to
surprise and capture the Filipino president, Emilio Aguinaldo.

The problems of control were not, however, the issue in the Russo-
Japanese and Balkan Wars and, as a result, they appeared to have
more to offer those considering the likely nature of a major European
conflict. This was even more the case because the Russo-Japanese
War involved one of the leading European armies, while observers
also closely scrutinized the Balkan Wars. The Russo-Japanese War
was the first sustained defeat for a Western by a non-Western power.
There had been individual defeats, most recently the Italians by the
Ethiopians at Adua (Adowa) in 1896, and that had led to an end, until
1935, to Italian attempts at invading Ethiopia, but these had been
defensive victories on the part of those attacked by the Westerners. In
1904–1905, in contrast, the non-Western power took the initiative,
and it was also victorious at sea (an unprecedented achievement since
early sixteenth-century Turkish successes in the Mediterranean), as
well as on land. The Japanese did so by Westernizing their military,
by outfighting their opponents, and by narrowly beating Russia in the
struggle to avoid the non-battle factors limiting both sides' ability to
fight on successfully.

In response to Western power projection and the clear-cut capabilities they displayed in Asia in the 1850s, the non-Western powers
had made varied efforts to emulate Western military methods. In part,

they were involved in a race not only with the development of Western expeditionary proficiency, but also with the growing ability of Western powers to recruit and move large numbers of Western-trained native forces. The "native" component in the British Indian Army rose from 137,299 troops in 1880 to 176,455 in 1910, and the net military expenditure as a percentage of the total expenditure of the government of India was 52 percent in 1884–85 and 1889–90. It subsequently rose in total, though generally falling in percentage, such that in 1912–13, it was 50 percent more than in 1884–85, though only 43 percent of the total expenditure.[20] The British force that invaded Zululand in January 1879 included at least nine thousand Africans, mostly in the Natal Native Contingent. Local white residents had not wanted them armed with firearms, but the military's view to the contrary prevailed.[21]

Furthermore, the reputation and industrial capability of the leading Western military powers were such that their weaponry, methods, and systems were emulated elsewhere in the West. This was particularly apparent in the Americas and Eastern Europe, lessening the degree to which distinctive military traditions developed there.[22] The profits of economic growth, not least for resource producers, enabled states to finance military borrowing, although this process also owed much to the ready availability of credit, as well as to a dominant social politics in which there was scant public investment in social welfare, while the ability of workers to gain a greater share of the profit derived from their work was limited. Foreign sales, in turn, were important to the profitability, even existence, of the armaments firms of the leading Western producers. For example, foreign sales, much of them to the Balkans in 1879–86, were responsible for 58.5 percent of the rifles sold by the major Austrian manufacturer, Steyr. Krupp's arms exports as a percentage of its annual armaments production was 54–65 percent in 1904–1909, with Eastern Europe being a key market for its artillery. Turkey was its leading customer.[23]

The most successful borrower of Western technology had been Japan, in large part because a combination of political will, central direction, and industrial capacity was linked with a willingness to remold the entire military instead of adding, as in China and Persia, new-model Westernized units to elements of the old. More generally, it was necessary to introduce a large-scale process of social and cultural change in order to make military borrowing effective.[24] It was easiest to press for reform in the aftermath of failure, as with Japan after the humiliation of the enforced opening of the country, and Turkey after its defeat by Russia in 1877–78. Even so, the process of modernization in Japan was accompanied by large-scale conflict, including the Satsuma Rebellion.

Sultan Abdulhamit II of Turkey responded to defeat by creating a High Commission of Military Inspection and by seeking foreign assistance, particularly the foundation in 1882 of a German military mission. Colmar von der Goltz, the key figure in the latter, a veteran of the Austro-Prussian and Franco-Prussian Wars, who had worked in the Prussian General Staff, was an ardent modernizer, keen on an effective system of conscription and an advocate of effective supporting artillery fire. In 1886, the Turkish army was divided into seven military districts. Furthermore, as part of the reform program, the conscription system was made more comprehensive, the War Academy was expanded, and a staff system created. In 1900, a Ministry of War was established. From 1878, the Çatalca Line was fortified to protect Constantinople from the West, while modern artillery and rifles were purchased in large numbers.

The Japanese army was modeled on the French, and then the German, their navy on the British. Yet, the Russians underrated their ability, in part as a result of racist attitudes, an ironic counterpointing of German assumptions about the Russians during World War II. The extent to which the weaponry and tactics used in the Russo-Japanese War prefigured much that was to be seen in World War I has attracted attention. This includes trench warfare with barbed wire and machine guns, indirect artillery fire, artillery firing from concealed positions, a conflict that did not cease at nightfall, and a war waged with continuous front lines across which forces engaged for long periods. The heavy casualties of the ground fighting owed much to those suffered by the Japanese, who mounted frontal assaults on entrenched Russian forces strengthened by machine guns and quick-firing artillery, for example, at the battle of Mukden in February 1905. In this battle, each side deployed about three hundred thousand troops along a nearly fifty-mile front.

At sea, Japanese gunners, aiming big twelve-inch guns, scored hits on Russian battleships from unprecedented distances. This was an important feature of modern warfare between regular forces. Close-order fighting continued, often within the same building, as in the German-Soviet battle at Stalingrad in 1942, but there was also a distance that stemmed from the enhanced destructive role of firepower, particularly the longer range of artillery, and the use of high-explosive and shrapnel shells, in place of the older solid shot, and also from developments in sea and air conflict. As a result, on average, combatants saw each other less frequently and also far less distinctly than hitherto, a process enhanced on land by the greater use of entrenchments. The psychological consequences of this shift are unclear, and its extent has to be handled with care. Already, in the eighteenth century, it was more common for infantry to be killed or wounded by musket shot than by the bayonet. The continued cult of cold steel—seen in the emphasis on the bayonet in the French revolutionary wars, and again in some late nineteenth-century commentary—nevertheless indicated a belief that the capacity to advance with the bayonet and to close with the enemy was important in the struggle for will, instilling and displaying morale and overthrowing that of the enemy. Interleaved with this rationalized approach was a belief in socialization to combat: exposure to the sight of blood was seen as a key aspect of the "blooding" of troops, and this was widely believed to require close-order combat. If this was "real" conflict, then the distant firing of technicians appeared deadly, but in some way less potent as a test of will. This underlines the complexities surrounding the notion of war as a total experience.

The Russo-Japanese War was different to World War I in a number of important respects, particularly the brevity of the conflict and its restricted geographical scope. Albeit on a wider scale, this was a frontier war, like the Austro-Prussian War and the initial stages of the Franco-Prussian War, and unlike the War of the Pacific (1879–83), in which Chilean forces had occupied the Peruvian capital, Lima, from 1881, after defeating the Peruvians at Chorillos. Even then, the Peruvians fought on, until defeated at Huamachuco in 1883. The Japanese could not afford to pursue the locally out-numbered and poorly-supplied Russians deep into Manchuria, while the Russians lacked the capability to mount amphibious attacks on Japan or Japanese-ruled Korea or Taiwan. Strained economically and militarily by the conflict, the Japanese needed peace. As in 1941, when they attacked the United States and Britain, they were essentially prepared for a short war. Russia was economically more powerful than Japan, but in 1905, it had a revolution to confront, one partly fostered by Japanese military intelligence. Indeed, the conflict indicated the importance, and fragility, of political determination, as much as, if not more than, the willpower of troops to take heavy casualties that exercised military commentators. The latter concluded from the war that frontal assaults were still feasible. The Russian commanders' lack of determination in the face of Japanese willingness to attack repeatedly and take heavy casualties was a serious problem for them and led to unnecessary retreats by the Russian forces.

The conclusion that attackers could win, and that offensives were still war-winners, was also drawn from the Balkan Wars. As with the conflicts in the 1990s that caused, and arose from, the collapse of Yugoslavia, so the key in 1912–13 was the fall of the Turkish Empire in Europe. The First Balkan War (1912–13) saw Turkey attacked by its neighbors—Bulgaria, Greece, Montenegro, and Serbia—and most of its European empire was conquered. At the tactical level, effective artillery played a crucial role. Conversely, in the absence of artillery superiority, the Bulgarian attack on the entrenched positions of the Çatalca Line was defeated on November 17–18, 1912, saving the remaining Turkish positions in Europe near Constantinople (Istanbul), and prefiguring the tactical situation in World War I. The Turkish artillery was outnumbered in this battle, but its centralized command and control situation was better, enabling it to damage the Bulgarian artillery and to wreck Bulgarian attacks. The Bulgarian emphasis on élan and the bayonet cost them dearly, although an absence of surprise was important, as was the extent to which the Turks had defense in depth. The Bulgarians suffered twelve thousand casualties. The strength of the defensive was also indicated at Scutari, a Turkish fortress besieged by Montenegro in 1912–13. Several costly attacks, which led to the death of close to ten thousand Montenegrin troops, were required before the fortress surrendered.

At the operational and strategic level, the First Balkan War demonstrated the risks associated with the absence of mass, as Turkish strategic dispersal—designed to prevent territorial loss in the face of attack from a number of directions—enabled their opponents to achieve key superiorities in particular areas of attack. This was similar to the problems that faced Poland in 1939 and Yugoslavia in 1941, as a result of the dispersal of forces to protect long perimeters, when they were successfully attacked by Germany and its allies. Operationally, the Turks squandered the tactical advantage of the defensive by unsuccessful attempts to encircle their opponents. This was an instructive guide to problems that were to arise in World War I, as the Turkish doctrine of encirclement and annihilation reflected the dominance of German concepts. In the Turkish case, a lack of rehearsal in annual maneuvers greatly lessened their effectiveness.[25] The rapid change of power politics led the victors to fall out, and in the Second Balkan War (1913), Bulgaria unsuccessfully fought its recent allies, as well as Romania and Turkey. The military use of the new technology of air power in the Balkan Wars was novel, but had little effect on operations or impact on outside opinion.[26] Furthermore, this use did not suggest that these conflicts were different to those covered in chapter 3.

At sea, with regard to the period covered in this chapter, contemporary observers emphasized the firepower and armor of battleships, although, in hindsight, naval capability may appear to have been transformed—first, by the development of powered torpedoes, then of submarines, and finally of radio, a crucial tool in command and control.[27] In 1864, the modern self-propelled torpedo originated, with the invention of a submerged, self-propelled torpedo driven by compressed air and armed with an explosive charge at the head. The British pioneered steam torpedo boats, launching HMS *Lightning* in 1876. France completed a submarine powered by an electric battery in 1888. However, the capability of large surface ships dominated attention. The naval force that could be applied was amply demonstrated at Alexandria in 1882. Although many of their shells missed, fourteen British warships with powerful guns, including HMS *Inflexible*, which had four sixteen-inch guns, inflicted great damage, with few British casualties: the shore batteries were not particularly well handled by the Egyptians, and the British warships did not have to face mines or torpedoes. There was a clear contrast to the difficulties the British had faced from Turkish shore batteries when forcing the Dardanelles in 1807. Launched in 1881, *Inflexible* was the first battleship fitted with vertical compound engines, as well as electric power for lighting, including searchlights, although these features led to its hitherto unmatched cost, £812,000, and to a construction period of seven years. It was the prototype for four other British battleships laid down in the late 1870s.

The spread of imperial systems provided the vital strategic network of naval bases, as steamships required coaling stations. The extension of the British network, advocated in reports produced in 1881–82 by the Carnarvon Commission, was particularly striking. Global range and rapid responsiveness were further enhanced by the use of the Suez Canal, opened in 1869, and deepened in 1898. This offered a speedier route from Britain to India, and then on to Singapore.

As earlier in the 1680s and the 1780s, competition between the major powers enhanced their aggregate naval strength, and therefore the gap between them and weaker states. This process was accentuated because the extent of new naval technology ensured that fresh investment was required in order to avoid obsolescence. In 1889, the British Naval Defence Act led to the expensive commitment to a two-power standard, so that Britain could be in a position to fight the second- and third-largest naval powers combined, a goal that arose from an apparently more threatening international situation. In the 1890s, the British built nine battleships of the *Majestic* class, followed by the laying down, in 1896–1901, of twenty battleships modeled on the *Majestic* class, while ten armored cruisers were laid down in 1898–99. The eight battleships of the *King Edward VII* class followed, starting in 1902–1904, as did twenty-two armored cruisers laid down in 1899–1904. HMS *Dreadnought*, which was the first of a faster and more heavily gunned type of battleship, was launched by the British in 1906.

On land and at sea, all powers sought to integrate new weaponry, improved weapons, such as new artillery, and organizational means and systems, into their militaries, their maneuvers, and their plans, as part of the process by which they responded to advances and to apparent deficiencies.[28] A sense of new opportunities stemmed from technological advances. In 1909, Colonel Frederick Trench, the British military attaché in Berlin, reported that the Germans were proposing to subsidize power traction vehicles "of a type suitable for military use," and in 1910, that they were aiming to build "large airships of great speed, endurance and gas-retaining capacity."[29] Developing links between centralized state procurement of large quantities of weaponry and the foundation and development of large industrial concerns, such as Krupp's in Germany, that were able and keen to produce such quantities and investing to create the capacity to do so, were significant.[30] So also were the major improvement of communication and logistical infrastructures and systems, including railway systems designed to strategic and operational effect,[31] telegraph, cable, and radio networks.

Yet, the mechanization of the Western militaries should not be exaggerated, and multiple deficiencies became apparent once a major war involved sustained conflict. This was a matter of drawbacks in recruitment, training, equipment, officership, and doctrine. The extent to which militaries corresponded to civil society was a major problem. In part, it compromised long-service professionalism, most obviously with the widespread dependence on reservists, but also due to the impact of political loyalties and tensions. Thus, the French officer corps was politicized, in particular with a major tension between "clerical" and "republican" generals, with patronage affected accordingly. In Britain, volunteer service in auxiliary forces ensured that, despite the absence of conscription, many had received some type of military training, but the hopes placed on the creation by this means of a "real national army, formed by the people," had not been realized.[32]

More generally, the nature of military culture, not least the role of social hierarchy in command and military ethos, was such that the enhanced effectiveness that might have stemmed from the spread of general staff systems was not fully realized.[33] In Russia, the lack of adequate governmental supervision and financial support were such that much of the army devoted its time to surviving rather than enhancing effectiveness, which particularly entailed the troops doing outside work, while the officers were primarily concerned with the nature of the regimental economy.[34] This is an under-researched field, but the same situation, at least in part, was true of other forces, not only the Balkan and Latin American armies, but also some units in the Austrian, Italian, Spanish, and Portuguese forces. The widespread use of troops as gendarmeries for policing purposes further sapped combat effectiveness.

A very different form of restraint arose from the belief in the greater potency of modern weapons and the enhanced destructiveness of warfare, although a humanitarian current was also very important. They combined to encourage an attempt to legislate restrictions in the use of military capability.[35] The willingness of governments to endorse this policy was a sign of reaction against the notion of total war. International conferences sought to secure the position of prisoners, wounded soldiers, and civilians. The Geneva Convention was particularly important for the latter, while the Brussels Conference of 1876 sought to protect civilians in towns that were under attack. The Conference stated that unfortified towns should not be bombarded, while the population of fortified towns should be allowed to leave, as it was difficult to fulfill the desired goal of only firing on the fortifications. Explosive bullets were also banned.

In essence, moreover, the Western militaries were prepared for difficult and costly conflicts, but expected them to be short. To that extent, despite talk of the need for a blooding to restore societies allegedly enervated by consumerism, and to revive true masculinity and traditional patterns of leadership, commitment to a total conflict that would transform societies was largely absent. This was understandable because, however much they might see international competition as inevitable or even (whether or not Darwinian in concept) natural, neither governments nor military leaderships sought large-scale social transformation or restructuring. Indeed, it was not until the Communists gained power in Russia in 1917 that there was a government committed to such transformation. This seizure of control was an unintended consequence of the strains of war and the resulting play of contingency in a volatile political environment. Similarly, although with the stress on totalitarian politics, not social transformation, the risk of defeat led German generals in World War I, such as Ludendorff, to press for a military-authoritarian regime able to focus all resources on the war.

Those most willing to consider war in 1914 had been the socially and culturally conservative elites that ran the monarchical empires of Austria, Germany, and Russia. They did not seek what was to be defined as total war, and, despite the Russo-Japanese War, did not appreciate the risks that would arise or the pressures for change that a major war would lead to. Instead, they looked back, hoping to refight a conflict akin to the Franco-Prussian War, albeit with the addition of more modern weapons. It was not to be.

# CHAPTER 5
# World War I, 1914–18

A world war was not the goal sought by the combatants in 1914. World War I began, indeed, as a conflict in the Balkans and, in part, was a continuation of the assertiveness and ambitions revealed there, particularly over the previous decade. Like the First and Second Balkan Wars, the ethnic and territorial rivalries of a Balkan world, where violence was the principal method of pursuing disputes, were important. World War I, however, was different because a great power, Austria, was one of the original combatants, while others intervened forcefully and from the outset. Yet, the fact that intervention by these powers had been very different in type and intention in the two previous Balkan wars, and also in earlier crises, such as those of 1876–78 and 1908, indicates that the course of events was far from inevitable. Indeed, tension over the position of Serbia had led Austria and Russia to deploy troops in threatening positions from the autumn of 1912 until March 1913, but the forces were then withdrawn.[1]

Austria felt under threat: from Russian-supported Serbian assertiveness, and Serbia's challenge both to Austria's international position in the Balkans and to the stability of Austria's Balkan possessions. War with Serbia seemed the answer to domestic problems for Austria, and in particular, the way to ensure this stability. The Russians, in contrast, were both encouraged by Serbian assertiveness and ready to see Serbia as a crucial protégé. Any clash between Austria and Russia would have been very serious, involving conflict from Poland to the Balkans, and much of the diplomacy of the previous century had been designed to prevent such an eventuality. In 1914, however, the prospect of German support emboldened the Austrians, and made more likely the prospect of war and also of a more widespread conflict.

In the early 1910s, powerful figures in the German political and military elite felt threatened by the buildup of Russian power and by encirclement by the Russo-French alliance. Growing Russian military strength, not least the development of her strategic railway net, led to pressure in Germany for a pre-emptive war. This railway system benefited from French investment specifically designed to improve the ability of Russia to mobilize, and to act once mobilized, an infrastructure that served strategic and operational goals. In the event of war, this made it less likely that Germany would be able to defeat France before confronting slower-moving Russian forces, and the railway system was therefore seen by German planners as likely to constrain Germany. A feeling of being under threat encouraged pressure for war within Germany, and this sense of threat was exacerbated by Turkey's defeat in the First Balkan War, which made Russia relatively stronger, and, more generally, by a widespread belief in the inevitability of conflict, which strengthened the desire to begin it at the most opportune moment.

The values of the period were important. Distrust of other states, and a willingness to fight, owed much to cultural and ideological factors, although that did not explain why war broke out in specific crises but not others. The Social Darwinism of the 1870s and beyond, with its emphasis on natural competition, encouraged a belief in a world that was necessarily red in tooth and claw. Militarism appeared natural. Late Romanticism glorified war and struggle as a means to discover identity and purity through commitment and pain. The bulk of the educated elites believed in the moral value of striving, self-sacrifice, and war; and the role of nationalism ensured that war between nations was seen as natural. Despite the popularity of pacifism in some circles, there was little interest in internationalism, except among the unempowered Left.

These cultural and ideological assumptions do not explain the outbreak of World War I, but they help account for the way in which small groups of decision makers were able to respond to the crisis without much pressure being exerted on them to maintain peace. At the same time, it was a limited war, not a total one, that was sought. When Austria declared war on Serbia on July 28, it believed that the prospect of German support would deter Russia from intervention. On July 29–30, both the German and the Russian governments responded hesitantly to the declaration. On the 29th, the Germans, concerned indeed that it would not be possible to localize the struggle, suggested to the Austrians that they stage a limited war in which they restricted themselves to the occupation of Belgrade, Serbia's capital. The Austrian government, however, was not interested. On July 30, Russia ordered a general mobilization against both Austria and Germany, although only after Tsar Nicholas II had been persuaded to reverse a decision to rescind the order. This general mobilization led Germany, whose army wanted war, to decide on war against Russia and its ally, France, which it was confident of beating. As with its Austrian ally, the German government did not seek the full range of conflict that was to break out: the Germans hoped that Britain would remain neutral, and Britain was a minor concern to German planners. The British government, however, was unwilling to see France's position in the balance of power overthrown, and was unprepared to accept Germany's violation of Belgian neutrality, of which Britain was a guarantor.

Britain's entry ensured that the war was global to an extent that no earlier one had been. This was not so much a matter of the range of combat, as of the intensity of links. If British and French warships and forces had fought across the world in 1754–63, 1778–83, and 1793–1815, the units had generally been small, and there was no equivalent to the intensity of links shown in 1914–18. The latter included the large-scale movement of troops to Europe, particularly Algerians (from the French Empire), Australians, Canadians, Indians, New Zealanders, and South Africans (British Empire), and from 1917, Americans to the Western Front in France and Belgium, and Australians, Indians, and New Zealanders (British Empire) to the Mediterranean theatre. As such, the war represented the most intensive, wide-ranging and effective military articulation of the European colonial empires hitherto; the troops deployed along the Suez Canal in 1915, to protect it from Turkish attack were "a revelation of Empire" to John Monash, an Australian brigade commander.[2] In some respects, indeed, alongside the display of mutual interdependence and related concessions, the collective effort represented by the war led to a strengthening of empire. In London, an Imperial War Cabinet, including representatives of the Dominions, met from 1917, and provided a public sign of cohesion in decision-making that countered the emphasis on distinctive interests, although the Dominions had grown less, not more, dependent on London by the end of the war. Britain's role as a market for imperial goods was fostered by military needs and political preference. The impact of the war on food imports to Britain from Continental Europe ensured that the British market increased for imperial exporters, such as South Africa.

The global dimension was also seen in conflict outside Europe. Part of this matched the earlier pattern of Anglo-French conflict, with British and British-allied forces directed against German colonies. One major difference, however, was a consequence of the recent enhancement of Western power for, whereas, prior to 1815, the British essentially had to capture a few bases, principally port cities, in order to secure the conquest of French colonies, now the German colonies enjoyed control of extensive interiors that posed a more serious military challenge to conquerors, and one that amphibious operations were less able to secure. This was made abundantly clear in the lengthy struggle to defeat German forces in East Africa, a struggle that continued to the end of the war. In Africa, this challenge also meant that Allied forces faced formidable logistical hurdles. Confronting them required the recruitment of large numbers of African porters, and this was an aspect of the acute disruption caused by the war. Many porters died, while their recruitment itself was very disruptive. The war also represented the last major stage of the partition of Africa, and certainly led to an intensification of European control there. The distribution of German territories among the victors, however, did not always match military events. For example, French strategy in West Africa was designed to ensure that France gained more of the Cameroons than the extent of French operations justified. British concern to satisfy France ensured that this goal was realized: Africa serving to permit (by offsetting advantages) the furtherance of European goals.[3] Force was also available to enforce imperial authority, as with the British expedition of 1918 against the Turkana of Kenya.

Transoceanic conflict included the struggle with German surface raiders, which were hunted down in the early stages of the war. It is possible to see this in terms of one of the definitions of total war, namely range. The East Asiatic Squadron under Vice Admiral Maximilian Graf von Spee, the leading German naval force outside Europe at the outset of the war, sailed across the Pacific to Chile, where a weaker British force was defeated off Coronel on November 1. Spee then sailed on to attack the Falkland Islands, a British colony, off which he was defeated by a stronger British force on December 8. Individual German warships elsewhere were eventually hunted down, although not before the *Emden* had inflicted some damage, and more disruption, to shipping in the Indian Ocean, and had shelled Madras.

Yet, the *Emden* was lost to the combination of naval fire and a reef in the Cocos Islands on November 9, 1914, and the threat from German surface raiders was essentially restricted to the opening months of the war. Indeed, Allied success in blockading the North Sea, the English Channel, and the Adriatic, and in capturing Germany's overseas colonies, ensured that, after the initial stages of the war and despite the use of submarines, the range of German naval operations was smaller than those of American and French privateers when attacking British trade between 1775 and 1815.

This was also the first European war in which a major East Asian and a major New World power had intervened. That both Japan and the United States supported the Allies was very important to the success of the latter, and a measure of the failure of German strategy at the world scale. China also declared war on Germany, although its impact was obviously less. However ably the Germans operated in Europe, they had not adequately planned for a global struggle, but this was an aspect of their expectation of a short conflict, one that, at least in terms of duration, was not seen as total. Bound to Britain by treaty, Japan was a bellicose state that saw ready opportunity from entering the war in the shape of gaining German positions in China and the Western Pacific, and it did both, capturing them speedily and easily. This served as a prelude to activity and expansion in the 1920s and 1930s in pursuit of imperial ambitions to replace European nations as the dominant power in these areas.

In the United States, in contrast, there was active hostility to the idea of participation in the European war because it was seen as alien to American interests and antipathetic to her ideology. The United States had a strong tradition of neutrality and isolationism, but that did not mean a pacific culture or an aversion to war and the use of force, as Spain had noted in 1898. The commemoration of the War of Independence and, even more, the Civil War in the United States lent heroism and purpose to the notion of conflict. Wars against the Native Americans had also played a major role in the definition of national identity (for those not of Native ancestry), contributing to a society that was violent and bellicose, even if its politics were not particularly belligerent.

The recent American background, however, was of small-scale expeditionary warfare that required neither conscription nor industrial mobilization. In 1905, President Theodore Roosevelt proclaimed the "Roosevelt Corollary," a supplement to the Monroe Doctrine, by which the "wrongdoing" or "impotence" of any state in the Western

Hemisphere could justify and require American intervention. As a consequence, Nicaragua was occupied in 1912, Haiti in 1915, and the Dominican Republic in 1916, and troops were sent into Mexico in 1916.[4] The focus was not on great-power confrontation. Indeed, when war with Germany was declared in 1917, the American navy had no appropriate war plan for the Atlantic, a key symptom of a more generally poorly-prepared force.[5] The major shipbuilding program authorized in 1916 had not yet come to fruition.

Concern over German intervention in Latin America, specifically apparent willingness to encourage Mexican revanche against the United States for losses in the Mexican-American War of 1846–48, played a major role in the deterioration in relations that led the United States to declare war on Germany in April 1917. Alongside Germany's crass wartime diplomacy, her actions, especially the unrestricted submarine warfare that sank American ships, led to a major shift in attitudes, in which Americans became persuaded of the dangerous consequences of German strength and ambitions, but also did so in a highly moralized form that encouraged large-scale commitment. Brazil, the largest state in Latin America, also suffered from the unrestricted submarine warfare and, in October 1917, it declared war on Germany. The Brazilian contribution was more modest than in World War II, when about twenty-five thousand troops were sent to fight as far as part of the Allied army in Italy in 1944–45. In World War I, instead, only a small naval squadron was eventually dispatched, and it did not see active service.[6]

In contrast, both American and Japanese warships were deployed in European waters in co-operation with Britain. Five American dreadnoughts (large battleships) joined the British Grand Fleet in December 1917, four sailing with it on April 24, 1918 when it failed to intercept a German sortie into the North Sea. The key American naval contribution was in destroyers, fast enough to track submarines and to keep them submerged. From May 1917, American warships contributed to anti-submarine patrols in European waters. To assist convoying in the Mediterranean, American warships were based in the British base of Gibraltar, and Japanese ones in the British base of Malta.

Another aspect of the global dimension represented a continuation of earlier patterns of imperial conquest of the non-European world, with Britain and Russia seeking to conquer parts of the Turkish Empire. As with earlier Western pressure on the Turkish and Chinese Empires, this, however, was more a matter of successes on the periphery than a triumphant overturning of the empire, akin, for example, to the Spanish conquests of the Aztec and Inca Empires in the sixteenth century. Indeed, the major blow aimed at the heart of the Turkish Empire, the attempt in 1915 to force the Dardanelles so that naval pressure could be brought to bear on the Turkish capital, Constantinople (modern Istanbul), was a total failure.

The campaign illustrated the strength of the defensive. An Anglo-French attempt to force the Dardanelles was stopped by minefields, shore batteries, and an unwillingness, in the face of the loss of ships, to accept the risk of further operations. There had been a belief that the Dardanelles could be taken by naval power alone because of a serious underestimation of the strength of the forts and of the Turkish ability and willingness to resist attack. Subsequently, troops were landed in an attempt to gain control of the landward side of the Turkish position, but advances were held as a result of a combination of poor Allied planning and generalship, Turkish fighting skills, and the general strength of defensive firepower in this period, particularly when un-suppressed by artillery fire. The fighting rapidly became static. In May 1915, Lieutenant-General Sir William Birdwood of the Indian army, the commander of the Anzac force, reported that deficiencies in the attacking force had ensured that he was pushed back onto the defensive and "practically reduced to a state of siege."[7]

More generally, the war was important in the shifting of power away from Europe. In part, this was a matter of the heavy human and financial costs of the conflict, which were relatively more serious than the physical devastation inflicted because, compared to World War II, far less of the continent served as a battlefield and far less was bombed, let alone bombed heavily. In absolute and relative terms, this shift away from Europe was partially a matter of the rise of the power of the United States and, to a lesser extent, of Japan. Relations within the Western empires also changed, with an upsurge in nationalism that influenced the nature of imperial relations.[8] In part, the experience of different military conditions established disruptive norms. Birdwood noted in Gallipoli in 1915, that the Martinique and Guadeloupe troops in the French forces "are treated in precisely the same way as if they were Frenchmen, which from our Indian Army point of view strikes one as curious."[9] Because they did not wish to divert national troops from the Western Front, the French deployed a considerable number of troops from their empire at Gallipoli, their division in the original assault being part of the *Corps Expéditionnaire d'Orient* and including North African and Senegalese troops.

Even though tensions within empires increased, opposition to imperial control was generally suppressed, as in French West Africa in 1916, and the French Sahara the following year, although the Italians encountered serious problems in Libya. In response, the Italians used gas and aircraft from 1917. In 1916, there was a major rising in Russian Central Asia as a result of attempts to conscript large numbers of Muslims for war work, particularly digging trenches. The brutal suppression of the rising led to very heavy casualties, not least of which resulted from both large-scale deportations and flight in harsh conditions.[10] More generally, the war represented an opportunity, and more so a need, to expand imperial control in order to contain possible discontent, pre-empt exploitation by rivals, and tap resources. This was particularly apparent in the Islamic world. In 1914, Britain annexed Cyprus and made Egypt a protectorate, while, in 1916, Qatar became independent from Turkish rule under British protection, and, in Sudan, British control increased with the 1916 conquest of the territory of Darfur, whose sultan, Ali Dinar, had heeded Turkish calls for Islamic action. The British used aircraft and light lorries (motor-trucks) to provide speedy firepower and mobility in Darfur.

The Gallipoli operation encapsulated much of the problem with the offensive in World War I. Tim Travers has concluded that the Allies failed primarily at Gallipoli because of their inexperience of modern war, especially because the 1915 campaign took place early in the war, "before the learning curve, greater experience, and vastly improved technical ability provided solutions to the trench stalemate later in the war. In fact, tactics ate strategy at Gallipoli."[11] The British lack of trench warfare munitions led to improvisation in the Dardanelles, as on the Western Front, of hand grenades and mortars. Major-General Alexander Godley's explanation for failure at Gallipoli underlined the need to consider both sides, "the lack of fresh reinforcements, both in April and in August, the strength and superiority of the enemy, in troops, guns and positions, were the true causes of why we did not get across the peninsula and that it was not on account of bad plans, or failure of the troops, or bad orders, or want of water, or want of co-operation with the Navy."[12] As commander of the Anzac (Australian and New Zealand) Division, in fact, he showed questionable leadership.

Gallipoli was an example of how, repeatedly, during the war, strategic conception was not matched by tactical and operational success. This was partially a matter of the absence of marked capability gaps in combat effectiveness between the combatants, and thus not the product of military failure, but rather of the fact that there was no failure creating such a gap. This absence of marked capability gaps was related to the tactical and operational strength enjoyed by the defensive, particularly the role of entrenched firepower.

Much of the literature on the war deals with the consequences of the latter, particularly on the Western Front. Trench warfare stands as a model for the futility of the war, indeed, for some commentators, of war as a whole. Such warfare had not been sought by any of the participants. Instead, while anticipating heavy casualties, all had sought to stage, and win, a war of maneuver. This was seen in 1914, as all the major armies launched offensives intended to gain decisive advantage and also to win the psychological advantage. The German invasion of Belgium and France engages most attention, but should be seen alongside the French invasion of Lorraine, the Austrian of Serbia, and the Russian of East Prussia. All failed, ending the chance of a rapid military end to the war, or any part of it. These failures partially reflected the strength of the defense, particularly in the case of the failure of the French attacks, but more was involved, not least because some of the invasions were checked by counter-attacks within maneuver warfare. The limitations that invading powers faced in maneuver warfare were serious, particularly in sustaining mass and maintaining the tempo of attack, and helped to cause the failure of the German offensive. The question is whether maneuver warfare as conceived prior to World War I was, in fact, a real possibility for European armies fighting each other in the early twentieth century, or whether it was an illusion, so that a quick victory from out-maneuvering the enemy was not plausible. In short, was trench warfare inevitable, or could it have been avoided by better planning, better generalship, or better tactics? Trench warfare certainly had not been avoided in Manchuria in 1904–1905, or in the Balkans in 1912–13.

Stopped in the battle of the Marne in September 1914, the Germans did not regain the freedom to stage a wide advance on the Western Front until the spring of 1918, and the strategic and operational situation then was less promising for them and the width of the advance far narrower. The last opportunity for open, mobile warfare on the Western Front, before the closing stage of the war, occurred in Flanders in October–November 1914, as the Germans struggled to break through to the English Channel. The fighting in the resulting First Battle of Ypres was transitional, with hand-to-hand combat still taking place and "with riflemen being as significant in its outcome as artillery," but all combatants were also increasingly aware of the shell shortages resulting from the failure to anticipate and meet the production demands of modern, mass-industrialized warfare. The opening campaign of the war in the West was instructive for all concerned, as pre-war plans largely fell apart, a product both of their deficiencies and of mistakes in execution.[13]

The Allied success on the Western Front in 1914 was one of defense. Yet, although the superiority of the defensive emerged clearly, the Allies did not have that option. The opening campaign ended with Germany in control of most of Belgium and much of France, and, in order to regain losses, it was necessary for the Allies to drive the Germans out because the German government was unwilling to accept a compromise peace that did not include substantial gains. This underlined the failure of the German 1914 offensive. It obliged the Allies to try to regain the territories lost, at great cost, but also encouraged German expansionism, and therefore nullified the strategic option for the Germans of a good compromise peace. As a result, their efforts were devoted to a goal that was not worth the costs and risks it entailed, one that ultimately proved fatal for German stability and territorial integrity, and those of their allies. Intransigence over war goals was scarcely novel, but its consequences were particularly deadly.[14] As a result, total war has been seen as a development of World War I, not its cause.[15]

If this set the strategic context, there was also the military conviction, held for example by Douglas Haig, appointed British Commander in Chief in December 1915, that the German error had been to abandon their offensive prematurely (which was probably correct in the case of first Ypres), and that it was instead necessary to persist in attacks.[16] This may appear foolish in light of the heavy casualties resulting from such offensives, but there was a finer line between success and failure than is often accepted by discussion of this war (and indeed other wars). A recent defense of Haig's role, focusing on one of his most controversial operations, third Ypres, claims "had he decided to halt the Flanders offensive after 4 October 1917, historians would undoubtedly have had a field day in blaming Haig for throwing away the opportunity to capitalize on the crisis in the German Army created by Plumer's offensives."[17] While a reasonable point, Haig's performance in command was patchy, and only pretty good on occasion. Nevertheless, the contrast between the hesitant initial German response to the Russian invasion of East Prussia in 1914, and the more confident sequel, in which the initiative was successfully seized and the Russians defeated, is more generally instructive.

As trench lines were dug in late 1914, maneuver gave way to static warfare in Belgium and France. In Eastern Europe, however, force-space ratios were different. The Eastern Front was double that of the length of the Western Front at the close of 1914, and the trench systems lacked comparable sophistication.[18] Despite lower force-space ratios in Eastern Europe, it was still possible, if troops could be massed, to mount offensives successfully, and these led to the conquest of Serbia in 1915 and of Romania in 1916, both by Austrian, German, and Bulgarian forces. The conquest of Romania was particularly rapid.

The entry of Bulgaria (1915) and Romania (1916) into the war, like that of Italy in 1915, reflected not a depth of commitment, but the continued determination and perceived need for second-rank powers to make assessments of opportunity. Far from the perceived ideology of either alliance playing a role, the key element was the gain of territories—small in themselves, but made important as a result of nationalist public myths, and their gain seen as a sign of success. Italy was offered gains at the expense of Austria,[19] the Bulgarians were promised Macedonia and most of Thrace, and Romania sought Transylvania from Austria (more accurately, from Hungary, which was also ruled by the Habsburgs and is for reasons of brevity subsumed as part of Austria). Success in the war was less important in eventually making gains than the very fact of intervention on the right side. This was conspicuously so in the case of Romania, which was largely overrun, but gained Transylvania in the eventual peace settlement and which—after an interlude in 1940–45, when it was returned to Hungary at Germany's behest—still holds it today. Similarly, Belgium, although also very largely overrun by the Germans in 1914, made gains from Germany in Europe and Africa in the eventual peace treaty.

There were also major advances in the Eastern Front struggle between Austria-Germany and Russia. In 1915, the Germans overran Russian Poland, outfighting the indifferently-led and poorly-supplied Russians. Operations included the storming of fortified towns, such as Kaunas, which fell to the Germans in August 1915. The Russians were more successful against the Austrians, although not consistently so, and, in countering Russian attacks, the Austrians benefited from German support. The Russian army proved inadequate to the challenge, in part because its command culture remained anachronistic. Although the Russian General Staff Academy graduates were a meritocratic group, exposed to a scientific approach to war,[20] they were also a small one. In general, an emphasis on lineage, connections, and character did not guarantee an informed response to the problems posed by machine-guns and entrenched defenders.[21] This failure of response owed much to the continued conviction of the role of will in victory.

Russia was knocked out of the war in 1918, partially a consequence of its being outfought by the Germans, but also of the working through of the political turmoil that began with the overthrow of the tsar in February 1917. Soldiers played a major role in the overthrow, not so much that some units in St. Petersburg demonstrated for change, but rather that there was also a lack of willingness to fight for the tsar, in part because of divisions within the officer corps.[22] The same was true of the Communist coup that October, as the Provisional Government also was unable to rely on the military, because its willingness to fight on against the Germans compromised military co-operation.[23] Alongside disaffection among the soldiers, some of the senior commanders were unwilling to fight for the government.[24]

In this fashion, the Russian army made a key contribution to the history of the period, one that was more direct than issues of fighting quality. In contrast, although there was a short-term breakdown of control in part of the French army in 1917, the political reliability of other militaries that year remained high, despite heavy casualties and a lack of confidence in a speedy conclusion to the war. This aspect of the war still requires more study. Raising, supplying, and training large forces was of scant value unless they were prepared to fight on. Even in Russia, although the offensive launched in June 1917 was poorly-supported by many of the troops, which helped wreck it, the army served until February 1918, when the failure of attempts to negotiate peace led to a renewal of the German attack and to mass desertions.

Differing responses to failure on the Western Front characterize much of the widely-read literature on the war.[25] A major emphasis is on an impasse and indecisiveness that owed much to poor commanders and to antiquated command systems. The dominant tactical image is of machine-guns sweeping away lines of attackers. The power of the defensive, especially when firepower enhanced terrain advantages (in this case, higher ground), was captured by General Birdwood, who wrote from Gallipoli in 1915, "It seems quite ridiculous that we should be within some ten yards of each other, and yet I am unable to get into their trenches."[26] Failure on the battlefield is then seen as forcing decision to a different level, one of attritional conflict, in which the ability and willingness on both sides to accept horrific casualties, while causing the same, and also to mobilize fully the resources of society, led to a competitive race of death.

This account of what is presented as total war is taken further with an emphasis on the role of anti-societal strategies designed to weaken the capacity of the rival society to support conflict. The emphasis here is on unrestricted submarine warfare by Germany, and on the Allied block-ade of Germany. This account adds a race to starvation to that of attritional conflict, and culminates with the claim that Allied victory stemmed from the indirect approach: blockade causing growing prob-lems within Germany, culminating in the widespread disaffection in late 1918 that led the German government to accept an armistice. Prefiguring this, there is an emphasis on how the war in the East came to an end because of the successive overthrowing of Russian govern-ments in 1917.

In short, the emphasis is not on the development of conflict or on how the war was won at the front. This leads to an underrating of the ways in which both sides confronted the challenges of conducting large-scale war against heavily-armed opponents and, specifically, of overcoming the constraints of trench warfare. Much of the interesting work in re-cent decades actually has been devoted to these subjects, has been revisionist in character, and has indicated the willingness and ability of both sides to address the problems of trench warfare.[27] At the same time, there were important constraints, not least of which was the difficulty of adapting to the large numbers of new officers and troops, most of whom were poorly-trained, as well as the problems of providing the appropriate equipment, especially the heavy artillery pieces required when bombarding opposing trench lines, and the very large number of shells necessary to maintain bombardments. These were problems for all of the combatants from 1914, and the difficulties the Western Allies had experienced were revisited by the Americans in 1918, and helped to contribute to the heavy casualties they experi-enced. Writing from Gallipoli in December 1915 to the Commander-in-Chief for India, Birdwood emphasized the problem with new troops:

I have only one regular division, viz. the 29th, which as you know came out here as a most magnificent force of old soldiers from India. I fancy that about 80% of these have disappeared for one reason and another, so it now consists of a vast proportion of young soldiers. With the exception of my own [Anzac] corps, the other divisions are Territorial and New Army, and I am sorry to say that the former include certainly one so called division, which is to all intents and purposes, useless, while all are very short of artillery.[28]

A lack of sufficient fire support was a major problem for many of-fensives, including the British one on the Somme in 1916. The key indicator in weaponry was the production of shells, and this was fully understood by contemporaries. There were important qualitative as well as quantitative improvements in the production of munitions. It was increased in Britain by involving the trade and by introducing cooperative group manufacture, whereby each manufacturer within the group made some of the components of the munition. This allowed inspection to be carried out at one location, the premises where the components were put together, instead of at the premises of each manufacturer, thereby speeding up production. The increased skill of the trade reduced rejections, and the inspectors from the Outside Engineering Branch of the Ministry of Munitions ensured that production increased to meet demand. In 1916–17, various unnecessary components in shells were eliminated, which also speeded up production. One of the problems faced by the British in 1915–16 was the poor quality of their shells. So great was the improvement brought about by better working practices, greater experience, and the inspectors, that prematures fell to 0.0004 percent, one in 250,000, the best rate in the Allied armies, and a formidable achievement of industrial application.

A focus on shells, however, did not preclude an emphasis as well on infantry weaponry. A combination of technological and tactical improvements helped in the provision of improved fire-support. By mid-1916, this was beginning to be provided for the British by the three-inch Stokes light infantry mortar. By mid-1917, the Stokes had become a reliable infantry support weapon that could be quickly used to engage German strongpoints, mortars, and machine guns. At the same time, rifle grenades were used in similar support and suppression roles. These tactics became effective during 1917, but developed during 1916. The British also used the Vickers machine gun to suppress enemy troop movements behind the front by indirect fire into map references over the heads of friendly troops.

Production had to rise rapidly to meet demand. For example, in the last quarter of 1914, only 2,164 hand and rifle grenades were produced in Britain, and, although the figure had risen to 65,315 in the first six months of 1915, it was still well below demand. Only in October 1915 did the output of the Mills No. 5 grenade meet demand when it passed 300,000 a week. Already, in 1915, the monthly demand for percussion grenades alone had risen to 252,000. British output of mortar ammunition rose from 50,000 rounds in April–June 1915 to 2,185,346 million rounds for April–June 1916. A total of 11,052,451 grenades were delivered from Britain in the second half of

1916.[29] Deliveries of trench mortars from Britain rose from 12 in the last quarter of 1914 to 2,145 in the last quarter of 1917.

The problems of maintaining firepower were not only a matter of providing and transporting sufficient supplies to the artillery and infantry—no easy task in the chewed-up terrain of the battlefield—but also of dealing with problems arising from wear and tear, particularly, for the artillery, the mechanical difficulties arising from worn barrels, faulty recuperator springs, and other defects. Usage thus contributed to greater inaccuracy, which considerably reduced the effectiveness of massed artillery.[30]

Political constraints were also serious in helping explain failure, as they ensured that under-prepared forces had to act. Concern about the stability of alliances proved particularly important, leading, for example, to Allied attacks on the Western Front in a necessary but ultimately unsuccessful effort to reduce pressure on Russia, while the Russian General Staff pressed for the offensive, finally launched in June 1917, in order to reduce German pressure on France and Britain.[31] Given military limitations and political constraints, it is not surprising that many commanders, such as Haig and Robert Nivelle, the French commander in 1917, emphasized willpower. This was linked to an often misplaced confidence in the continued capability of the offensive, which led, for example, to the maintenance of appreciable cavalry forces, especially by the British, designed to achieve and exploit a breakthrough. Haig has been criticized for mistakenly clinging to notions of decisive battle and cavalry sweeps, and this has been presented in terms of a failure to accept the attritional logic that, rather than gaining large amounts of territory, "industrial war" required breaking enemy resistance by killing large numbers, a goal achieved by massing the firepower to blast them from their defensive lines.[32] Subsequently, Haig was to argue that the Allied offensives of 1915–17 on the Western Front were a crucial preparation for the final victory in that they wore the Germans down, but at the time, he wanted them to be far more decisive—tactically, operationally, and strategically.

Despite the problems encountered in confronting the nature and circumstances of trench warfare, there was also a willingness to rethink the situation. In part, this was strategic and operational. A good example is provided by the new understanding of German strategy offered by Erich von Falkenhayn, who became Chief of the German General Staff in 1914, after the failure of the initial campaign. Appreciating that Germany did not have the resources to defeat its enemies in the rapid, decisive campaign required by pre-war doctrine, he instead sought a negotiated peace, albeit on terms favorable to Germany. This built on earlier discussion, by Moltke the Elder and the academic commentator Hans Delbrück, of the limitations of the concept of decisive victory. To develop a matching new operational method, however, proved difficult, not least because of firm opposition within the officer corps, which revealed the difficulties of implementing policy. In 1915, Falkenhayn's attempt to force Russia into a separate peace failed, in part because breakthroughs at the front did not produce strategic results. In 1916, Falkenhayn accepted that a breakthrough in the West was impossible, due to the defensive strength of modern weapons. Instead, he sought in the Verdun offensive, launched that February, to break the French will by forcing the French army to mount costly counter-attacks to a successful German attack with limited objectives. As with the German use of defensive positions—for example, the retreat to the Hindenburg Line in 1917—this reflected a traditional practice in warfare, the attempt to exploit an understanding of ground. In his plan, the strategic, operational, and tactical dimensions of the war were in concert.

Yet, as so often happens with planning, there was over-determination, with everything depending on the 5th Army achieving its goals and on the French doing exactly what Falkenhayn wanted. In the event, the Germans were unable to profit from the offensive they launched. Instead of rapid results, Falkenhayn increasingly had to rely upon the effects of a steady hemorrhaging of the French army brought about by a near-continuous German offensive. This, however, engaged most of the German reserve, and led to heavy German casualties, while French willpower remained strong despite serious losses. There was also a basic strategic flaw, in that any peace on German terms was politically unacceptable to Germany's enemies, while the Allies could afford the costs of wearing down the German army.[33]

In 1918, the Germans were more successful tactically on the Western Front, thanks to their abandonment of attacks by massed formations, in favor of the use of infiltration tactics that they had already employed with effect on both the Eastern and the Italian Fronts. Elite storm-troopers were used to penetrate opposing positions, isolating strongpoints and disrupting the cohesion of opponents. This proved very effective at the tactical level, but the Germans were poor at exploiting their advantages. In local battles, the British sometimes fought the German attackers to a standstill by not falling back and by counter-attacking, so that the advantages of infiltration were lost. The German army failed to adapt to such situations because the highly-trained storm-troopers had moved on, leaving the lesser-trained follow-up troops to deal with resistance. The tail was a drag on the head. In addition, instead of maintaining the tempo of the individual advance, in 1918, the Germans mounted a sequence of attacks on different sections of the Western Front, none of which achieved the necessary military or, even more, political affect. Furthermore, the cumulative impact of casualties hit German combat effectiveness and morale.

American entry into the war in 1917 has led some scholars to argue that the Americans were instrumental in the defeat of Germany in 1918.[34] This interpretation misunderstands the American contribution, which was greatest in the shape of industrial capacity and credit, and was crucial in that respect to the Allies from the outset. In 1914, neither Britain nor France had an industrial system to match that of Germany, which had forged ahead of Britain in iron and steel production; and the Allies were dependent on the United States for machine tools, mass-production plants, and much else, including the parts of shells. By 1914, American industrial output was equivalent to that of the whole of Europe. By the time the United States sent its army to France, American production was so committed to producing munitions for the Allies that U.S. industry was unable to supply the American army. Thus, the French and British had to equip the Americans with French- and British-designed artillery and other munitions.

The Allied, principally British, ability to keep Atlantic sea-lanes open and to blockade Germany ensured that America made a key contribution before formal entry into the war. Once the latter had occurred, the American navy, thanks to their vital escort vessels, contributed to the effectiveness of convoying, and thanks to their battleships, made any idea of a decisive German naval sortie less credible. On land, however, the Americans were limited by the small size of their pre-war army and by its lack of training for trench warfare. Combined with an overly-confident failure to appreciate the nature of the conflict and to learn from allies (although the Americans reproduced British and French manuals about, among other things, grenades and mortars, and their tactical use), this led to heavy American casualties in 1918.[35] It cannot be said that American attacks inflicted key defeats on the Germans. From July 1918, the Americans came to play a significant part in Allied operations, but they were not instrumental to victory. Nevertheless, the American role would have been more important had the war continued into 1919, when large numbers of trained American troops would have made a major difference. Furthermore, the knowledge that they would be a factor both helped stiffen Allied resolve and influenced the German high command in 1918. Nearly two million American troops were in Europe by the armistice.

It is necessary to focus on the breakthrough campaigns of 1918, which pose a classic problem in military analysis, as two contrasting factors have attracted particular interest. The most noteworthy in public attention is new technology. In a series of articles for the *Daily Mail* published in 1913, the novelist H.G. Wells predicted that science and engineering would be crucial to winning the next war, which would be more mechanized than any hitherto, putting a premium on "the best brains." World War I indeed witnessed important advances in this sphere, although the problems of using innovations to effect in a conflict of this scale were considerable, particularly with the size of the forces deployed. These factors tended to lessen the impact of change, and to ensure that it was easier to be effective where the number of units was more limited: at sea, the sphere in which machines were more significant compared to land, as man does not fight naturally on the sea. Nevertheless, the war saw the first use of new weapons, particularly the tank, but also poison gas and mobile flamethrowers, the first large-scale military use of recently-developed weapons, particularly aircraft, and also major developments in older but still relatively recent weapons, especially submarines. All of these weapons, however, faced serious limitations. For example, the Germans, British, and French experimented with one- and two-man flamethrowers, as well as wheeled and static models. None was mobile in the way that backpack models of the 1930s and 1940s were, and they were also severely hampered by being capable of only short-range bursts.

Aircraft played an important role, not only in fighting other aircraft, but also in influencing combat on the ground (and at sea), with reconnaissance aircraft proving especially valuable, particularly in helping direct artillery fire. Aircraft were used for spotting and reconnaissance in 1914, which was how the fighter evolved: as an armed reconnaissance plane for protection, followed by armed aircraft for shooting down spotters. Critical of the initial plan for Gallipoli as a purely naval attack, General Callwell remarked, "As a land gunner I have no belief in that long range firing except when there are aeroplanes to mark the effect."[36] "Seeing over the hill" altered the parameters of conflict, but despite capabilities including strafing troops and tanks, aircraft were not yet a tactically decisive or operationally effective tool. Their role had been grasped, but execution was limited.[37] German Zeppelin (airship) and aircraft raids, particularly on

Britain, however, inflicted damage and led to an appreciable devotion of military resources to anti-aircraft defenses. The impact on society, especially blackouts to make targeting harder, helped underline the "total" character of the war, in the shape of its consequences for civilian life. Monash wrote back from London in 1916:

You can hardly imagine what the place is like. The Zeppelin scare is just like as if the whole place was in imminent fear of an earthquake. At night, the whole of London is in *absolute darkness*...All games and museums are closed—nothing but war-work everywhere...everything is at famine prices. Nothing is going on—in the ships, in the streets, anywhere—that has not a direct bearing on the war. Martial law everywhere—no private motors allowed, no functions, no racing...Nothing I had read conveyed to me any idea of how the war had taken hold of the whole British nation, and how every man, woman and child were bent on the one sole purpose, to prosecute the war in every form of activity.[38]

The Germans launched bomber attacks in 1917 because they believed, possibly due to reports by Dutch intelligence, that the British were on the edge of rebellion. As a result, the attacks were intended not so much to serve attritional goals, but rather to be a decisive war-winning tool. The use of bombers, the German Gotha, reflected the rapid improvement of capability during the war, as science and technology were applied in the light of experience: Zeppelins had been revealed as vulnerable to aircraft interception, as well as to the weather. In contrast, the Gotha Mark Four could fly for six hours, had an effective range of 520 miles, could carry 1,100 pounds (or 500 kg) of bombs, and could fly at an altitude of 21,000 feet (four miles or 6,400 meters), which made interception difficult. Furthermore, the crews were supplied with oxygen and with electric power to heat the flying suits.

The first (and deadliest) raid on London, a daylight one on June 13, 1917, in which fourteen planes killed 162 people and injured 432, not least as a result of a direct hit on a school that killed sixteen children, led to a public outcry and was met—in the rapid action-reaction cycle that characterized advances during the war—by the speedy development of a defensive system involving high-altitude fighters based on airfields linked by telephone to observers. This led to heavy casualties among the Gothas, and to the abandonment of daylight raids. More seriously, the rationale of the campaign was misplaced because, far from hitting British morale, the bombing led to a hostile popular response. This remained the case even in the winter of 1917–18, when the Germans unleashed four-engine Zeppelin-Staaken

R-series bombers, able to fly for ten hours and to drop 4,400 pounds (or 2,000 kg) of bombs. They required, however, a major logistical support system and failed to inflict sustained serious damage.[39] The alarm raised in sections of British civil society by German air attacks encouraged post-war theorists to emphasize the potential of air power. During the war itself, however, the consequences of strategic bombing—either to disrupt industrial life or to cause civilian casualties—was limited. For 1919, the British had planned long-range bombing raids on German cities, including Berlin, but the war ended before their likely impact could be assessed, although one of the planes successfully flew the Atlantic in 1919.

If Monash's account of London in 1916 was one definition of total war, it was very much war as an expression of the state. Alternative narratives of modernity, in which the state played a smaller role, and of modern warfare in which the people played a less-subordinate role, were far less pertinent. In 1917–18 Russia, however, successive breakdowns of government control led to the collapse of the war effort, while, in 1918, the failure of the June offensive on the Italian front led to a marked fall in the morale of the Austrian army and encouraged a breakdown of the military establishment, with mutinies and large-scale desertions. The collapse of the ethnic cohesion of the Habsburg army was followed by that of the empire.[40] In all the combatants, state authority had increased during the war, often, particularly in Germany, with the military playing a major role,[41] not least in seeking to control economies: from managing resources to dictating production priorities. Any diminution of control was very unwelcome to military authorities, and this included any move toward warfare outside military control. In October 1918, the German military successfully resisted proposals within the War Cabinet for continuing the war by staging a popular uprising.[42]

Yet, in a precursor of strategy that was employed by the Allies during the Second World War and, even more, as a means to wage indirect warfare during the Cold War, there was interest in inciting popular opposition elsewhere. The Germans sought to do this in the Islamic world, in particular, undermining the British in Egypt and India. Indeed, in 1918, Edmund Allenby, the British commander in Palestine, was concerned about the loyalty of Muslim soldiers in units newly arrived from India. The Allies tried, with far more success, to elicit Arab support against the Turks, and also to tap disaffection within the Habsburg (Austro-Hungarian) Empire. This by no means exhausted the range of options. The Germans tried to arm Irish nationalists, and in 1917, trained Finns in preparation for an attack on Finland (then part of the Russian Empire), while, in 1915, an Allied intelligence report recommended attempting to stimulate an Armenian rising and then landing British troops to exploit the situation.[43]

The large-scale massacre, and genocidal mistreatment, of Armenian civilians by their Turkish rulers in 1915–16 constituted the most prominent instance of atrocities as an aspect of policy. Elsewhere, combat units also engaged in atrocities. In the case of German forces in Belgium and France in 1914, this reflected anger with opposition, particularly unexpected resistance by Belgium, as well as indiscipline and inexperience. The energy the Germans devoted to denying their atrocities reflected their lack of official acceptance of this aspect of war, but also the role of such episodes in Allied propaganda.[44] The desire to maintain civilian morale in a lengthy struggle, as well as to appeal to public opinion in neutral countries, particularly the United States, encouraged such propaganda. It can be seen as an aspect of total war, but was far from new. The development of printing had ensured that lurid propaganda about atrocities had reached a mass audience during the European Wars of Religion, and, certainly, the slaughter of prisoners and civilians was more common at that time than in World War I.

The end of the war also ensured that Allied plans for a large-scale tank assault in 1919 were not brought to fruition. Although plans for armored land vehicles were scarcely new, the development period for the tank was shorter than that for aircraft. Tanks were not in use in 1914; indeed, the British and French invented them independently in 1915, and they were not used in combat until September 15, 1916.[45] Furthermore, problems with sustaining mobility made them of limited value for rapid advances. They were suited more for transforming static into maneuver warfare, rather than for the latter itself. Certainly, tanks seemed to overcome one of the major problems with offensives against trenches: the separation of firepower from advancing troops, and the consequent lack of flexibility. By carrying guns or machine guns, tanks made it possible for advancing units to confront unsuppressed positions and counter-attacks. They offered precise tactical fire to exploit the consequences of the massed operational bombardments that preceded attacks. The value of tanks and their likely future consequences attracted much attention from commentators. Commanders had to decide how best to employ tanks, and to combine them with infantry and artillery. This was an issue made dynamic by the variety of tank types, and by developments in them.

A memorandum of June 1918 from the British Tanks Corps Headquarters claimed:

Trench warfare has given way to field and semi-open fighting...the more the
mobility of tanks is increased, the greater must be the elasticity of the co-operation
between them and the other arms. The chief power of the tank, both material and
moral, lies in its mobility, i.e. its pace, circuit, handiness, and obstacle-crossing
power.

Now the tank commander had to make sure he was not too far in
advance of the infantry:

whilst formerly he merely led the infantry on to their objective protecting them, as
best he could now he must manoeuvre his tank in advance of them zig-zagging from
one position to another, over-running machine guns, stampeding away and
destroying the enemy's riflemen and all the time never losing touch with the infantry
he is protecting.

   This increased power of manoeuvre of the Mark V Tank demands an increased
power of manoeuvre on the part of the infantry. By this is not meant a higher rate of
advance, but skill in the use of ground and formations suitable to the ground and the
tactical situation...demands more and more initiative on the part of the infantry
leaders...Though the effect produced by tanks leading forward infantry may be
compared to that of the artillery barrage, the infantry should not look upon it as such,
but should regard the tanks as armoured fighting patrols or mechanical scouts thrown
out in front of them, not to exonerate them from fighting.[46]

   Edward Heron-Allen was impressed by tanks when he saw them
crossing a road on October 16, 1918, his account descriptive of the
subordination of terrain by the new weapon:

really a fearsome sight...The road was on a slope of the hill, and the tanks just
crawled up the slope, up the right bank nose in air, down with a bump into the road
and across it—almost perpendicularly up the left bank, and down with a bump
behind it and so onward up the hill without a moment's pause or hesitation.[47]

   Tanks were indeed important, but their value was lessened by their
limitations—especially durability, but also firepower and speed. The
British light infantry mortar in practice was more effective, more reliable, and more capable of providing flexible infantry support than
the tank, which was under-powered, under-gunned, under-armored,
and unreliable. Moreover, it was difficult for the crew to communicate
with each other, let alone with anyone outside the tank, and this made
it harder to get a tank to engage a target of opportunity. The value of

tanks was also affected by the difficulty of providing sufficient numbers of them, which reflected their late arrival in wartime resource allocation and production systems, and by the ability to devise anti-tank tactics. German anti-tank measures were quite effective. Wherever tanks met real resistance, they did not do nearly as well as anticipated. The use of artillery against tanks was particularly important in this respect, and reflected the extent to which the incremental nature of improvements in artillery was a matter of tactics as well as technology and numbers. To operate most effectively, tanks needed to support, and to be supported by, advancing infantry and artillery, a lesson that had to be learned repeatedly during the century in the face of pressure from enthusiasts for tanks alone.[48] British successes at Cambrai and Arras provide misleading examples of the usefulness of tanks because they did not meet organized resistance, and most of the tanks engaged in these battles subsequently broke down or were otherwise immobilized within a few days.

Had tank production been at a greater level, then tanks might have made a greater contribution in 1918, but the idea that massed tanks would have made a significant difference to Allied capability had the war continued into 1919 is contentious. Assuming that the tank could have been mass-produced in order to manufacture the huge numbers required, which was not the case hitherto, the same basic problems of unreliability—slow speed, vulnerability to anti-tank measures and field guns, under-gunning, poor inter-communication capabilities, and poor obstacle-crossing capability—nevertheless would have remained. There is little to suggest that the tanks would have performed well. If the British tanks of the 1920s are considered as an extension of the line of development from World War I, it is difficult to see how they would have been decisive. Furthermore, this approach ignores the anti-tank technologies that would have been developed by the Germans. Indeed, the chances are that anti-tank guns would have been superior to the tanks.

Artillery-infantry tactics were far more crucial to the Allied success in 1918. In particular, well-aimed heavy indirect fire, ably coordinated with rushes by infantry who did not move forward in vulnerable lines, played a major role. Such tactics were necessary because German defensive tactics had improved during the war, particularly as a result of the repeated bludgeoning on the Somme in 1916. In place of deep dugouts and continuous trench lines packed with infantrymen came mutually-supporting concrete bunkers surrounded by obstacle belts able to provide a flexible defense in depth.[49] Similarly, in

Palestine, British successes against the Turks in 1917–18 owed far more to infantry and heavy artillery than to cavalry or the use of airplanes and armored cars.[50] Cavalry in Palestine, as elsewhere, offered mobility, but lacked the force necessary to overcome defenses. Some commentators have seen changes in the use of artillery and infantry that occurred in 1917–18 as so important that they have been treated as ushering in the "modern system," one requiring initiative and leadership way down the command hierarchy so that technology and tactics are brought into appropriate harmony.[51] This, however, describes much combat, and it is more appropriate to argue that 1917–18 saw tactical and operational realignments that responded to the particular problems of World War I, and to what these problems indicated about a certain stage of industrial warfare in particular circumstances, rather than to claim that the problems and/or the solution defined industrialized war as a whole, let alone modern warfare.

This argument can also be made about naval warfare. Alongside a focus on dramatically-new technology and doctrine—including submarines, radio, aircraft, airships, and anti-submarine warfare—it is necessary to note the role of traditional practices, such as blockade, as well as incremental improvement, less-spectacular technology, and manufacturing capacity. Mines provide a good example of this; their role tends to be seriously underrated. As well as being responsible for the loss of many merchantmen and surface warships, mines sank more submarines than other weapons, and mine barrages limited the options for submarine warfare. Massive barrages that reflected industrial capacity and organizational capability were laid across the English Channel at Dover in late 1916, and across the far-greater distance of the North Sea between the Orkneys and Norway from March 1918. As an example of incremental development and of the application of scientific knowledge, by the end of the war, magnetic mines had been developed, and were being laid by the British. The complex relationships between tactics, technology, manufacture, and operational experience were more generally shown in anti-submarine warfare. Aircraft and airships supported convoys in coastal waters, forcing submarines to remain submerged, where they were much slower. Furthermore, one of the advantages of aircraft in dealing with submarines is that viewing submerged objects is far easier from above than from sea level. However, aircraft were not yet able to make a fundamental contribution to anti-submarine operations, because key specifications they had by World War II were lacking during World War I, while the anti-submarine weapons dropped by aircraft were fairly unsophisticated compared to those of World War II.

Much of the recent British literature on the Western Front has focused on the development of the appropriate artillery and infantry tactics, a development to which the ability to overcome shell shortages—itself a product of "total" economic war—greatly contributed. This led to important advances in the last months of the war, particularly by British, Australian, and Canadian forces.[52] Improvements in the French army also enabled it to play a major role in the closing offensives.[53] In his report on operations from August 8, 1918, to the end of the war, Thomas Blamey, Chief of Staff to Monash and the Australian Corps, noted that the campaign:

differed from similar operations carried out in 1916 and 1917...

a) Every possible effort was made to obtain surprise both strategically and tactically. It was, therefore, determined that there should be no preliminary bombardment or attempt at destruction of enemy defence systems.

b) Careful concealment of our intentions...

c) Emplacement of a large proportion of artillery within 2,000 yards of the front line which enabled the advance to be covered by an effective barrage to a depth of 4,000 yards into enemy country, and thus ensured that the advance of the infantry beyond the line of the enemy's field guns should be protected by a barrage.

d) No registration of guns in new positions. This was made possible by the careful calibration of guns as new artillery came into the area.

e) The employment of a large proportion of smoke shell in the barrage with the object of enabling the infantry to appear suddenly before any enemy defences and rush them before the enemy was able to realize what was happening.

f)  i) The employment of Tanks...All infantry engaged was given an opportunity of training with tanks prior to the operations.

ii) The 17th Armoured Car Battalion, Tank Corps, was placed at the disposal of the Australian Corps. It was given an independent mission to move direct against enemy centers of communication, headquarters etc. Its operations were brilliantly successful and its exploits read like a tale of the old days.

As a reminder, however, of the danger of selective quotations, the details provided on particular operations indicated the vulnerability of tanks to strong resistance, and the continued problems encountered from unsuppressed machine guns. More generally, there was still considerable pessimism in August 1918 that the war could be won that year; as well as considerable debate over what victory would mean. Blamey recorded that, on August 9, 1918, tank support was "with very reduced numbers owing to casualties suffered on the 8th...Direct fire [on the 9th] was responsible for considerable casualties among the tanks supporting the 1st Australian Division." The need to resort to artillery emerged clearly. On August 11, Blamey wrote, "Owing to the greatly increased enemy resistance in the Lihons Ridge and the fact that there were but few tanks available to support the advance, it was decided to employ a creeping artillery barrage." Indeed, on September 18, the accuracy of the barrage helped in capturing the outer defenses of the German Hindenburg line.

The Germans, however, still fought hard, and Allied casualties were very heavy in the last offensives. Near Peronne, on September 2, the attack was "met by hurricane machine gun fire," while in the main attack on the Hindenburg line on September 29:

on the 27th American Division front, trouble from hostile machine guns inside the barrage was experienced from the start. A number of the tanks supporting the 27th American Division were put out of action by enemy shell fire and by anti-tank mines, and with this support gone the infantry in this sector of the attack rapidly lost touch with the barrage. Enemy machine guns were thus free to harass the main weight of the attack with the result that only isolated parties were able to get forward.

On the front of the 3rd Australian Division, "the tanks detailed to assist...suffered considerably from hostile shell fire." The capture of the Hindenburg defenses led to heavy casualties. On October 3, 1918, "considerable opposition was met with along the Beaurevoir-Masnieres Line which was too wide on the front of the right brigade for the Whippet Tanks to cross. The heavy tanks encountered much anti-tank fire but a few reached the line of La Motte Farm and ably assisted the progress of the infantry."[54]

Total warfare is sometimes confused with an account of modern warfare, and the latter understood in a (misleading) teleological fashion that sees World War II as the culmination of what came before. If so, then the emphasis on tanks, aircraft, and other ways to restore mobility is understandable. If, to adopt another criterion, total warfare is understood in terms of the experience of the soldiers, then a different analysis is possible. Here, the emphasis is rather on the extent to which troops were part of an industrial process, and also on the continual nature of exposure to the pressure of conflict. In May 1915, Monash wrote back to his wife from Gallipoli:

We have been amusing ourselves by trying to discover the longest period of absolute quiet. We have been fighting now continuously for 22 days, all day and all night, and most of us think that absolutely the longest period during which there was absolutely no sound of gun or rifle fire, throughout the whole of that time, was ten seconds. One says he was able on one occasion to count fourteen, but none believe him.[55]

Yet, as a reminder of the variety of the conflict, and specifically of the punctuated intensity—or, looked at differently, disturbed stasis—of trench warfare, Monash wrote the following year from the Western Front, where he commanded the 3rd Australian Division, "compared with Anzac [Gallipoli], the people here don't know what war is. It is true they get an intensive bombardment now and then, and that is pretty bad for anyone who gets in its way, but in between time you'd hardly know there was a war on at all."[56]

Monash also captured the specialization of function and intensity of organization among the military that matched (and connected with) features of contemporary industrial society, writing from Gallipoli in 1915:

We have got our battle procedure now thoroughly well organized. To a stranger it would probably look like a disturbed anti-heap with everybody running a different way, but the thing is really a triumph of organization. There are orderlies carrying messages, staff officers with orders, lines of ammunition carriers, water carriers, bomb carriers, stretcher bearers, burial parties, first-aid men, reserves, supports, signalers, telephonists, engineers, digging parties, sandbag parties, periscope hands, pioneers, quartermaster's parties, and reinforcing troops, running about all over the place, apparently in confusion, but yet everything works as smoothly as on a peace parade, although the air is thick with clamour and bullets and bursting shells, and bombs and flares.[57]

The extent to which the Germans were outfought on the Western Front in 1918 was not one that was to attract adequate subsequent attention at the popular level. The Germans preferred the "stab-in-the-back" legend, attributing defeat to left-wing disaffection at home; while post-war opposition among the Allies, particularly Britain, to the human cost of the war and, to a lesser extent, to post-war diplomacy, tarnished the presentation of victory. More recently, academic study of the warmaking, specifically of improvements in British fighting techniques, and an emphasis on the challenge posed by German aggression and expansionism, have had scant impact on popular views.[58] As a result, the conflict continues to be one of the most misunderstood of all major wars, which leads to more general problems with the assessment of military capability, effectiveness, and development in the period covered by this book.

Raymond Aron saw World War I as ensuring a shift, from a situation in which the conditions for total war existed, to one in which such a conflict could develop, and he suggested that "the approximately equal strength of the opposing forces" provided the key opportunity.[59] This approach captures the contingent nature of developments, and also the extent to which wartime policies were a response to problems. For this reason, it is misleading to see the nature of the conflict as the culmination of pre-war thought, planning, and preparations. Most wars do not develop as anticipated, but this was particularly true of World War I. The cult of the offensive, which had led to the deliberate under-estimation of the impact of firepower in pre-war maneuvers,[60] is too readily read forward into the course of the conflict. There is a failure to note the degree to which pre-war planning saw attacks as an aspect of maneuver warfare and indeed urged the value of mobile defense; while wartime experience forced a rethinking of the attack as the way to overcome static warfare, specifically the impasse of trench conflict.

This led, as discussed in this chapter, not only to a number of expedients, but also to a rethinking of combined-arms operations. The emphasis on strong firepower support reflected a need to suppress defenses that were stronger than those generally anticipated prior to the conflict. This gave point to interest in new technology, particularly (but not only) gas, aircraft, and tanks. If a tactical and operational perspective is thus taken, then the shift toward a new type of warfare occurred during the war, not with its outbreak.

At the strategic level, Aron's perspective is a valuable one. The ability of both sides to sustain the struggle forced a mobilization of resources on a scale that differed from preceding conflicts. This returns attention to the causes of the conflict and its continuation, and why neither side was willing to compromise to avoid the war or to end it. Here, in terms of the causes of war, the context was to change greatly and in a generally unpredicted fashion, from the close of World War I, as more overt ideological factors came to play a larger role in international relations, first with the Soviet Union and the response to it.

The play of overt ideological factors in domestic politics from the close of World War I also ensured that the context within which industrial mobilization occurred was to change. During World War I, however, the degree of such mobilization had already encouraged large-scale governmental and social change. In many respects, this was less novel than it might appear, because such change had also arisen from earlier conflicts. For example, British participation in the French Revolutionary and Napoleonic Wars, from 1793 to 1802 and 1803 to 1814, and again in 1815, had led to a major increase in government activity, the results of which included an expansion in the information that it sought to deploy. The Ordnance Survey to map the country was complemented in 1801 by the first British national census, while income tax was introduced and the rights of workers to take industrial action were curtailed. Living standards were also affected by economic problems that in part arose from the war, although the government could not control harvests.

The economic context was different in World War I, because of the key role of manufacturing, and therefore of large organized workforces. Pre-industrial forms of deference and social control, in terms of the rule and role of landlords and clerics, were no longer pertinent for the bulk of the population, although in rural areas they remained more relevant than is sometimes appreciated. The social politics of the period gave the state a greater role than a century earlier, in the sense that the organization of economic mobilization was necessarily on a larger scale, and also required more central direction.

Economic mobilization was accompanied by the overthrow of globalization. John Maynard Keynes reflected in *The Economic Consequences of the Peace* (1919):

What an extraordinary episode in the economic progress of man that age was which came to an end in August, 1914 ... life offered, at a low cost and with the least trouble, conveniences, comforts, and amenities beyond the compass of the richest and most powerful monarchs of other ages. The inhabitant of London could order by telephone, sipping his morning tea in bed, the various products of the whole earth ... he could at the same moment and by the same means adventure his wealth in the natural resources and new enterprises of any quarter of the world ... But, most important of all, he regarded this state of affairs as normal, certain, and permanent, except in the direction of further improvement, and any deviation from it as aberrant, scandalous, and avoidable.

In practice, there were already pre-war threats to the liberal economic order, not least due to tariffs, but it was a very dynamic capitalist world that was hit hard by the war. Aside from the destruction of manufacturing plant, there was tremendous damage to trade and economic interdependence. On the global scale, European powers, especially Britain, sold much of their foreign investment in order to finance the war effort. Furthermore, the disruption of trade (and its total collapse outside Europe in the case of Germany), and the diversion, under state regulation, of manufacturing capacity to war production, ensured that the European economies were less able to satisfy foreign demand. This encouraged the growth of manufacturing elsewhere, not least in Latin America and in European colonies such as India, although American exporters benefited most of all. The British war effort was heavily-dependent on the United States, while the Americans were well-placed to replace British exports to Canada and Latin America.[61] Import substitution and industrial expansion were also pushed in South Africa under a consolidated tariff for the entire Union introduced in 1914. The unprecedented global economic range of this war was facilitated by the extent of colonial empires. India, for example, provided large quantities of products for the British war effort, including food and textiles. This was true even for areas not well integrated into imperial economies. For example, food exports from the Anglo-Egyptian colony of Sudan rose to meet wartime demands, leading there and elsewhere to the disruption stemming from price and wage inflation. After the war, the British sought to re-create the liberal economic order, but with only limited success.

Alongside long-term disruption, the enforced reconfiguration of the international trading system brought considerable misery during the war. This was not simply a matter of inflationary pressures, but also of hardships stemming from the seizures of resources—the Germans taking millions of tons of food from Russia and Romania—and from the deliberate interruption of trade. The most potent was the Allied blockade of Germany. This may be seen as an aspect of total war, with its direction of pressure on an entire society, and reference can be made to economic warfare during the American Civil War,[62] but such blockades also preceded the period seen as the age of total war. During the Napoleonic Wars, France tried to stop continental Europe trading with Britain, which in turn applied a blockade. There was also a British blockade of the United States during the War of 1812, while the American response of privateering was another form of blockade.

Demographic growth, and the growing economic specialization and interdependence through trade that stemmed from the global development of Western capitalism, however, made the societies of the early-twentieth century more vulnerable to blockade. This was seen with the major strains on British and German society imposed by German submarine warfare and Allied blockade, respectively.[63] The nature of this pressure, however, was very different. Unrestricted submarine warfare, by attacking all shipping and by sinking without warning, violated international law, and it was unsurprising that American political and public opinion responded unfavorably. The Germans had anticipated a rapid victory through the economic warfare of unrestricted attacks declared on February 1, 1917, but the British did not sue for peace on August 1, as it had been claimed they would. The Germans had insufficient submarines to match their aspirations, in part because of problems with organizing and supplying construction, but largely because of a lack of commitment from within the navy to the submarine warfare, and a preference, instead, for surface warships.

Furthermore, more seriously, the operational flaws of German warmaking rested on a strategic misjudgment of British vulnerability. During the war, the Germans sank 11.9 million tons of, mostly commercial, Allied shipping at the cost of 199 submarines, but aside from the benefits that stemmed from the British introduction of escorted convoys in May 1917—in cutting shipping losses dramatically and in leading to an increase in the sinking of German submarines—the British were less vulnerable to blockade than had been anticipated. It proved possible to increase and reorganize food production in Britain, and to direct its distribution. In so far as total war is a helpful phrase in this context, it applied to the methods but not the capability of German submarine attacks, the means and results of the British institutional response, including the establishment of an effective Food Production Department, and the success of the traditional means of surface blockade as applied against Germany.[64]

The latter offered the British more against Germany than it had against France in the Napoleonic Wars, in part because of long-term developments in naval effectiveness, specifically the replacement of sail by steam, but also due to the nature of the international system. Germany was unable to dominate continental Europe, as Napoleon had done, while the United States was willing to accept the consequences of British naval power, unlike the anger displayed during the earlier period, which had culminated in the War of 1812. The results of the naval war were also seen in the peace settlement of 1919, with the merchant ships seized from Germany allocated to the victors in proportion to their wartime maritime losses.

The naval struggle had been important, but there had not been the major battle sought and anticipated by navalists. Although the battle of Jutland between the British and German fleets in the North Sea in 1916 was the largest clash of battleships in history, it was not the hoped-for Trafalgar, still less a repetition of the Japanese victory over the Russians at Tsushima in 1905: a total victory soon followed by the end of the war. The Allied fleets proved more effective at blockade than battle, but they had few opportunities for the latter. The role of resources and alliances were important in both. Because the Germans finished not one of the dreadnoughts or battle cruisers they laid down during the war, compared with the five battle cruisers laid down and completed by Britain, the Germans did not have the margin of safety of a shipbuilding program to fall back upon, nor did they have the prospect of support from the warships of new allies that the British gained with the entry of Italy and the United States. This helped accentuate the importance to the Germans of submarines, although, in combating these, the British benefited from their wartime shipbuilding program, which included fifty-six destroyers and fifty anti-submarine motor launches. The strategic advantages of the Allies nullified the capability the Germans derived from their submarines: fewer Allied warships were sunk than were added to the combined total.[65]

Aside from the varied nature of social change and disruption across Europe resulting from the war, which particularly hit those who benefited from pre-war prosperity and stability, there was a more immediate physical shock arising from the nature of the battlefield, specifically the way in which the terrain was devastated by conflict, with the scale seemingly dwarfing any opportunities for heroism. The direct exposure of large numbers to the conflict was accentuated by its impact on others via reporting and photography. The length of the conflict, the numbers involved, and the fact that so much of it occurred in Europe, ensured that it was not easy to treat it as a distant spectacle. Traveling the Bapaume Road, close to the Western Front, on October 20, 1918, Edward Heron-Allen, a visiting civilian, wrote in his diary, "The whole landscape seen on either side . . . was a scene of complete desolation. As far as one can see to the horizon, blasted woods and ruined villages." Two days later, he reached Ypres:

I thought I had seen absolute devastation and ruin at Bapaume, and Péronne, but Ypres by comparison is as the Sahara to a sand dune. I could not realize that we were approaching—much less in—the outskirts of Ypres. When, passing through some mounds of rubbish I asked where we were and was told "This is Ypres," it absolutely turned me cold. Even the streets are obliterated . . . there were not even bases of walls to show where houses had begun and left off . . . "The Hinterland of Hell" is the only phrase that in any way describes the road and the surrounding country between Ypres and Menin. Hitherto the desolation and devastation has seemed mournful—tragic— here it is fierce and absolutely terrifying. The whole landscape is ploughed up into "hummocks" like pack ice in the Arctic Floe-mounds and crevasses of blackened earth, dotted about with English and German graves, the entrances to dug-outs leading apparently into the bowels of the earth... shell holes and mine craters of every size.

As earlier with poison gas, retribution seemed the order of the day, "A flight of aeroplanes which passed overhead in battle-formation, off on a road to the east, seemed a fitting commentary upon the ghastly desolation."[66] In turn, in 1918, the Germans planned large-scale bombing attacks on London and Paris using more effective incendiaries, but, due to the imminence of defeat, they were not launched.[67]

Yet, alongside the emphasis on horror, it is necessary to note a more complex situation. As ever with scholarship, there are issues of emphasis. For example, lately there has been much stress on executions of those unfairly judged guilty of cowardice in the British army, but their relatively exceptional nature has received insufficient attention. There were 361 British military executions during the war, and they were primarily motivated by considerations of discipline.[68] This issue is related to the more general question of the response to "shell shock," which would now be referred to as post-traumatic stress disorder. As a result of World War I, there was a change of perception by some doctors who were treating psychiatric disorders, and the awareness of psychiatric pressures in wartime increased. The acceptance of shell shock and battle fatigue as a legitimate illness waned afterward, however, and the lessons of World War I had to be relearned in World War II.[69]

There was often a rise of such disorders, known by different names at different times, during and immediately after war. Furthermore, shell shock was not the fate of the majority of soldiers in World War I. Indeed, the morale of the British military seems to have been pretty good throughout,[70] and that also seems to have been the case with the German army until the summer of 1918. Also, the experience of terrible casualties in 1914–16 did not stop the French or Russian armies from fighting: large-scale mutinies in either did not occur until 1917, and there were particular precipitants for them. The morale of the French army recovered quickly after General Henri Pétain replaced Robert Nivelle as commander that May.

Reasons varied for the willingness of the majority of soldiers to fight, and much was due to commitment and group cohesion, but this willingness also partially reflected the extent to which the war was less terrible an experience than is suggested in some of the sources. Factors to note include the degree to which fronts were relatively quiet, other than during offensives, while the latter were episodic and restricted to sections of the front. The consistency of conflict did not match that on the Eastern Front in 1941–45, or the Western Front in 1944–45. In addition, the material condition of the troops was frequently better than at home, particularly in terms of rations. Accommodation was no worse than slums at home. In some respects, indeed, conditions were better than at home, and this was particularly true for the British army, which benefited from frequent rotation out of the frontline, and from organized rest and recreation while out of it.[71] French troops were not treated as well, although Pétain introduced important reforms, not least of all in the leave system. There were particular problems for the Allies, where the front lacked depth, most obviously at Gallipoli,[72] but this was unusual.

The subsequent perception of the war was an important aspect of its wider impact. This was partly a matter of the presentation of the experience of conflict, and also of the struggle to come to terms with mass bereavement. Both played a major role in inter-war collective memory.[73] The scale of the sacrifice was indeed unprecedented, and this had a major impact on society, with the loss of so many sons, husbands, and fathers. Furthermore, there were large numbers of wounded. The impact was felt in family economies and the general economy, and in private and public senses of grief. A major revival in interest in spiritualism and the occult was one consequence, prefiguring a similar, but less pronounced, revival after World War II. The world-wide nature of the grief was unprecedented, and a major consequence of its global scope. New Zealand, the most distant large dominion of the British Crown, participated fully in the war (introducing conscription in 1916) and lost heavily: forty percent of military-age men (nineteen to forty-five) served overseas; of this 120,000, more than 50,000 were injured and 18,000 died, many at Gallipoli. Among the 332,000 Australian troops who served overseas, 58,460 died, while 56,119 Canadians died. Grief and remembrance therefore reached out to distant corners.[74] The commemoration of the struggle, for example, the design of cemeteries and the staging of anniversaries, provided an opportunity to underline national identity by offering a history of sacrifice and an emphasis on the casualties, that was, at the same time, a call for the sacrifice not to be in vain. Thus, past, present, and future were linked.

This provided a context for public discussions about how best to consider the war. The large number of casualties provided the prism within which perceptions and ideas were discussed. Much of the portrayal of the conflict was very critical. A more complex view, not least one which attempted to put costly battles, such as the Somme, alongside other aspects of the war, including eventual Allied success in 1918, found little favor. The same was true of the peace settlement. Just as, by the start of the 1930s, British confidence in the conduct of the war was being sapped by critical publications that focused on the horrors of trench warfare and the mistakes of generals, also at that time, criticism of the peace settlements that had ended the war, particularly as unfair to the Germans and/or inopportune, was well-established. Focus on the reparations demanded from Germany, as an aspect of its war guilt, proved a particular source of criticism, encouraging the view that the peace had been mainly retributive. In short, a mishandled, if not misguided, total war had led to a harsh peace, the latter a consequence of the former.

This was an inappropriate judgment of a conflict that was far from harsh on Germany, and of peace terms that were certainly far less severe than those of 1945. Germany lost territory in 1919, but there was no attempt to return it to the situation prior to unification under Prussian control. Talk in France of a different future for the Rhineland led nowhere. Partly, this was because of a concern to prevent the spread of Communist revolution to Germany, and partly because the military verdict was as if World War II had ended in September 1944. At the time of the armistice in 1918, Germany was not yet overrun by the Western powers. Furthermore, she was still in occupation of large territories in Eastern Europe. The terms of the peace were designed to prevent Germany from launching fresh aggression, and thus to serve as a form of collective security. This was true of the limitations on the German military, the occupied area along the French and Belgian frontiers, much of it occupied until 1930, and the demilitarized zone that Germany had to accept.

Austria suffered far more severely from the peace, in large part because the Habsburg Empire was far more vulnerable than Germany to the principle of national self-determination actively pushed by President Woodrow Wilson of the United States. The treaty settlements imposed on Austria by the French Revolutionaries and Napoleon had been drastic, with Austria losing the Austrian Netherlands (modern Belgium and Luxembourg) in 1797; Lombardy in 1797; Venetia (which she had gained in compensation in 1797) in 1805; Tyrol in 1805; her territories in southwest Germany in 1806; West Galicia (in Poland), Cracow, and much of Carinthia and Croatia in 1809; and Salzburg in 1810. Yet, Austria had retained control of Bohemia, Moravia, Slovakia, Hungary, Transylvania, most of Galicia, and part of Croatia. After World War I, in contrast, all of these were lost, as were territories Austria had regained in 1814–15 and others gained subsequently: Galicia went to Poland; Transylvania to Romania; Trentino and Istria to Italy; and Croatia, Bosnia, and Slovenia to Yugoslavia; while Bohemia, Moravia, and Slovakia became the independent state of Czechoslovakia. Hungary became fully independent. This was a settlement without compromise. Insofar as total war was a matter of outcomes, this was total war.

Turkey also suffered far more severely than Germany. It was vulnerable to the idea of national self-determination, as some Arabs, Armenians, and Kurds sought nationhood, but, far more, to the international ambitions of the victorious powers, in this case Britain, France, Italy, and Greece.[75] Furthermore, unlike Germany, the war ended with much of its empire conquered, although Turkey rebounded under Kemal Atatürk in the 1920s. Moreover, the victors, and the League of Nations they established in 1920 as a pan-national organization with a mission to prevent war and to deal with any unresolved peace settlement issues, introduced and maintained very different logics of territorial legitimacy outside and within Europe. Whereas local consent, in the form of plebiscites, was used to determine some European frontiers, for example, those between Denmark and Germany, and between Germany and Poland in East Prussia in 1920, such consent-frontiers were not granted outside Europe. The Treaty of Sèvres of 1920 established particularly harsh terms on the Turks, but the Turks were able to defeat the Greeks in 1922 and to force the other Western allies to accept more lenient terms in 1923.

The Versailles settlement and the international system it established worked better in the 1920s, at least from the perspective of Western interests, than was generally appreciated in the 1930s. There was domestic instability and international tension in Europe, but this had been the case prior to 1914, and World War I and the collapse of the European dynastic empires had left many disputes. Having launched the war in the West in 1914, and then been defeated, it was understandable that Germany suffered, but the terms it had to accept scarcely justified any sense of a peace that can be used, in itself, to substantiate the description total war.[76]

# CHAPTER 6
# Between the World Wars, 1919–38

The caveats already expressed about inter-war periods are also valid for this one. Indeed, discussion about the lessons to be drawn from World War I, and about the anticipation of the next major conflict, so dominates attention of 1919–38 that it is apt to drown out other aspects of military history, not least of all the many conflicts of the period. This reflects the developmental model of history: events are of significance if they exemplified and contributed to the key pattern of development, a singularly teleological view. As far as 1919–38 is concerned, this leads to a focus on anticipations of World War II, particularly the Spanish Civil War (1936–39). Such an approach is a misreading of the specific conflicts that are considered—the Spanish Civil War, for example, being very different from World War II, and not being largely waged within the techniques and tactics, particularly the terror-bombing of cities, that attract attention.[1]

More seriously, the approach matches the general pattern of much scholarship during the inter-war period, with its focus on the last years before World War II and its general neglect of the 1920s. This is unfortunate for a number of reasons. The 1920s saw a working through of the experience of World War I by military commentators and, of course, by civilians coming to grips with grief and with the varied experience of the war,[2] who were keen to ensure that future war be different or, indeed, never occur.[3] Furthermore, the conflicts that followed 1919 indicated the extent to which war was total, not as suggested by World War I in terms of the experience of fighting—massed forces in conflict in a concentrated area, supported by the panoply of industrial munitions—but rather as an aspect of bitter struggles, some heavily ideological, in which there was little contrast between the military and civil society. Two obvious, and related, consequences were the relatively high rate of atrocities against civilians, and the extent to which militias and irregulars played a major role in conflicts, a situation that had not been true of the recent world war.

The deliberate targeting of civilians was encouraged by the extent to which national self-determination played a major role in the politics that spanned the closing stages of the war in Eastern Europe with the post-war period. As new states based on notions of ethnic homogeneity strove to define their boundaries, it proved attractive to turn on minorities. In what had been Russia, tensions were not only ethnic-nationalist but also ideological, with the Communists seeking to use class identity to bridge ethnic divides and, instead, to isolate and destroy what were seen as internal enemies. The consequences were brutal, with war overlapping with pogroms, for example, by Cossacks against Jews in Ukraine, and also with the killing of those seen as social enemies and, therefore, political traitors.

The multi-dimensional nature of struggles made them complex in causes, course, and consequences. In Central Asia, for example, there were struggles in the autonomous emirate of Bukhara and khanate of Khiva, with their autocratic rulers successfully resisting local reform movements, and the Russian Communists intervening. They established a People's Soviet Republic in the latter in February 1920, and, after a first expedition had failed that March, a second overthrew the emir of Bukhara in September. This led to a People's Soviet Republic of Bukhara. Both, however, were unilaterally ended in 1924 when the Moscow authorities reorganized the governmental system in Central Asia.

Ideological rivalry was also a feature of conflict in post-war Germany, as radical attempts to seize power were contested by right-wing paramilitaries. In the warlord period of 1916–27 in China, atomization also reflected the strength of local military figures and this led to a spread of militarization as local communities sought to respond to the dominance of administration by overt force.[4] The instability of the warlord era was a legacy of pre-war change, specifically the overthrow of the Manchu dynasty in 1911, but this had been accentuated during the war by the subsequent failure to create a popular and successful replacement, not least in the face of Japanese demands for gains as a result of its support for the Allies.

Wartime problems also helped lead to post-war instability in Portugal. British pressure had led the Portuguese government in 1917 to the unpopular and expensive decision to support the Allies, a measure bitterly criticized by the trade unions, and it was overthrown that year by a dictatorship under Sidónio Pais, which responded to riots by force, only for Pais to be assassinated. The liberal republic returned, but was overthrown by an army coup in 1926 that created a conservative order that lasted until a radical army coup led to its overthrow in 1974.[5]

The fighting after World War I in Europe and the former Russian Empire was far more confusing than that during the conflict. In place of clear-cut adversaries came shifting alignments and uncertain interventions, for example, those of the British in the Baltic republics, and instead of regular forces, readily apparent command structures, and clearly demarcated front lines, there were irregulars, complex relations between civil and military agencies and goals, and fluid spheres of operations. The force-space ratios were very different from those of World War I, particularly on the Western Front, the subject of most military discussion.[6] As a consequence, these were conflicts in which the emphasis was on activity, raids, and the seizure of key political positions, rather than on staging battles from prepared positions. The difficulty of sustaining operations encouraged this emphasis. As a result, the balance swung back toward the offensive, as in February 1918, when the newly-established Communist government in Tashkent sent a small force that rapidly seized Khokand, overthrowing the Muslim government that had been established there.

The defensive remained important at the tactical level, and, in some respects, more so than in World War I, because the artillery necessary to suppress fire was in limited supply and not really useful for fast-moving operations over large areas. At the same time, the absence of continuous fronts made it easier to outflank defensive positions, as was also amply demonstrated in China, and this encouraged the stress on maneuver. In addition, defensive positions could be stormed, and there were short battles, such as the Red Army's victory over Czech and White Russian forces at Samara on October 8, 1918, and the White storming of Tsaritsyn (later Stalingrad) on the second attempt in June 1919; unlike the long battles, resting on repeated attacks, seen so often in World War I.

A stress on maneuver was also encouraged by the need, after World War I, to establish control rapidly in contested areas in order to present peacemakers and other powers with faits accomplis. This was a response both to the failure of peacemakers to accept the complexity of situations on the ground and a rejection of the attempt by outside bodies to dictate developments. The process began in the former Russian Empire as authority collapsed in 1918, prior to the end of World War I further west, for example, in Finland from January when Red (Communist) Finns seized Helsinki. The resulting conflict involved them, White (conservative) Finns, Germans who allied with the Whites, taking Helsinki in April 1918, and Communist Russians. The presence of German forces in the western parts of the former Russian Empire, and their active role in political struggles there, ensured that there was no clear divide between World War I and post-war struggles. Similarly, Turkish forces advanced in the Caucasus, capturing Kars, only to be heavily defeated by the Armenians at Sardarapat in May 1918, a key event in modern Armenian nationalism.

Conflict spread as the Austrian Empire collapsed later in the year. Before the end of 1918, Germans and Czechs were clashing in the Sudetenland, as were the Carinthians and Slovenes in what became the Austrian-Yugoslav border area. Pre-war disputes became post-war clashes. As the number of "players" in conflict rose, the notions of a clear-cut definition of military forces, and of war as the prerogative of the state, were put under severe strain. This obliged regular militaries to confront situations in which goals and opponents were far from clear, and atrocities, terrorism, and terror became more than the small change of war.

In part, this was a matter of the projection into Europe of the small-wars techniques hitherto employed as an aspect of imperial conquest, but there was the added element of political terror. Imperial conflicts—of which there were several in 1919–29, including between Britain and Afghanistan and between France and Spain on the one hand and local opposition in Morocco—did not involve war with compatriots determined on a different political outcome, except insofar as the Western power recruited local support. As a consequence, the similarity in means of conflict with Europe was not matched by that of goals. Civil warfare was different to imperial wars. One obvious distinction was in intensity of control. In imperial policing, there was much delegated rule (and use of violence), and not the need perceived in Europe to ensure dominance of the localities. The latter was often less complete in Europe than might be imagined, for example, the Albanian government having little control over mountain tribes. Nevertheless, there was an obvious contrast between the relatively light British policing of Burma and Sudan, and the attempt of new or newly-extended states and governments in Europe to enforce their authority. This was taken furthest when those who followed different social practices were seen as enemies, irrespective of their degree of political activism, and this was most apparent with the Communists who seized control in Russia.[7]

As a consequence, civil war understood as military operations, over-lapped with civil war that dealt with those defined as social enemies. White victory in Finland was followed by the establishment of a prison camp on the island of Suomelinna. It held 8,500 Red prisoners at the peak and about 1,000 died there between April 1918 and March 1919. This overlap was not a novelty. Specifically, in some respects, Soviet policy was a revival of the military politics of internal conflict in revolutionary France, while the notion of war as an aspect of politics was central to civil conflict. The nature and frequency of civil warfare in the period covered by this book, particularly in 1918–22, helps ensure a situation in which the violence associated with revo-lutionary (and counter-revolutionary) politics was frequent in the West, but that had also been the case over the previous century and a half, especially with the civil warfare of 1787–98, 1830, and 1848–49. The nature, scale, and intensity of the Taiping and Boxer Rebellions and their suppression in China and of the Chinese civil wars in the 1920s–1940s, suggest that a Western-centric narrative and analysis of the problem is limited. Even within the West, it is unclear that the paranoia and violence associated with the ideological warfare of 1917–45 were different in type to the Wars of Religion in Europe in 1560–1648.

As with many other civil wars, military necessity also led toward internal violence, because it was necessary to create and sustain forces without a clear-cut, coherent, and uncontested governmental struc-ture, or the possibility of eliciting consent through established political channels. In Russia, the Communists nationalized businesses, seized grain, and imposed a firm dictatorship, while opposition was brutally suppressed. The Communist mind-set was very much one of un-constrained struggle, a notion that was also seen in Fascist ideology. Analysis of Communist Party internal language indicates that their self-belief readily permitted a rationalization of the use of force, not least in the absence of the mass support anticipated or hoped for be-cause of their proclaimed role as vanguards of the people.[8] The geo-graphical extent of the Russian Civil War and of the related struggles was greater than that of World War I in Europe, although there was neither a naval nor a transoceanic dimension. The length of the struggle was also noteworthy, although this was partially a product of the sequential character of Communist offensives against opponents who found co-operation difficult. Thus, once Poland had made peace in 1920, it was possible for the Red Army to turn south against the Whites based in the Crimea. Civil war lasted from 1918 until October 1922, when the Red Army captured Vladivostok. Related struggles were waged in those sections of the Russian Empire that sought independence. Foreign intervention on behalf of the Whites was affected by a lack of consistent political support in the metropoles, as well as by the absence of a coherent White command structure and strategy with which to co-operate. For example, the Franco-Greek force that landed at Odessa in December 1918 made scant contribution to the White cause, and was evacuated the following spring in the face of the Communist advance.

On a smaller scale, there were also conflicts across much of Eastern Europe. Ideology played a role, as when the Romanians and Czechs suppressed a Communist regime in Hungary in 1919, after the Romanians had conquered Transylvania and after bitter fighting between Czech and Hungarian forces in Slovakia. Nationalism was also crucial, for example, in the Polish seizure of Vilnius from Lithuania in 1920, the Lithuanian seizure of Memel from a French garrison in 1923, and the 1919 occupation of the town of Fiume by an Italian volunteer force (undermining the authority of the state), angry that it had not been allocated to Italy in the peace settlement and determined to force a different outcome. The implementation of the peace settlement in the former Turkish Empire involved more large-scale conflict, particularly for the Greeks in Turkey and the British in Iraq. In Syria, however, the new colonial power was more successful. Faisal, the son of Hussein ibn Ati, king of the Hijaz, had joined with the British in capturing Damascus in 1918, but his ambition to be ruler of Syria was thwarted by France, which gained a League of Nations mandate to govern it. In 1920, Faisal's forces were defeated at Maisalun, France seized Damascus, and Faisal took refuge in Iraq.

If this wave of conflict was over by 1923, there was no guarantee that it would not revive. Territorial claims, for example, by Hungary on Romanian-held Transylvania, remained an issue, as irredentist parties continued to be influential. Indeed, particularly at the level of second-rank powers such as Hungary, Italy, and Bulgaria, this was a key element in affecting participation in World War II. These concerns, and the frequently related social politics of military service, not least the emphasis on conscription and social control, helped account for the force structures and doctrines of many armies during what became the inter-war period. Rather than emphasizing state-of-the-art weaponry or fortification, there was a stress on numbers, and the conflicts prepared for were not too different from those waged in 1912–23.

As a result, the shadow of World War I, although powerful, was less pronounced than is generally believed. This was understandably so because, although, as far as the previous century was concerned, participation in a large-scale conflict nearby was unprecedented for Britain, the war had been part of a sequence in areas such as the Balkans and Poland. If different largely in type and scale to what had gone before, World War I was less so for Bulgaria, Romania, and Greece than for Britain and France. Similarly, in Latin America, the years after World War I saw a continuation of earlier patterns of conflict, much of it insurrectionary in character—for example, the failed invasion of Costa Rica in May 1919 by exiles based in Nicaragua; the Liberal revolt in Nicaragua in 1925; and the Cristero rebellion in Mexico in 1926–29, a Catholic rising against the revolutionary state and its agrarian reform and attack on the church, which led to guerilla warfare.[9]

When combined with the continued role of colonial warfare for Britain, France, Italy, and Spain in the 1920s and 1930s, this civil and insurrectionary warfare underlines the extent to which concepts of total war did not dominate attention. Indeed, there is considerable anachronism in assuming that they should have in the 1920s. There was certainly conflict then involving the major powers, but it proved possible to contain. The Western powers and Japan intervened in the Russian Civil War, but were able to withdraw without a continuation of the conflict. The Soviet attempt to advance westward was stopped by Poland near Warsaw in 1920. The French provided military advice, but did not need to send troops to Poland to fight Russia, as they had done unsuccessfully in 1734.

France itself intervened in Germany, sending troops alongside those of Belgium into the Ruhr, the key German economic zone, in 1923, in an attempt to enforce the payment of reparations (money owed as part of the peace settlement), but this led to large-scale civil disobedience in Germany, not war. Germany had been restricted to an army of only one hundred thousand men with no advanced weapons in the Versailles peace settlement, and it was in no shape to contest the Franco-Belgian occupation. Civil disobedience did not lead to guerilla warfare, or the people's war pressed by some German commentators, and the crisis was resolved before conflict could break out.

Given these issues, and the heavy burden of debt and recovery left after World War I, it was scarcely surprising that investment in the armed forces did not match new military doctrine. Limitation agreements appeared to provide an answer, and were instances of the Great Powers trying to legislate against totality. The basis of such agreements varied. World War I led to restrictions on the defeated powers. This was most significantly seen with the provisions in the Versailles Treaty of 1919 restricting the size of the German military and limiting its force structure. There were also negotiations between the undefeated powers, particularly the agreements on surface shipping that led to the Washington Naval Treaty of 1922 and the London Naval Treaty of 1930. The Washington Naval Treaty also included a clause stopping the military development of American colonies in the Western Pacific and also of many of Japan's island possessions. There was also interest in regulating submarine warfare.[10]

If this was a response to what World War I had suggested about the dangerous consequences of large-scale warfare, the willingness to accept limitations scarcely suggested a welcoming of military capability. This was further seen with the major interest in the 1920s in disarmament and in the peaceful settlement of international disputes. The failure of the Wilsonian idealism that had influenced American policy in 1917–19 did not lead to the end of internationalism. Instead, new international institutions, particularly the League of Nations, acted as the foci for multilateral diplomacy, injecting a newly-strong, multinational dimension to the practice of traditional negotiation.

Large-scale war, whether defined as total or not, might then appear to have come to an end in the 1920s. Indeed, within Europe, the conflicts of 1919–22 did not recur, and the Locarno Treaty of 1925 appeared to indicate that Germany could be readily re-assimilated into the international system. Trotskyite interest in furthering world revolution became far less pronounced in the Soviet Union as Stalin, the dictator from 1924 until 1953, concentrated on domestic goals. Although Soviet propaganda, and the activities, both known and suspected, of the Comintern (the Communist international) and of Communist parties went beyond the confines of acceptable diplomacy, revolutionary aspirations were subordinated to the more pragmatic interests of the Soviet state.

The largest-scale warfare of the 1920s, the civil wars in China, did not engage world attention and anyway appeared settled with the success of the Kuomintang's Northern Expedition (1926–28). This achieved an uneasy unity for much of China. It was a stage in the struggles for unification that had begun after the overthrow of Manchu imperial rule in 1911 and continued when President Yuan Shih-Kai crushed opposition to his rule in 1913: his forces stormed Nanjing, the former imperial capital. It was to be stormed anew by Kuomintang (Chinese nationalist) forces in 1927. Much of the warfare of the 1920s can be seen in terms of the anarchic self-interest of the warlords, their kaleidoscopic alliances, and the growing power of the Kuomintang which, despite a measure of idealism, came under Chiang Kai-shek, its effective head from 1926, to act as a form of successful warlordism with national pretensions. China in the 1920s is a useful corrective against any assumption that the bases of politics and warfare were necessarily defined in terms of modern states. The same was true of Arabia, where, after the collapse of Turkish control and influence, tribal leaders operated rather like Chinese warlords. The most successful, Ibn Saud of Nejd, gradually extended his position, defeating the Hashemites in a dawn attack at Turabah in May 1919, and gaining control of Mecca in 1924 and Medina and Jeddah in 1925. This was a conflict of raids and loose sieges.

As a reminder that this is not an ethnocentric point, the Fascist glorification of war[11] and cult of the leader also offered echoes from the past. Unlike many contemporaries, the Fascists did not see the abolition of war as possible or desirable. Fascism created a history for itself in which struggle and martial images played the major role, most obviously with Mussolini's March on Rome in 1922. This was an unnecessary step, as his entry to power had already been accepted, but he was keen to show that he had taken power. Mussolini also showed that the cult of the leader was not a way to restraint. Like autocrats before and since, he surrounded himself with the trappings of unconstrained power, literally strutting a stage as he soaked up his own bombast.

Nevertheless, alongside continuity, the conflicts of the 1920s also demonstrated the extent of military modernization in China, with the use of World War I–type equipment, the large-scale production of munitions, especially in Mukden in Manchuria, and the ability to move troops rapidly by rail. As with the American and Russian Civil Wars, this helped shape the conflict, at least in operational terms, not least because, at a distance from railways, the communication system was very different, indeed heavily dependent on coolies: human porters, such as those the Europeans had used in Africa. As with the Russian Civil War, instead of continuous fronts, there was a stress on rapid advances on key positions, as with the Kuomintang storming of Shanghai in March 1927, and on seeking to build up support by winning over warlords, who were a major challenge to the central state's monopolization of legitimate force. However, the changing commitments of the warlords resulted in a lack of consistency in the forces engaged, suggesting that, whatever the scale of conflict and the degree of modernization, both of which were considerable in China in the 1920s, this was not total warfare. Ideological commitment was limited. Generals changed sides: Feng Yuxiang of the Zhili faction, for example, did so, thus enabling the Manchurian warlord to gain control of Beijing in October 1924. Armies lacked cohesion. Furthermore, popular mobilization for war, particularly in rural areas, was far less than during the conflict between the Kuomintang and the Communists in the 1930s.[12]

In the colonial world, meanwhile, the armed resistance to imperial expansion and control seen in the early and mid-1920s largely ended later in the decade. The British contained opposition in Egypt and Iraq by granting their independence,[13] France and Spain crushed the Moorish rebellion in 1925–26, and the French regained control in Syria and the Dutch in Indonesia in 1926–27. Furthermore, there were no large-scale rebellions in such key colonies as India and Algeria. The disturbances in Punjab in 1919, most prominently remembered for the Amritsar massacre by the British, were not a large-scale rebellion. In resisting these and other risings, the imperial militaries benefited from their ability to call on the military resources of empire and to deploy troops relatively rapidly. At Amritsar and in Iraq, the British used Indian troops, and in Syria the French employed Syrian and Malagasy troops. Western forces generally, although not invariably, proved effective in both attack and defense. Prepared units were able to hold off larger attacking forces, as in the OK Pass in British Somaliland in March 1919, where the British lost two men repelling an attack by about four hundred supporters of Mullah Sayyid Muhammed, who allegedly lost two hundred men. Resistance there ended in 1920. Such success contrasted markedly with the Western intervention in the Russian Civil War, indicating the difficulty of judging overall capability.

Despite the criticism that colonial militaries, such as the British Indian Army, sometimes received from reformers, not least of whom were those keen on mechanization, such as J.F.C. Fuller, they were engaged in their own action-reaction processes, as colonial warfare was far from being a static entity. Indeed, the challenges of counter-insurgency warfare led to theoretical discussion.[14] The capacity for mobility and tactical advantage offered by air power encouraged particular interest.[15] There was also a role for mechanized capability, as well as interest in the use of gas.[16]

If a "pull" factor of large-scale symmetrical conflict able to clarify the nature of modern military effectiveness was absent, the "push" factor of militaries (and politicians) certain that World War I had shown them the way forward was similarly lacking. The lesson of the war had been not only that such conflict was extremely costly, but also that it was easier to think in terms of industrial or total war than to execute it. This was true not only of economic management, which had repeatedly revealed constraints and limitations, but also of combat. Commanders had found it difficult to use effectively the unprecedented forces with which they had been entrusted. The year 1918 brought operational and strategic victories, but the campaigns of that time had also indicated the severe problems confronting particular policies, whether the German use of storm-troopers or even the combined-arms system developed by the British. Furthermore, the success of the latter in the last months of the war left unclear how far it would be able to cope with rapid post-war changes in weapons effectiveness.

The military situation of the 1920s prevailed for much of the 1930s, but the global depression that spread from 1929, the Slump and the subsequent Depression, increased domestic and international pressures. These exposed tensions in the international order, as well as the failure of policy makers to take advantage of the peace in the late 1920s in order to establish ways to co-operate. Competition was accentuated by the Depression, and co-operation did not seem the way to overcome differences.[17] The Depression accentuated a tendency for protectionism and led to a greater emphasis on economic self-sufficiency. It also encouraged social and political tensions, and helped lead to the rise of anti-democratic political movements which, by their very nature, relied on crisis and violence, to waves of strikes, and to coup attempts, as in Finland in 1930 and Austria in 1934. There had also been such attempts in the 1920s, but those in the 1930s were more common and often more serious. This was seen in Brazil, where the military revolts in 1922 and 1924 were small-scale and suppressed by the loyal majority of the army, while, in 1930, the government was overthrown when the army proved unwilling to resist a rebel army advancing on São Paolo, and, instead, seized power before handing it to Getúlio Vargas, the leader of the revolt. In turn, federal forces suppressed a three-month-long revolt against Vargas in 1932, which was supported by forty thousand troops largely from the São Paolo militia. As so often, this episode in Latin America is ignored in military history, even though the government deployed more than seventy-five thousand troops, and also used air attacks. In comparison, the risings by pro-Communist troops in Brazil in 1935 were small-scale and rapidly suppressed.[18]

In Japan, the focus on self-sufficiency seen in the Depression encouraged a determination to control the raw materials, first of Manchuria and, eventually, of Southeast Asia. Nevertheless, the Japanese invasion of Manchuria in 1931 did not lead to full-scale war with China until 1937, or to more than short-term clashes with the Soviet Union. Appeasement, first of Japan over Manchuria, then of Italy over Ethiopia, and finally of Germany over Europe, partially rested on concern about Great Power warfare, and also ensured that it did not occur until 1939 when appeasement of Germany (but not of the Soviet Union) ceased. As a result, the consequences repeated the situation during the age of Western imperialism prior to World War I: the major wars of 1931–36 were not the result of opposition to the expansionist policies of Japan, Italy, and Germany, and it is important that the military history of the period is not dominated by planning for, and forecasts of, such a conflict. Even in 1937–38, the area of major conflict was China, not Europe. Furthermore, war between Japanese invaders and Chinese forces[19] could be placed in a continuum stretching back long before the interventions that had started in the late-nineteenth century. There were echoes of the major Japanese attacks on Korea in the 1590s, attacks that had been resisted with Chinese assistance.

Prior to the full-scale war from 1937, there were large-scale operations in conflict between Kuomintang (Chinese nationalist) regulars and Communist forces.[20] These included an attempt to control civilian populations, which prefigured insurgency and counter-insurgency campaigns in Eastern Europe during World War II. In their 1933 offensive, the Kuomintang moved peasants in order to deprive the Communists of local support, particularly of food and information, and also sought to control the countryside through the establishment of large numbers of blockhouses. Serious pressure was brought to bear. In 1937, the Communist leader Mao Zedong published *Guerilla Warfare*, a pamphlet in which he argued that, in response, unlimited guerilla warfare offered a new prospect that was more effective than what was presented as more primitive guerilla warfare. Indeed, Mao offered a prospectus for a major, not an ancillary, effort:

In a war of revolutionary character, guerilla operations are a necessary part. This is particularly true in a war waged for the emancipation of a people who inhabit a vast nation . . . the development of the type of guerilla warfare characterized by the quality of mass is both necessary and natural... We consider guerilla operations as but one aspect of our total or mass war... All the people of both sexes from the ages of sixteen to forty-five must be organized into anti-Japanese self-defense units.[21]

Operationally, the emphasis included words used to describe conventional warfare in the period, such as "mobility, and attack... dedeliver a lightning blow, seek a lightning decision."[22] Yet, in what truly was a prospectus for total war, general revolutionary wars were defined in terms of "the whole people of a nation, without regard to class or party, carry on a guerilla struggle that is an instrument of the national policy." Furthermore, this was seen in accordance with the historical process, "All these struggles have been carried on in the interests of the whole people or the greater part of them; all had a broad basis in the national manpower, and all have been in accord with the laws of historical development,"[23] the last a key ideological justification for Marxists. This type of "true" guerilla war was contrasted with its use by counter-revolutionaries, which was seen as directly contradicting "the law of historical development."[24] At the same time, Mao did also leave a major role for regular operations, and the history of the post-1945 Chinese Civil War, and also of the Vietnam War, particularly the conquest of South Vietnam in the 1975 campaign, revealed that this was indeed appropriate.

The key role of regular forces certainly had been the lesson of conflict in Europe. The Russian Civil War had shown the value of volunteer enthusiasm, as the Communists seized the initiative and pursued military and internal agendas. At the same time, the problems of such units, the limitations of irregular warfare for offensive operations, and the need to be able to use mass effectively, encouraged the resort to a regular military, albeit one that had its political identity and loyalty secured by political commissioners. This seemed necessary in order to protect the revolution from internal subversion and external aggression, both givens in Communist analysis.[25] A similar engagement with enthusiasm was seen in the Fascist states, but it was contained due to a reliance on the regular military. Mussolini organized Blackshirt legions, but they proved to be of limited effectiveness in combat roles. In Germany, the SA was not allowed to take the role of the army, and was speedily suppressed. The SS gained an eventually large-scale military role, but it was organized to that end more like regular units.

Elsewhere in Asia, there was no war in the 1920s and 1930s on the scale of what occurred in China, but imperial policing continued there to lead to the large-scale deployment of forces. This was particularly true for Britain, with substantial forces sent to contest the risings that broke out in Waziristan on the northwest frontier of India (modern Pakistan) in 1936, and in Palestine, "the Arab Rising," in 1937. More than sixty thousand troops were deployed against the first in 1937 and fifty thousand against the latter in 1938.[26] Yet, these were also contained struggles. The Waziristan risings did not spread to Muslims elsewhere in British India, while the British did not respond to their difficulties by invading Afghanistan, in which the Faqir of Ipi, the leader of the resistance, was apt to take refuge. Although European imperial authority was not involved, inter-war struggles between tribes and state authority in Ethiopia, Iraq, and Persia were similar in origin: the authority of the central government opposed by autonomous forces, frequently in border or remote regions.

There was no rebellion on the scale of the Arab Rising against established imperial control in sub-Saharan Africa. In Libya, however, the Italians completed the subjugation of the interior. Insofar as total warfare refers to brutality, this was a total war, more so, for example, than the German conquest of Poland in 1939, although the consequences of the latter for Jews and other Poles were soon to be particularly brutal. In Libya, where the Italians were opposed by irregulars, they resorted to anti-societal warfare. More than fifty thousand civilians were probably killed as the result of a ruthless suppression of the population in which wells were blocked and flocks slaughtered, both effective forms of economic warfare. The native population was disarmed and resettled in camps in which large numbers died. Italian tactics included the dropping of gas bombs, and large-scale executions. Despite the use of aircraft and gas, the subsequent Italian conquest of Ethiopia in 1935–36 can also be seen in the context of the wars of European imperialism beginning in the early nineteenth century. It was characterized by brutality similar to that used in Libya. If the Italians deployed large numbers of troops in Ethiopia, the French had done the same conquering Algeria the previous century.

The conquest of Ethiopia was designed in part to increase Italy's weight in Europe, as well as to strengthen Mussolini's position at home. This is a reminder of the extent to which imperial military commitments were an aspect of a strategy that included Europe, rather than detracting from it. At the same time, British commitments in the late 1930s indicated the problematic nature of that approach. Aside from the need to secure colonial government from internal opposition, there was also the threat to imperial security—both colonies and sea-lanes—posed first by the rise of Japanese naval power and subsequently when an increase in Italian military strength in Africa and the Mediterranean complemented Mussolini's aggressive bombast.

Similarly, rather than seeing other conflicts of the 1930s simply as anticipations of World War II or as characteristics of a new military system, it is pertinent to locate them in a longer time span. This was true of the major war in Latin America, the Chaco War of 1932–35 between Bolivia and Paraguay, and of the Spanish Civil War of 1936–39. Each owed much to long-established causes and practices of conflict in particular environments. The Chaco War looked back to that of the Triple Alliance in the 1860s. Understanding terrain and logistics proved key factors in both conflicts.

The Spanish Civil War is more commonly seen as a harbinger of World War II, and the ideological divisions between the two sides are emphasized. Caution is required on the first head, while the ideological dimension was scarcely new. It had played a role in the civil war aspect of the Peninsular War of 1808–13, and even more in the Carlist Wars. The Spanish Civil War began as an attempted right-wing Nationalist military coup against the Republican government, but the coup was only partially successful, and this launched the war. It was mostly fought in Spain, but there was also a naval dimension. As a result of the nineteenth-century loss of most of the Spanish Empire, the overseas dimension of the rising was slight, although there was initial fighting in Spanish Morocco, with Republican resistance in the town of Larache having to be overcome after hard fighting. The Balearic Islands also saw conflict.

As far as land conflict in Spain was concerned, the Spanish Civil War was different from the Western Front in World War I, as well as from the initial campaigns in World War II. In contrast to the former, there was no density of defensive positions, so that, as a well-developed system, the front line was only episodic. This made it possible to break through opposing fronts relatively readily, but, in contrast to the German successes in 1939–41, it proved to be very difficult to develop and sustain offensive momentum. As a result, exploitation was inadequate; a pattern seen in the failure of Republican attacks in the battles of Brunete (1937), Belchate (1937), Teruel (1937–38), and the Ebro (1938), and of Nationalist attacks at Jarama (1937) and Guadalajara (1937). This was a product of the nature of the armies, which were poorly-trained and inadequately-supplied, but also of a lack of operational art, seen particularly in inadequate planning. This helped give an attritional character to the war, much of which lacked the more fast-moving maneuverist dimension of the Russian and Chinese civil wars of the 1920s. This attritional character ensured that resources, including vital foreign support, were crucial. It also meant that much value accrued to the side that was better able to manage its economy, maintain morale, and retain political cohesion. On all three heads, the Nationalists under Franco were more effective. The Republicans were particularly unfortunate in the timing of the conflict because if it had occurred during World War II, the Western Allies probably would have provided them with support in response to German backing for the Nationalists.[27]

Once Franco had won the Civil War, the military and paramilitary were the key defenses of the regime. This replicated the situation in many countries, particularly in the 1930s, when the Depression led to the rise of more authoritarian governments that were readier to use, and to threaten, force.

Foreign interest in what the Spanish Civil War suggested about the potential of contemporary military methods reflected the changing international situation, particularly concern about Germany. The move toward a major war between leading powers had been hesitant on the part of many states. Under the Ten Year Rule adopted by the British in 1919, it had been argued that there would be no "great war" involving the empire for another ten years, that therefore there was no need to prepare for one, a major restraint on expenditure demands, and that the army and air force should focus on imperial control. This rule was renewed until suspended in March 1932. The American military similarly was not prepared for a major conflict. In 1938, the army could only put six divisions in the field while, with the exception of cruisers and aircraft carriers, the navy was smaller than it had been in 1925.[28] Instead, with its major investment in the fortifications of the Maginot line along their common frontier, France was better prepared for war with Germany. This was part of a pattern of expenditure, which was exceptionally high for a major power in terms of the percentage of gross national produce. In the event, however, the French army was outmaneuvered in 1940.

Under the pressure of growing German, Italian, and Japanese strength, ambition, and unpredictability, the other powers rearmed in the 1930s, although their ability to do so was affected by limitations in industrial capacity and capability, by fiscal problems, and by a lack of certainty over tasking, and over appropriate force structure. The latter could be seen in such debates as those over emphases between investment in, and doctrine stressing, battleships or carriers, fighter planes or bombers, mechanized or non-mechanized forces, and so on. Considering the likely threat from German submarines, British policy makers, for example, failed to understand the lessons of World War I and to appreciate the need to focus aircraft and surface convoys on convoy protection; instead, they preferred to emphasize the value of attacking the Germans, by air attacks on submarine bases and yards, and by hunting groups at sea.[29]

Discussion over the future character of conflict focused greatly on the response to improvements in weapons systems, a trend that had characterized speculation and planning over the previous century.[30] There was particular interest in the capacity of air power, with a conviction in Britain and the United States that strategic bombing would have a major impact,[31] although this commitment was not shared in France, Italy, or Germany. Instead, they put a heavier emphasis on tactical air power. The British played the key role in developing the concept of strategic bombing. This was based on optimism, institutional need (in the shape of the requirements of the Royal Air Force), and the wish to have a Great Power capability in European warfare without having to introduce conscription or incur the casualties seen in World War I. The British assessment of strategic bombing was not based on any informed analysis of the impact of bombing in World War I or of subsequent developments in capability.

The British were also interested in the role of tanks, but, due in part to imperial commitments and to financial constraints, there was considerable uncertainty over the extent to which they should play a role in force structure and doctrine.[32] This was a problem that also partly arose from differences over the assessment of their role in 1918, and this was accentuated because Plan 1919 was not mounted. The extent to which large-scale tank attacks were not mounted in the last two months of the war encouraged officers who emphasized the role of more traditional weaponry, particularly artillery.[33]

Conflict involving tanks and aircraft had at least been extensive during World War I. In contrast, there was very little experience to draw on with regard to aircraft carriers. Raids by aircraft launched from early carriers had been staged by Britain in the last phase of the war and soon thereafter during the Russian Civil War, but there was no experience with conflict between aircraft carriers. Nevertheless, there was considerable confidence in their potential. In 1920, Rear Admiral Sir Reginald Hall MP argued in the *Times* that, thanks to aircraft and submarines, the days of the battleship were over. This was of scant interest to the British Admiralty, which remained committed to the battleship, but, despite financial stringency, there was an important commitment to naval air power. The number of planes in the Fleet Air Arm rose to 144 by the end of the 1920s, and five new carriers entered service in 1922–38, while hydraulically reset transverse arrester gear were in use by 1933 to handle landing. Aside from being used in the Russian Civil War, carriers were sent far afield, the *Argus* being stationed near the Dardanelles during the Chanak crisis in 1922. There was a carrier on the China Station in the late 1920s (first *Hermes* and then *Argus*), and another, *Furious*, took part in the major naval exercises in the late 1920s.[34] In the 1930s, however, the lead was increasingly taken by the United States and Japan, in part because they would be the key powers in any struggle for control of the Pacific. Indeed, War Plan Orange, the plan for war with Japan, was a key element in American strategic planning.

No naval power was as acute a threat to Britain in the 1920s as Japan was to the United States, while in the 1930s, the need for British deep-sea air capacity in any war with Germany appeared lessened by the vulnerability of German naval power to land-based air attacks. The lesson of World War I was that the Germans could be bottled up in the North Sea. In 1940, however, they transformed the situation by seizing first Norway and then France, and by basing powerful warships and submarines in both.

The character of any future conflict, at least in part, would be set by the respective combatants involved, and in the 1930s, the identity and alignment of the latter were far from clear. Despite alliances, the position of Germany, Italy, Japan, and the Soviet Union was particularly uncertain in the late 1930s, and in fact Italy did not enter World War II until 1940. The Americans, who had been involved in planning for hypothetical wars since 1919, had plans for war with Japan, but also for conflict with Britain and Mexico, and for intervention in China. None of the last three occurred.

A lack of clarity about allies and enemies made it difficult to produce effective strategic plans. Some strategic conceptions supposed the identity and policies of allies and enemies, revealing a degree of naivety in assuming that they could be determined,[35] but others lacked that false precision. Furthermore, for much of the 1930s, it was by no means clear to many commentators in Western Europe whether Nazi Germany or the Soviet Union was more of a threat, and indeed, in early 1940, there was pressure in Britain and France to send military assistance to Finland, which had been attacked by the Soviet Union. The eventual outcome for Britain—alliance with the Soviet Union from

1941 and then cold war with her—was far from inevitable, and was possibly less likely for much of the 1930s than conflict with the Soviet Union.

Despite the buildup in expenditure in the late 1930s, there were still serious deficiencies in the armed forces of the major powers. In part, this is an inevitable product of the process of investment and diffusion to ensure that the best practice is adopted, particularly when the rate of change is high. Furthermore, the nature of the sources has to be borne in mind: military leaders are not prone to say that they have adequate resources. At the same time, particular problems arose from the range of commitments of the major powers. This was especially the case for the imperial ones, but Germany and the Soviet Union each also had to consider challenges on two fronts. Furthermore, the large size of the militaries made the cost of improving them especially high; indeed, the burden of sustaining forces that were so numerous—in particular, feeding, clothing, housing, and arming such numbers—was a serious problem.

This issue accentuated the tendency to focus on key sectors, which helped encourage debate about their identity. In contrast, the bulk of the military lacked comparable investment and improvement. This pattern was abundantly clear with the most far-flung of the imperial militaries, that of Britain. Alongside cutting-edge investment, for example, in aircraft carriers (five of which were laid down in 1935–37), fighters, and radar, there was a failure to invest in the bulk of the army, as well as in fixed defenses. As a result, colonies such as Burma, Ceylon (Sri Lanka), and Malta were seriously vulnerable. The course of World War II would show, however, that the consequences of this were far from inevitable: Burma was swiftly overrun by Japanese forces in 1942, but Malta withstood air attack and attempts to blockade the island.

The emphasis on the leading sectors of mass militaries was an attempt to reconcile the apparent needs for both quality and mass in modern warfare. This was seen, for example, in the French army, where the development of mechanized and motorized divisions were intended to provide a mobility capable of countering the German advance in Belgium, as a prelude to an engagement by the mass army with its infantry and artillery. This did not work in 1940, largely due to poor French command decisions,[36] and to the German ability to sustain a breakthrough. French planning was not a product of any unwillingness to engage with the likely nature of conflict, but the emphasis on carefully-controlled operations failed to provide sufficient room for decision-making at lower levels, and therefore gravely compromised flexibility. German training and practice was far better in this respect, a consequence both of methods developed by Moltke the Elder in the mid–nineteenth century, and of the emphasis in the 1930s on employing flexibility to ensure mobility by making best use of armor. Like the French, the Germans emphasized elite units as a force multiplier ahead of the mass army.

In the case of the Soviet Union, the primacy of politics was shown at both the external and the internal levels. In the former case, the policies both of the Soviet Union and of other states ensured that the enemies in 1939–40 were Poland, Finland, and (at a contained level) Japan; while in 1941, the situation abruptly altered and a major war broke out with Germany. At the internal level, Stalin's decision to turn against the high command[37] wrecked the latter's attempt to build up a well-equipped military capable of waging effective offensive warfare, using concepts of operational conflict to combine mass and maneuver.[38] The purges of the high command and officer corps gravely weakened the Soviet military, and removed the cadre committed to operational warfare, helping ensure that fighting quality and, even more, general effectiveness was inadequate in 1939–40 and still flawed in 1941.[39] At the same time, the purges served as a reminder that one of the key roles of the military was as a reliable arm of the state. This entailed issues of effectiveness different from those of combat readiness. As Stalin managed to avoid a major conflict in 1939–40, the consequences of deficiencies in the latter were limited. Japan's willingness to negotiate a non-aggression pact in 1941 further secured the situation for Stalin, but his position rested on an assessment of Hitler that seriously underrated the latter's irrationality and misunderstood his goals.

# CHAPTER 7
# World War II, 1939–45

Fighting quality—a constant factor in conflict rather than a characteristic of total war—was a key element that plays too little a role in the assessment of why the Allies won World War II, but it is one that demands attention, however it is defined. Indeed, a stress on Allied fighting quality reverses the emphasis in much of the literature, where the focus is on Allied resources and, in particular, the ability to outproduce the Axis (Germany, Italy, and Japan). This factor is seen as the key element in the total war interpretation of the conflict. This latter emphasis reflects a number of factors, but particularly the dominant interpretations of the nature of conflict that put a stress, first, on material factors, such as the number of tanks—more/better resources apparently beats fewer/worse resources—and, second, on war and society. The eventual Allied resource base was indeed impressive, the United States spending $82 billion on the military in 1944 alone, and contrasted with German, Japanese, and Italian deficiencies in economic mobilization.[1]

The war and society approach, which enjoyed much favor in academic circles from the 1960s, placed much of the explanation for victory on the "home front" and specifically on the ability to mobilize the factors of production, particularly labor, for wartime production of weaponry. From this perspective, the Allies won because their more integrated and benign societies enabled them to take part in a total mobilization; while the conservative, not to say reactionary or worse, attitudes of the Nazis and Japanese—for example, toward the employment of women and conquered peoples—ensured that they lost. "Rosie the Riveter," and her equivalents in the United States and Allied countries, thus won World War II.

This was an interpretation that brought together Western democratic and Soviet Communist public myths and, like most public myths, rested on a degree of accuracy, although it underplayed the cruelty of the highly authoritarian Soviet war economy, as well as, albeit less systematically and viciously, the extent of anti-union activities and segregation in the United States. Nazi racism and Japanese oppression made it difficult for Germany and Japan to derive the benefit that might have been anticipated from their extensive conquests, and even led to a degree of popular resistance, especially in Eastern Europe and, less clearly, China, that soaked up a lot of Axis military resources. The Allies did not encounter comparable resistance, with the important exception of the Soviets in areas they brutally conquered or reconquered, at the same time as they drove out the Germans, such as Poland and Lithuania. Resistance to Soviet occupation in these areas was weakened by divisions and by a lack of Western support, but the NKVD (People's Commissariat of Internal Affairs) was also successful in striking at the leadership of the Underground, and was greatly helped by war weariness on the part of the population in these countries and by offering a number of amnesties to dissidents. The last amnesty in Poland in 1947 led most of the remaining Underground to surrender.[2] In contrast, the weakness of popular resistance on behalf of the Nazi regime during and after the Allied conquest of Germany was a demonstration of its *eventual* unpopularity and sense of failure, although the formal surrender of the German regime after the death of Hitler was also important in undermining the legitimacy of any resistance.

Valuable as it is to look at resources and home fronts, and it would be very foolish to neglect either, these interpretations will not suffice. Like all-too-much analytical work on military history, they risk taking the fighting out of war, although an important link is provided by the extent to which the protection, or destruction, of resources did play a major role in strategic and operational planning. This was mostly the case with naval and air warfare, the former focusing on communications, and the latter on production, but was also seen with land warfare. A British strategic review of August 1941 noted, "Iranian oil and the Abadan refinery are essential to us. Our present positions afford a defense in depth to the shores of the Indian Ocean and Persian Gulf."[3]

In the case of World War II, the focus on home fronts and resources, however, underrates the extent to which the Axis was also outfought: on land, in the air, and at sea. In doing so, this focus on home fronts also appears to support self-serving Axis interpretations that emphasise their fighting quality and suggest that they lost only because they were outnumbered. This, indeed, takes up themes of the period, for example, the Nazi argument that they were defending civilization against Asiatic "hordes," in the shape of the large Red (Soviet) Army. To this day, on the German side, there is still a tendency to regard their defeat as due to being beaten in resource production by the Allies, and to minimize or ignore the extent to which they were outfought. This is a parallel to the earlier tendency, after 1918, to blame defeat on everything other than the Allied ability to defeat German forces on the Western Front.

For World War II, all-too-much of the work on the German side is based on post-war analyses of their own campaigns by German commanders and staff officers, which place the responsibility for defeat on resource issues, as well as the size and climate of the Soviet Union, and, above all, Hitler's interventions. Hitler indeed was a seriously flawed commander, in attack, as seen in the inconsistently conceived and executed offensives against the Soviet Union in 1941 and 1942, and the poorly-coordinated pressure on Britain in 1940, but especially in defense, due to his unwillingness to yield territory, and his consequent preference for the static, over the mobile, defense. In large part, this attitude was a reflection of Hitler's obsessions with willpower and with battle as a test of ideological and racial purity, as well as his suspicion about the determination of subordinates. By concentrating decision-making, and being unable to match Stalin's ability to delegate, Hitler ensured that there was no alternative way to provide sound command decisions, and, by 1944, his diminished grasp on reality exacerbated the difficulties of German command and undermined support from within the senior ranks of the military. Generals who withdrew to escape encirclement, as Kleist did across the Dniester in the spring of 1944, risked dismissal.

It is important, however, to stress that Hitler's deficiencies were part of a more general failure of German warmaking, not least a dysfunctional system of civilian-military relations that echoed similar failures in the Wilhelmine period. There was a misplaced emphasis on will. As in 1914, the will to win could not be a substitute for a failure to set sensible military and political goals, specifically the inability to make opposing states accept German assumptions. There were also serious shortcomings within the Japanese high command. Post-war German (and not only German) analyses also ignore archival evidence that highlights battlefield mistakes by German commanders, and, in particular, do not consider the issue of Soviet fighting quality, a subject emphasized by excellent recent American work, especially by David Glantz, that has benefited from the widespread (although not complete) opening of Soviet archives after the fall of the Communist regime.[4]

An understanding of German deficiencies in the war with the Soviet Union, with which the bulk of the German army was engaged from the opening of hostilities on June 22, 1941 until the end of the war, is in line with the tendency to offer a reading of the early German campaigns that emphasizes the extent to which they were not easy victories.[5] The advantages the Germans derived from poor strategic choices on the part of their opponents—for example, the French dispatch of their strategic reserve toward the Netherlands in May 1940—rather than from a totally different quality of conception and fighting, are now general to the literature.[6] Germany's enemies made the mistakes Germany needed them to make, as Japan's also did in the winter of 1941–42. Weaknesses on the part of the Germans can also be stressed. For example, although planning for an invasion of Poland was well-developed, the conquest of Denmark and Norway in 1940 was far more improvised and, indeed, the latter attack that April was particularly vulnerable to maritime interception by the stronger British naval force. Far from a pre-determined result, the Germans benefited from comparative advantage: both less-flawed planning than the Allied forces that intervened, let alone the poorly prepared Scandinavians, and a greater ability to respond, indeed improvise, under pressure. Furthermore, an emphasis on the ability of well-led Allied forces to create problems for the Germans by mounting appropriate defense operations can also be found.[7]

German warmaking rested on a greater willingness than their opponents to center operational planning on the tactical potential of combined arms, and joint (air-land) operations, the two joining to make maneuver warfare possible. This potential, which was enhanced by generally good tactical and operational command and by a high level of tactical skill did not, however, mean a certainty of success. Furthermore, this potential should not lessen an awareness of the large-scale improvisation that characterized German warmaking and military support systems, indeed a widespread failure to appreciate the role of supply and logistics. It is also necessary to note variations in

German effectiveness. For example, in the Battle of the Bulge offensive of late 1944, the infantry's low morale and lack of tactical skill contrasted with the higher fighting quality of the German tank units. The problems of military support systems were seen not only with the German army, but also with the German navy and air force. The delay of focusing on submarine warfare was a major problem, as was the management of the *Luftwaffe* (air force).

Nevertheless, the views of both victors and defeated combined to endow the German military with extraordinary strength and proficiency, not least overwhelming mechanised forces. This helped boost German confidence and the sense of being at the cutting edge of progress,[8] and also assisted the defeated in dispelling attention from issues relating to their own fighting quality, morale, and command skills. In practice, there was no such general superiority in weaponry, and other aspects of German effectiveness were also exaggerated. Subsequent claims that, in 1940, the Germans had many more modern tanks than the Western Allies (Britain and France) were unfounded, and, indeed, the Germans had fewer heavy battle tanks suited to fight other tanks, whereas the French were relatively well-provided with them. American major Paul Raborg's account of sixty-ton German tanks equipped with flamethrowers and communicating by radio directly with Stuka dive-bombers was inaccurate for 1940, when the heaviest German tank weighed nineteen tons, there were no flamethrower tanks, and as yet, no such communications.[9]

A belief in Axis effectiveness was a key element in the contest over morale. This was seen not only as important in a strategic sense, with reference to the maintenance of war economies via popular support on home fronts—but also operationally, specifically for countries that were invaded. The extent to which Germany had been helped in ensuring that its victory over France led to a willingness to surrender by a lack of French determination raised concern at the time, and has been controversial since. This was not only an issue there. In April 1941, General Henry Wilson, the commander of the British Expeditionary Force in Greece, then under successful attack by the Germans, was concerned about Greek morale, writing about "The question how to raise the morale of the people as well as that of the Greek forces who are showing signs of disintegration."[10]

The focus on morale ensured that the combatants made major efforts to try to influence both domestic and foreign opinion. Due to the need for popular support for war efforts dependent both on large-scale economic mobilization and on conscription, these efforts could be seen as instances of total and modern warfare, although a concern with morale was scarcely new. The means might be different, but the radio was a secular pulpit with new characteristics, rather than a new departure in psychological manipulation. As with many facets of the total/modern war debate, the criteria discussed are more pertinent if the contrast is drawn with the pre-Revolutionary eighteenth century than with earlier periods of, in particular, religious partisanship. The emphasis on public opinion back at home in some instructions to commanders, nevertheless, is notable. In June 1941, Robert Menzies, the Australian prime minister, wrote to Blamey, then commanding the Australian forces in the Middle East, "A disaster at Tobruk [in Libya, at the hands of the Germans] coming on top of those in Greece and Crete might have far reaching effects on public opinion in Australia and a reverse in Egypt itself would, I think, produce incalculable difficulties in Australia."[11]

The German tendency to underrate Soviet fighting quality in the analysis of the conflict in Eastern Europe is not simply a matter of technicalities, but, rather, an aspect of a more wide-ranging modern German failure of perception. For example, most German commentators do not appreciate the extent to which the German army was involved in atrocities and, indeed, that military violence against unarmed civilians was not a matter of rogue commanders, but, instead, was integral to its conduct from the outset of the war.[12] This is, in part, because this argument challenges the sanitization of the Wehrmacht's reputation during the Cold War when West German rearmament was seen as crucial to the defense of the West.

There is a parallel between the assessment of German effectiveness and the treatment of Japan. It is clear that its attacks in 1941–42 benefited from poor Allied operational command, particularly in the Philippines, Malaya, and Burma, but also from strategic inadequacies that in part stemmed from the range of British commitments. Concerned about the war with Germany, the British mistakenly hoped that the defense of Malaya and Singapore would benefit from the strength of the American fleet in the western Pacific, and also seriously mishandled their own naval units. At the same time, Soviet success in earlier clashes with Japan along the borders of Manchuria, particularly near Nomonhan in 1939, indicated deficiencies with Japanese warmaking.[13]

The Japanese equivalent in explaining failure includes an overemphasis on Allied bombing, especially the dropping of the atom bombs. There is also an unwillingness to address the issue of comparative fighting quality in the field in 1944–45. Furthermore, the military and political reasons why the Japanese had failed earlier to knock out China (on which they had launched a full-scale assault in 1937) from the war, also repay consideration. They indicate why an ability to plan and execute major advances (equivalent to German *blitzkrieg* offensives) did not lead to victory.

Before turning to consider fighting quality in greater detail, it is important to understand that an emphasis on it does not imply that resources played little role. Instead, such an approach is partly a matter of a shift in focus. Clearly, both resources and fighting were crucial. For example, the extent of American shipbuilding capacity, and the consequent ability to do far more than just replace losses, was central to the American ability to secure, and then exploit, naval superiority in the Pacific. Yet, in addition, the Japanese navy had to be both repeatedly beaten in battle by the Americans from 1942, and weakened by their air and submarine assault on the Japanese war economy. More generally, although it is a factor, the strength of a state does not explain the operational successes of its forces. Japanese defeats, in part, reflected the balance of fighting quality, command skills, and luck in particular battles; as well as flawed Japanese doctrine, for instance, in the less successful use of submarines compared to that by the Americans.

It is also necessary to direct attention to the idea of a synergy between resources and fighting quality. More and better weapons themselves are not sufficient until victory. They can increase fighting quality, for example, by enhancing confidence and morale. Conversely, they can also compromise it, by encouraging a misguided confidence in the weapons themselves, or by leading to tactics in which there is a reluctance to close with the enemy for fear of affecting aspects of the weapons' performance. Rather the relationship is the opposite: instead of more resources increasing fighting quality, better quality can make a more effective use of resources. This implies that forces with superior fighting quality will benefit disproportionately from enhanced (in both quality and quantity) resources, as the Americans did in the Pacific in the latter stages of the war. Militaries need men trained to use new weapons, something the Americans did well in 1943–45. Also, in the absence of such resources, forces with superior fighting quality can use it to lessen, indeed, sometimes close, the capability gap.

In World War II, the general trend was that a gap in combat effectiveness and fighting quality at the outset that favored the Axis

(Germany and Japan, but not far more lackluster Italy) was overcome by advances in Allied proficiency that the Axis did not match. Initial Axis successes—by the Germans in 1939–41 and by the Japanese in 1931–42—were not simply due to fighting quality, although it was important, as the success of German *blitzkrieg* attacks amply demonstrated. Other factors also played a role, from the tactical/operational—for example, the impetus stemming from the surprise nature of the German assault on the Soviet Union in 1941, and that of the Japanese on Britain and the United States later that year—to the strategic/geopolitical.

Crucial to the latter was the sequential nature of Axis warmaking. Japan was able successively to invade Manchuria (1931) and to launch a full-scale attack on China (1937), without the intervention of other powers, despite the fact that they were not otherwise engaged in warfare. Japan was also able to fight a limited border war with the Soviet Union (1939) that did not escalate, and to attack Britain and the United States in 1941 without having to fear Soviet entry into the war with her. Germany engaged first in rearmament, and then in sequential aggression against Austria and Czechoslovakia in 1938–39, without any united hostile response. Hitler then successively attacked Poland, Denmark, Norway, Belgium, the Netherlands, Yugoslavia, and Greece, with the Soviet Union at least neutral (and in the case of the attack on Poland, an active participant), and with the United States unwilling to come to the aid of fellow neutrals, although, in late May 1940, Roosevelt requested planning for support to Brazil in the event of German attack. Similarly, Norway and Sweden refused to help Finland when it was attacked by the Soviet Union in 1939–40, and also refused to allow transit for any Anglo-French relief force, a major factor discouraging an intervention that would probably, anyway, have been unsuccessful.

The combination of the skill and success of German military operations, and the wider geopolitics of the conflict, ensured that, by the end of May 1941, Germany had apparently won the war as then conducted. Most of the powers attacked by Germany had been in effect isolated: Soviet backing was crucial to Germany's ability to gain control of Eastern Europe, as it removed any effective counter, for Anglo-French military support against Germany was ineffective. This was true not only of Poland, but also of the German ability to dominate the Balkans. At the end of May 1941, Britain and her empire fought on, but, despite sending an expeditionary force, had been unable to save Greece when Germany attacked that April. With Germany dominant in Europe, and linked to the Soviet Union, and the United States neutral, there appeared no way in which Britain would be able to reverse the verdict of recent defeats. Indeed, the British were concerned that German successes in the Mediterranean, successes that might be enhanced if the Germans advanced through neutral Turkey, could compromise their position in the Middle East. This encouraged interest in fall-back positions in Iraq and Persia (Iran), and therefore in the occupation of both. These concerns were to be accentuated when the Soviet Union did badly in the early stages of the war.[14]

Prior to the German attack on the Soviet Union on June 22, let alone the Japanese attack on Britain and the United States on December 7, 1941, the war was far from global, even if German naval operations, the contributions of the British Empire, and the impact of Italian entry together ensured that it was more wide-ranging and varied than the conflict between Japan and China. Nevertheless, the absence of any German invasion of Britain (or British landing in France) meant that the British and German armies did not fight between June 1940 and March 1941 (the British fought the Italians in Africa). This followed on from the very different Phoney War between the major powers the previous winter. Each situation can be variously explained, and involved more than habitual winter pauses and preparations for spring operations, important as both were, but they scarcely match any definition of total war. In contrast, year-round campaigning was to be the characteristic of the German-Soviet war launched in 1941, while, in Burma, the British came to fight through the monsoon.

The impact of Soviet, and then American, entry into the war on its eventual outcome is well rehearsed, but that of improved Allied fighting quality is less fully discussed. Take, however, either the German-Soviet conflict or the war with Japan. In 1941, the Germans had been able to inflict very heavy casualties on the Soviets, not least by being more successful at the tactical level in linking firepower and mobility, while operationally, they out-maneuvered Soviet defenders, and were more successful in imposing their tempo on the flow of conflict. Yet, with time, the Red Army learned to cope with German tactics (for example, by negating the impact of German tank attacks with the skilful use of anti-tank guns) and operational methods (coping with breakthroughs by establishing defenses in depth). This ability to respond was also seen in changing British doctrine. General Claude Auchinleck, the perceptive Commander-in-Chief in the Middle East in 1941–42, drew up instructions in October 1941 in which he stressed the value of engaging the Germans in maneuver warfare, but also offered "general principles governing all the strategy of the defense" that reflected the challenge posed by the greater mobility of contemporary warfare:

All main communications, road or rail, will be denied to the enemy by a series of defensive areas sited astride of them, and arranged in depth.

These defensive areas will be made tank proof, and capable of all round defence, and stocked so as to make them self-supporting for at least 60 days...In no circumstances will a garrison abandon its area, unless ordered to do so by a superior commander.

Adequate air support for these defensive areas is essential and whenever possible they will contain one or more landing grounds to enable communication to be maintained with them by air and, when feasible and desirable, to enable air forces to be operated from within their perimeter.

It will, however, certainly be necessary to operate air forces from aerodromes situated outside these defensive areas. The general protection of these aerodromes should be assured by the action of mobile reserves operating between the defensive areas.

It is essential that all idea of maintaining a linear defence in the face of superior enemy armoured forces be abandoned. Penetration between the defensive areas...must be expected and accepted...so long as these areas hold firm and thus deny to the enemy the use of the main arteries of communication, he can not continue for long to press forward with large forces.

The garrison of each defended area will include anti-aircraft artillery and should, if possible, include infantry tanks for counter attacking purposes, but the bulk of such armoured and motorised forces...will be held...to bring the enemy to battle on ground of our choosing and to make the fullest possible use of the defensive areas as pivots of manoeuvre.[15]

Aside from their growing success in defense, the Soviets also developed an eventually effective offensive doctrine that could cope with the resilience of German defenders. The Soviet determination to learn from mistakes had already been demonstrated after the end of the winter war with Finland (1939–40), an aggressive opportunistic campaign launched in order to enhance the Soviet defensive zone. In this war, the Red Army had initially done very badly, before concentrating on an artillery-led breakthrough of the Finnish defensive positions in Karelia, the Mannerheim Line. The Soviets held a secret, high-level analysis of the conflict that has recently been published as a result of the opening of their archives. It led, in May 1940, to the issue of Order No. 120, which pressed for changes, including better training, more fluid infantry tactics, and better all-arms coordination.[16]

An improvement in Soviet fighting quality was clearly demonstrated in the war with Germany, not least in the differences between successive Soviet offensives. At the same time, effectiveness has to be considered not in the abstract, but relative to the fighting capability of the opposition. This can be seen in Operation Uranus—the encirclement of the German Sixth Army, in and near Stalingrad—in November 1942. The Soviets benefited greatly in this operation from their buildup of forces, not least as a consequence of the recovery and development of their munitions industry, for example, in tank production. The earlier evacuation of Soviet industrial plants in the face of German advances was a major achievement, which reflected the control wielded by the Soviet government. Soviet advantages in Operation Uranus were also magnified by the success of their planning and preparations, and thanks to the poor quality of German command decisions, including the allocation of what became key flank positions to weak Romanian forces, a flawed decision but a predictable one. A poor German response to the Soviet breakthrough was also crucial.

Earlier, the large-scale Soviet counter-offensive in the winter of 1941–42 had eventually run out of steam, in part because, like the German offensives on the Western Front in 1918, it was on too broad a front. The Soviet counter-offensive in early 1943 was eventually stopped by Manstein's successful fighting defense. Thereafter, however, the Germans proved far less successful in stemming Soviet advances. Instead, the major constraints on the Soviet forces in both 1944 and 1945 proved to be logistical, specifically the re-supply of advance units, especially with fuel. The Soviets showed, for example, in Operation Bagration—the 1944 overrunning of Belarus and the destruction of Army Group Centre—as well as in their advance into the Balkans the same year, and, finally, in the Manchuria campaign of 1945 against Japan, that they had mastered the capabilities of their weaponry and fighting systems, learned how to outfight their opponents, and acquired not only a Deep War doctrine but also the ability to maintain the pace of a fighting advance. The provision of American trucks helped to operationalize Soviet concepts for the offensive.

In 1944, the Red Army proved adept at developing good co-operation between armor, artillery, and infantry, and at making the latter two mobile, successfully executing encirclements. The Germans were outnumbered, particularly in artillery and aircraft, although not so much as to make the verdict obvious. They suffered, however, from the consequences of "no retreat" orders, which robbed them of mobility.

The campaign was less well handled by German commanders than that of early 1943, although the different verdict also reflected an increase in Soviet operational effectiveness and tactical skill: as a consequence, German counter-attacks were less successful than hitherto, which affected the flow as well as the tempo of the Soviet advance. The Soviets used their reserves well to maintain the pace of the advance and to thwart counter-attacks, and were helped by the combination of simultaneous attacks and the breadth of the front, which made it difficult for the Germans to move forces so as to block breaches.

The Germans were more successful in delaying Anglo-American advances in Italy and (initially) Normandy,[17] as the fronts there were more constricted, and because Anglo-American forces were less adept at switching to the exploitation phase of battles and, subsequently, in maintaining the advance when it encountered resistance. Both problems were seen in Italy and France. This reflected a lack of understanding of operational art, as well as less experience than the Soviets in large-scale maneuver battles with the Germans.

At the same time, it was only possible for advancing Soviet forces to achieve so much before exhaustion, losses, and supply difficulties had an impact and led, first, to the slackening and, then, the stopping of the offensive. Until 1945, there was to be no one-campaign end to the war. This gave the conflict an attritional character, and led to an emphasis on the quantity as well as the utilization of resources. Indeed, British planners considering post-war scenarios, and the risk that the Soviet Union would resume pre-war hostility to the West were troubled by the resilience and extent of the Soviet military-industrial base, as well as by Soviet fighting quality.

In Manchuria in 1945, the Japanese were outnumbered, particularly in artillery, tanks, and aircraft, but they were also badly outfought: the Soviet forces were better trained and many had experienced combat in Europe. Aided by skilful deception techniques, they seized the initiative and advanced rapidly to envelop their opponents. Although the Japanese fought tenaciously, including using suicide tactics, such as carrying explosives and detonating them against tanks, their planning was disoriented by the speed of the Soviet advance. The Japanese had failed to appreciate the advances the Soviets made in 1943–45 in developing and sustaining Deep Operations. In particular, the Japanese underrated Soviet mobility and inaccurately assumed that the Soviets would need to stop for re-supply after about 250 miles, providing the Japanese with an opportunity to respond to the Soviet advance.[18] The Soviets were able to move faster than the Japanese had done in

Operation Ichigo in late 1944 when, in an offensive from both directions, they successfully opened the land route from Japanese China to Vietnam.

Soviet skill in deception—particularly in deceiving the Germans about the axis of advance in 1944 and the Japanese about the likelihood of attack in 1945—matched that of the Western Allies in Operation Overlord, the invasion of Normandy in 1944. This suggests that the Germans had also lost the intelligence war, and thus the capacity to out-think their opponents. This argument, however, has to be employed with care. The German success in gaining surprise at the Battle of the Bulge in December 1944 was significant. Furthermore, British failures on Crete (1941) and at Arnhem (1944) indicated that the use of intelligence information was as important as its availability; the British ULTRA system was a strategic resource that had varied operational consequences.

The Western Allies also improved their fighting quality. In initial clashes, they had been found seriously wanting: the British conspicuously so in Norway in 1940, and the Americans in the 1943 battle of the Kasserine Pass in Tunisia. With time, however, improved Allied training and the benefits of experience told, especially at the command level. The Allies also became far more skilled at integrating their forces. Thus, air support played a major role in the eventual success in the Battle of Normandy, although, arguably, a lack of appropriate direction and coordination at the strategic level ensured that too many air resources were directed into the bombing of Germany. This was an instance of the way in which the range of available resources and policies, which had grown greatly with large-scale air capability, created particular demands on command and control skills, and therefore enhanced their role.

At the same time, the difficulty of making general statements about effectiveness is underlined by the different conclusions of detailed studies. For example, American fighting quality in the winter of 1944–45 has been affirmed in a study of the Vosges campaign, but work on the Huertgen Forest operation has been less positive due to a questioning of command skills. Such differences reflect not only scholarly emphasis,[19] but also the frequently underrated issue of variations between units, as well as the extent to which particular command decisions could accentuate the nature of such differences. The relatively small size of the American army also ensured a lack of reserve divisions, and the resulting duration of combat without a break for individual units in 1944–45 created serious difficulties.

A comparable process of improved Allied fighting quality occurred in the war with Japan. In the winter of 1941–42, the Allies were outfought: the British and Australians in Malaya and Singapore, the Americans in the Philippines, and the Dutch in modern Indonesia, all conspicuously so. Training and experience, however, helped lead to a major improvement in quality, seen, for example, with the Australians in New Guinea, the British in Burma, and the Americans in Pacific operations. British training now emphasised the need to patrol the jungle aggressively, instead of handing it to the Japanese, and, if flanked or enveloped, the importance of not retreating in disorder (as in Malaya in 1941–42 and Burma in 1942), but of forming defensive boxes with all-around fields of fire and standing firm. In contrast, Japanese tactics did not change, as was noted in both New Guinea and Burma.[20]

Resources, obviously, were part of the equation, as with the ability to air-drop supplies into British defensive boxes on the India-Burma border in 1944, and into advancing Australian forces in New Guinea the same year. Yet, more significant was the ability to fight successfully on the ground, and this was the prelude to the reconquest of Burma, a feat that involved the defeat and outmaneuvering of a Japanese field army,[21] as well as to the reconquest of New Guinea. The Americans displayed the same improvement between their two campaigns in the Philippines. Blamey, the Commander-in-Chief of the Australian army and commander of Allied land forces under MacArthur in the Southwest Pacific area, who took personal command of the Allied operations in New Guinea in September 1942, produced a report on them in July 1943, in which he argued that "the chief reason for our success in this campaign was that our ground troops proved to be better led, better equipped and better trained than those of the enemy and were man for man better fighters." In his report, Blamey drew attention to the role of resources, arguing that air support in particular was crucial, but his stress on the difficulty of the terrain underlined an emphasis on human resilience and effort, "Throughout the region the tangled undergrowth, broken ground and ever prevailing damp made movement off the track difficult and arduous in the extreme . . . Beyond Nauro the track is inches deep in mud while whole leeches abound everywhere."[22]

A subsequent report, by General Stanley Savige on the operations of the 3rd Australian Division in the Salamanca area of New Guinea in 1943, again emphasized air support, but also underlined the need for physical fitness on the part of the troops and for very good junior officers and NCOs (non-commissioned officers). The stress was on greater Australian effectiveness in fighting on the ground, and on the role of training and determination in achieving this:

> All companies must retain their mobility and be capable of dealing with enemy parties endeavouring to infiltrate between the companies . . . Standing, reconnaissance and fighting patrols must be constantly active . . . At least three days food, water and ammunition must be placed in each perimeter. It is inevitable that, when attacked by large and determined forces, perimeters will be surrounded, but defenders must hold out. In every instance where this was done the enemy were beaten off and the defenders were relieved . . . On occasions when withdrawals were attempted the casualties suffered were heavy . . . the rules of hygiene and sanitation and anti-malarial precautions must be strictly observed at all times, no matter how hard the fighting, or how weary the troops . . . Patrolling must be aggressive and continuous and is the key to success in the jungle . . . A high standard of training is necessary.

In contrast, the Japanese were reported as reliant on simple and inflexible tactics, as disliking moving in small patrols, and as lacking accuracy with small arms.[23] In Burma, the British found that Japanese inflexibility provided opportunities to achieve flanking attacks.[24] Accounts of greater Australian effectiveness, however, were at once accurate and also aspects of the creation of a distinctive myth. There is also the danger of over-emphasizing the individual soldier as the pendulum of historical interpretation shifts from an emphasis on resources.

The quality of disease prevention and medical care was particularly important for jungle warfare. Work on medical care has shown, again, that resources and technology were important, but so was the way in which these were employed. In the British army, the care of the sick and wounded was transformed during the war by new medical practices and drugs, such as active immunization against tetanus, sulphonamide drugs, and penicillin. In contrast, the Germans lacked antibiotics, so that many of their wounded suffered from severe sepsis. Penicillin permitted a British offensive, not only against wound infections, but also against the debilitating inroads of venereal disease. Yet, at the same time, the use made of resources was important. The significance of administrative advances was particularly the case with the British system for blood transfusion established after the foundation of the Army Blood Transfusion Service in 1938. In contrast, the German collection and storage of blood in forward areas was inadequate. The British showed a capacity to learn during the war, leading to a marked improvement in the provision of their medical care.

Defeat in the early years of the war led to many problems, not least of all because the level of care available in the field was affected by the disruption attendant on defeat and rapid retreat. These early campaigns, however, provided some valuable experience: It became apparent that blood transfusion apparatus needed to be available in all forward units, and not just in specialist ones. The early campaigns also indicated that larger field hospitals were of limited use in mobile warfare, and this led to a later emphasis on field ambulances and mobile specialist units, which had actually been used by the Americans as early as the battle of Shiloh in 1862. By 1944, most British casualties were receiving treatment within hours of wounding. Resources and organizational culture were also complementary in disease prevention. Rates of admission to hospital from disease on the part of British troops fell in Southeast Asia, the Middle East, and the Central Mediterranean, and the British had an important comparative advantage, with rates of sickness considerably lower than those in the German, Italian, and Japanese armies. Anti-malarial drugs, for example, complemented an emphasis on hygienic and anti-malaria discipline.[25] This situation contributed to the retention of troops in, and re-entry of troops to, combat formations and to morale.

In addition, at sea, more than resources were at stake. For example, there was an important development in Allied anti-submarine tactics, weaponry, and doctrine in the Atlantic. This was necessary in response to the challenge from U-boats. In 1942, 1,664 merchantmen, amounting to nearly eight million tons, were sunk by U-boats, while the losses of the latter were less than new launchings—fifty-eight lost in July–December 1942, when 121 were completed—and, for the first time, there were enough U-boats to organize comprehensive patrol lines across North Atlantic convoy routes. Accumulated experience, however, increased Allied operational effectiveness, both for convoy escorts and for aircraft. Incremental steps included not simply better weapons, such as improved radar and more effective searchlights, but also the development of more appropriate sailing formations and tactics.[26] The greater availability of escort carriers also helped, as did even more so that of merchantmen. Whereas, thanks to shipbuilding, the British had replaced most of their merchantmen sunk during the First World War, they were unable to do so in World War II. Instead, the merchant fleet in 1945 was 70 percent the size it had been in 1939, and it was American shipbuilding, with its more effective prefabrication and flow production methods, that played the crucial role. Equally, this ensured the strategic failure of the U-boats. In the first quarter of

1943, the Allies built more ships than the U-boats sank, and, by the end of the third quarter, they had built more than had been sunk since the start of the war: riveters were indeed important. Defeating the U-boat attack ensured the Allied ability to move and apply resources. Nevertheless, Allied success simply spurred Karl Dönitz, Commander-in-Chief of the German navy from 1943, to become steadily more radical in his pursuit of victory, demanding fanaticism from his men and accepting increasingly more hazardous operating conditions, which led to a very high rate of fatalities in the submarine service.[27]

In the Pacific, it was necessary to develop carrier warfare techniques, a formidable task because of limited pre-war experience in this field, although, by the mid-1930s, many American admirals had carrier experience. These techniques and doctrines also had to include the unfamiliar sphere of co-operation with other surface warships. A variety of factors, aside from carrier numbers, were involved in American victory. In the crucial Midway campaign of 1942, Japanese failure reflected factors particular to the battle, as well as more general issues. In the campaign, the Japanese were seriously hit by flawed planning and preparation. They under-estimated American strength, while their deployment in pursuit of an overly complex plan and their tactical judgment were both very poor. Admiral Yamamoto also exaggerated the role of battleships in any battle with the Americans. In contrast, although there were serious deficiencies in the American force—for example, problems with the torpedoes carried by the torpedo bombers—American preparation was superior. This included the ability to intercept and decipher coded Japanese radio messages, enabling them to out-think their opponents: the American intelligence failure of Pearl Harbor was more than rectified. Furthermore, the Americans were able to mount an effective repair effort, returning to service the carrier *Yorktown*, damaged at the battle of the Coral Sea in 1942. Despite these systemic advantages, the battle of Midway still had to be won. Far from being an inevitable result, it reflected American tactical flexibility, as this was a battle in which the ability to locate opposing ships and planes, and to respond to both, proved crucial; while, as with combined arms operations on land, the combination of fighter support with carriers (in defense) and bombers (in attack) was important in order to minimize losses.

In the air war with both Japan and Germany, alongside the great increase in Allied airplane numbers, there was an improvement in such spheres as ground support. The training of large numbers of aircrew was a formidable undertaking, but it paid off, not least of all for the

Americans in the Pacific. There was a growing disparity in quality between pilots, a matter of numbers, training, and flying experience, and, as a result, the Japanese could not compensate for their growing numerical inferiority in the air. At the same time, it would be foolish to neglect the extent to which the Americans by 1943 benefited in the Pacific from better aircraft. Whereas the Japanese had not introduced new classes of planes, the Americans had done so, enabling them to challenge the Zero fighter, which had made such an impact in the initial Japanese advances. The Corsair, Lightning, and Hellcat outperformed the Zero, while, as their specifications included better protection, they were able to take more punishment than Japanese planes. The Japanese had designed the Zero with insufficient protection, in part because its light weight increased range and maneuverability, but also because the safety of their pilots was a low priority.

The contrast in resources in the closing stages of the war in the Pacific was readily apparent. Although the Japanese XIV Area Army in Luzon in early 1945 had more than a quarter of a million troops, its condition reflected the degradation of the Japanese war machine. There were only about 150 operational combat aircraft to support it, and their planes and pilots could not match the Americans in quality; indeed, most were destroyed by American carrier planes before the invasion of Luzon. The Japanese troops lacked fuel and ammunition, and the relatively few vehicles available had insufficient fuel. Nevertheless, although the Americans, with Filipino assistance, overran the key parts of Luzon and gained bases for an invasion of Japan, they suffered more than 140,000 casualties in their operations on the island.

Pacific operations exemplified a feature of World War II that was different from World War I: the extent to which, despite the lack of a single American commander for the Pacific, joint tri-service operations were a matter not only of tactical co-operation, greatly enhanced by radio, but also of operational and strategic importance. An emphasis on the value of air power for ground support, sea support (specifically anti-shipping and anti-submarine attacks), and strategic bombing led to a stress on the acquisition and protection of air bases. This helped determine operational and strategic options, leading the United States in 1944, in response to the Japanese overrunning of bases in China that had been designed for the bombing of Japan, to emphasize gaining control of islands, particularly Saipan, from which similar sorties could be mounted. This was also an issue in Europe, with, for example, the occupation of Iran in 1941 seen as the basis for British air attacks on the Baku oilfields if the Germans seized them from the Soviets,[28] and the capture of southern Italy in 1943 providing a base for Allied strategic bombing, including of the oilfields in Ploesti, Romania, the key source of oil in Europe.

The vulnerability of naval units and merchantmen also made air bases of particular importance in the war against Germany. The need to close the "air gap" in the Atlantic, in order to ensure air support to convoys, a crucial pre-condition to the buildup of Allied forces in Britain in preparation for the "Second Front," led to a stress on acquiring bases in Atlantic islands, particularly Iceland and the Azores. Air bases were also seen as crucial in the Mediterranean. Control of Malta threatened Axis lines of communication, and British planners for the same reason feared possible German advances into Turkey and Cyprus. In 1941, Blamey wrote about eastern Libya, "Cyrenaica is regarded as most urgent problem of Middle East as control to Benghazi would give fleet freedom of movement as far as Malta and advance air bases to allow cover of sea operations."[29]

Training was also an issue in the air war with Germany. Better familiarity with the potential of radar helped first the British and then the Germans in directing the interception of bombing attacks. In combat in the skies, the Germans did worse in the later stages of the war. In 1944, the *Luftwaffe* lost many planes over combat zones, while, thanks in part to the Mustang's superiority to German interceptors, the *Luftwaffe* lost large numbers of planes responding to American air raids. Pilots were very difficult to replace, largely because German training programs had not been increased in 1940–42, as was necessary given the scale of the war. This helped to ensure that, irrespective of aircraft construction figures, the Germans would be far weaker in the air. Toward the end of war, the Germans could not afford the fuel for training, while a lack of training time was also a consequence of the shortage of pilots. The net effect was a lack of trained pilots comparable in quality to those of the Allies. By the time of the Normandy landings in 1944, the Germans had lost the air war, and their ground units treated aircraft as probably hostile: Indeed, only two *Luftwaffe* pilots fired shots in anger on June 6, 1944.

One major area of Allied improvement, in which training and doctrine were both crucial, was close air support.[30] Blamey reported in 1941 that air support had become a priority for Allied forces planning to attack the Germans and Italians in North Africa:

Great advance in this in last two months. Attitude Air Force here most cooperative ... All suitable air squadrons to be trained in army co-operation and joint control organization for field co-operation being set up. During operations specific air units to be allotted to military organizations under control army commander with air controller on his staff.[31]

Aside from training and experience, there has also been insufficient attention to the geopolitics of the conflict, and, in particular, to the failure of the Axis as an alliance. It is unclear how best to integrate this factor into "total war" discussions, but it was important. This was a matter both of planning and of execution. Hitler's inability to direct his allies led to serious problems for him, most especially with their attacks on other powers, that of Italy on Britain and Greece in 1940, and of Japan on the United States in 1941. As a result of the failure of the unsuccessful attack on Greece, his timetable for launching an attack on the Soviet Union was overtaken, and the gap between his determination to impose his will on events and the pressure of reality became ever stronger. It had undoubtedly been a factor from the outset: Hitler had not wanted a major war in 1939, as he was not ready for one then. Instead, he had sought to coerce Poland.

The implementation of the Axis as a military alliance was also a serious problem. Germany and Japan were unable to create a military partnership, or to provide mutual economic assistance that in any way matched that of the Allies, strained as relations among the latter were. German plans for war with the United States made little of the prospect of Japanese assistance and preferred to focus on the possibility of using naval power to exploit bases in Vichy North Africa or the Canary Islands, or indeed on long-range bombers, multi-stage rockets, space bombers, or submarine-launched missiles. These schemes included attacks on New York City and Washington.[32]

The ineffectual German-Japanese attempts at naval co-operation, which included the dispatch of German technology, indicated that even where co-operation was possible, it did not achieve much. Furthermore, although their submarines met there, the Germans and Japanese failed to mount large-scale concerted operations in the Indian Ocean. The loss of Japanese offensive capability as a consequence of the sinking of so many of their carriers at Midway, made thoughts of joint action with the Germans implausible. This was significant because the major role that Japan played in the war was an important aspect of its novelty, obliging Allied planners to confront challenges on a far greater scale than in World War I. The operations of German warships then in the Indian and Pacific Oceans were no preparations for the challenge posed by Japanese advances in 1941–42. In 1942, for example, a successful Japanese naval raid on Sri Lanka led the British to withdraw their fleet to East Africa and Bombay, as it was now necessary to think about the need to protect the Arabian Sea, and thus tanker sailings from the Persian Gulf, as well as the route down the coast of East Africa to the Cape of Good Hope. That February, the Japanese bombing of Darwin, the leading town in northern Australia, had dramatized the extension of the war in another direction. Yet, the carriers that had mounted the raid on Sri Lanka were sunk by the Americans at Midway, and there was to be no repetition of this threat to the strategic resource and depth presented by British control of the Indian Ocean.

There were also serious problems with the German alliance system in Europe, which add a major caveat to any discussion in terms of total war. Italy did not join the war until June 1940, when Mussolini scented opportunities from German victory in the Battle of France. Moreover, the degree to which Italian resources were subsequently mobilized was not sufficient to maintain the Italian Empire, let alone to support Mussolini's expansionist ambitions against Greece, Egypt, and the British colonies bordering Italian East Africa: Sudan, British Somaliland, and Kenya. Conscription was readily evaded, rationing was limited, and the economy was not militarized. The totality of Italian Fascism was also frequently overplayed. Italy rapidly became a drain on the German military, as did many Eastern European allies.

Furthermore, the Allied invasion of Italy in 1943 led not to the fight to the finish that might be expected in total war, but to the rapid overthrow of Mussolini and the establishment of a government that sought peace with the Allies. Mussolini was rescued by a German airborne force, and Italian Fascists continued the struggle to the end, large numbers fighting the Resistance in a low-level counter-insurgency conflict that was more typical of the warfare of the period than is generally appreciated. However, the defense of central and northern Italy against the Allied advance rested on the Germans. Similarly, military, political, and economic support from Bulgaria, Croatia, Hungary, Romania, and Slovakia proved to be of limited value to Germany, and largely evaporated when the war went badly. A recent Hungarian study of the defense of Budapest against Soviet attack in 1944–45 contrasts the high morale of the Germans, even in this closing stage of the war, with the situation of the Hungarian soldiers, "For them the war was not an existential issue. In five hundred years of history, Hungary had lost every war, so that the Hungarians were more familiar with defeat."[33]

The Finns were more effective fighters than Germany's other allies, but Finnish involvement in the war as a German ally from 1941 was primarily to regain territory lost to the Soviet Union in 1940, and was indeed referred to as the Continuation War by the Finns. The Finns refused a full-scale commitment against partly-besieged Leningrad, despite repeated requests from the Germans. This represents one of the many "what ifs" of the war, as such an advance might well have cut the supply route across Lake Ladoga and brought the siege to an end, enabling the Germans to concentrate their forces further south. The Finns abandoned the Germans altogether in 1944, and, like the Romanians, joined the Soviets against them.

Elsewhere, Germany was able to draw on widespread anti-Communist and anti-Russian sympathies, and indeed on opposition to the Allies in the Arab world,[34] but it failed to exploit those opportunities, largely due to the brutality and racism of its military and governmental attitudes, combined with unpopular policies such as deportations to provide forced labor in Germany. This was particularly apparent in Ukraine.[35] The Japanese were equally culpable. Western colonialism was unpopular, but harsh Japanese direction of conquered colonies was cruel and unpopular, particularly the control of labor and the allocation of resources. Maybe two and a half million Javanese alone died in 1942–45 as a result.

There was no equivalent harshness within the Western empires, although a massive famine in India in 1943 did lead to a high death rate for which the British administration has received part of the blame. Although challenged, control over those sections of Western formal and informal empires that were not conquered by opponents was also enhanced in wartime. The French, for example, suspended the Syrian and Lebanese constitutions in 1939, arresting politicians associated with Germany and the Soviet Union. Vichy authorities subsequently used tanks against bread riots in Syria. The British intervened in Egypt in 1942, and more forcefully in Iraq and Iran in 1941, to displace pro-Axis leaders. Although the Congress Party's Quit India campaign of 1942 was successfully resisted by force, the British Empire faced no equivalent in India or elsewhere to the Irish nationalist rising of 1916. The Japanese-backed Provisional government of Free India that was formed by the Indian nationalist Subhas Chandra Bose in October 1943, was granted administrative control of the conquered Andaman and Nicobar islands the following month, while a pro-Japanese government was granted titular independence in Burma in August 1943; but Bose's Indian National Army made little impact, and pro-Japanese activity in India was very limited.[36] Having conquered Burma in 1942, the Japanese gave it nominal independence in 1943, but the Burma National Army provided Japan with scant assistance.

At the level of the major powers, there were important gaps in hostility. Despite Hitler's hopes, Japan did not attack the Soviet Union after he declared war on the United States following Pearl Harbor, and the two powers did not go to war until August 1945. This lessened the problem for both states of being over-extended on too many fronts. Although, in contrast to Japan and the Soviet Union, Germany could not have done anything, Hitler did not declare war on China.

There were serious tensions over both goals and means within the anti-Axis Alliance, and, on the specific point of the Far East, the Soviet Union neither declared war on Japan until August 1945, nor was willing to allow the use of its territory for American air attacks on Japan, which would have effectively ended its neutrality. There were also important tensions between Britain and the United States. This was specifically the case over the emphasis to be placed on the Mediterranean theatre, which was pressed by Britain, and also over the fate of Eastern Europe, where Churchill was much more concerned about the political consequences of Soviet advance than Roosevelt was. A more fundamental divide, however, was over the future of empire. The Roosevelt administration was opposed to colonial rule and, instead, in favor of a system of "trusteeship" as a prelude to independence. Roosevelt pressed Churchill on the status of both Hong Kong (which he wanted returned to China) and India, and British officials were made aware of a fundamental contradiction in attitudes. In 1943, at the Tehran conference, Roosevelt told Churchill that Britain had to adjust to a "new period" in global history and turn its back on "400 years of acquisitive blood in your veins."[37]

Indeed, American dominance of the Anglo-American alliance had important implications for the British Empire, as there was a marked increase in the American military presence in the Dominions and the colonies. This was a matter not only of bases and the presence of troops, warships, and planes, but also of defense planning. Although there was tension, not least over the role of the United States in the southwest Pacific, the war ended with closer strategic relations between the United States and both Australia and Canada.[38] At the same time, Britain only won security and success as part of an alliance system.

The character of the diplomatic web during World War II, specifically Japanese-Soviet neutrality for most of the conflict, is an instance of the far from total commitment of many of the participants. The argument has been advanced from a recent direction in *Armageddon*, a study of the war in transalpine Europe from September 1944 to the end of the conflict, in which Max Hastings argues that there was a major contrast between the "world of the Western allies, populated by men still striving to act temperately, and the Eastern universe in which, on both sides, elemental passions dominated."[39] Indeed, he claims that the soldiers of the Western Allies lacked "the energy, commitment and will for sacrifice of either the German or Russian armies."[40]

This is overly stark, and ignores the range of qualities and characteristics in all armies. Clearly, the notion of aggregate characters is particularly questionable for forces of this size, while it is not helpful to read simply from casualty figures to relative determination (or indeed fighting quality). Hastings also quotes critical remarks from British and American generals, although all generals are apt to criticize their troops. He neglects the extent to which the nature of the German and Soviet regimes ensured that comparable evidence is lacking.

Nevertheless, Hastings focuses attention on an important issue, differences in these factors, and this contributes to a major qualification of the "totality" of, at least, the fighting experience. He sees the British and American armies in Europe as preserving the "civilized inhibitions of their societies,"[41] thanks in part to the Soviet willingness to take very heavy casualties. The intensity of conflict on the Eastern Front led to average casualty figures on both sides that were higher than those in the Mediterranean and the Western European theatre. This intensity was matched by some Western Allied units—for example, American marines in such Pacific operations as the invasion of Peliliu in September 1944—but the preference for firepower, rather than frontal assaults and close-quarter engagement, that characterized much Anglo-American fighting in Europe was different in type to Soviet practice. This preference was a response to manpower shortages and also to concerns about morale. As far as D-Day was concerned, Montgomery was very conscious that he had under his command Britain's last army, and that shortages of manpower meant that heavy casualties could not be replaced. Furthermore, Major General Richardson, the chief military psychiatrist, pointed out problems with morale. At the same time, Eisenhower was receiving reports that, with the exception of the airborne divisions and the rangers, most American units were inadequately trained for the task that lay ahead. There was a particular problem with finding adequate space in Britain for training for action.[42] The nature of American warmaking also posed a serious problem, as its highly mechanised fashion helped ensure that there was an expectation of four support troops for every combatant.

The Americans also encountered the difficulty seen in World War I that a rapid expansion of the military posed major problems for training and combat effectiveness, particularly if compared in the field with more experienced forces. Blamey threw light on the consequences in terms of operational execution, when he wrote from New Guinea in 1942:

I had hoped that our strategical plans would have been crowned with complete and rapid success in the tactical field. It was completely successful strategically in as much as we brought an American division on to Buna and an Australian division on to Gona simultaneously. But in the tactical field... it was a very sorry story... the American troops cannot be classified as attack troops... from the moment they met opposition sat down and have hardly gone forward a yard. The action, too, has revealed a very alarming state of weakness in their staff system and in their war psychology... the American forces, which have been expanded even more rapidly than our own were in the first years of the war, will not attain any high standard of training or war spirit for very many months to come.[43]

However, as already indicated, the tendency to criticize American and British fighting quality needs to be contextualized. In place, for example, of the view of the British as the worst army in Normandy, it is necessary to note British fighting ability. Indeed, in terms of a learning curve toward greater effectiveness, the British position by 1944–45 can be seen to parallel that by 1918 in World War I. The breakout from Normandy and the Battle of the Bulge were also potent demonstrations of American capability.

As far as fighting to the death was concerned, there were major variations in ratios of prisoners to fatalities. The Japanese were least willing to surrender and many of those who were captured were wounded. The Army Field Service Order of 1941 that forbade being captured was in accordance with strong currents in Japanese public culture. Although there were signs of lower morale as defeats accumulated—for example, in Burma—the willingness of the Japanese to fight on meant that the destruction of their forces was the key objective.[44] This fed into both the character of Allied warmaking, in order to further the securing of what was seen as a uniquely difficult unconditional surrender, as well as into the Japanese leadership's attempt to leave no space for such a solution.[45]

In contrast, there was a far greater willingness in other militaries to accept surrender as a consequence of defeat. At the tactical and operational level, this is readily apparent and extended to a consideration of to whom it was best to surrender. This was not exactly a characteristic to be expected in a total war, or, rather, suggested that the Germans were waging a total war with the Soviet Union and not with the United States. At the strategic level, the definition of defeat was problematic. The Germans went on fighting after defeat in the Battle of Normandy, even though they had arguably lost all hope of winning; although, in September 1944, the German position was still better than that of Britain in June 1940 or the Soviet Union in November 1941, and both of them had continued to fight. Hitler's lack of realism was the key major factor in Germany fighting on; it focused on a flawed confidence in wonder weapons, such as the V2 rocket. The German proclivity to search for paradigmatic shifts in technology (as with jets) hampered operational effectiveness. Hitler also had a misplaced hope that, far from pursuing unconditional surrender (the Allied goal agreed at the Casablanca conference in January 1943), the alliance against Germany would split before the end of the war.

At the tactical level, the failure to use gas, other than by the Japanese in China, marked a more limited situation than the previous world war and, indeed, than had been widely envisaged in the interwar years. The gas masks distributed to British civilians at the outbreak of the war were not made necessary by German bombing, as had been feared, and American tests on the effectiveness of phosgene, hydrogen cyanide, cyanogens, chloride, and mustard gas were similarly not taken forward.[46] The Germans, however, used gas to kill large numbers in pursuit of the genocidal policies toward the Jews that were central to Hitler's vision of the German struggle.

As a reminder of the extent to which even the criteria of "total war" only fitfully applied to Germany, appointment to the officer corps was only comprehensively Nazified after the traditional military leadership had been compromised by the role of some generals in the July 1944 bomb plot against Hitler. Furthermore, Hitler's need to bring back generals, such as Gerd von Rundstedt, whom he had removed from command positions because he questioned their zeal when they recommended withdrawals (Rundstedt from Rostov in December 1941), was an indication of a pressure for pragmatism on a leader rarely noted for such. More generally, Hitler felt it necessary to bribe his generals with large amounts of tax-exempt money or seized Polish and German-Jewish property. Such bribery was in line with the frequently chaotic nature of German government under Nazi rule, but it also revealed the extent to which there was a military autonomy that scarcely accorded with notions of totalitarianism, or indeed with the practice of control, not least through political commissars, in the Soviet Union. The rivalries of the German intelligence systems also suggested a regime that found it difficult to focus key strands on its external enemies.[47]

This can be related to the wider question of the relationship between mobilization, economic, social, ideological, or otherwise, and effectiveness. Some of the language of mobilization was designed to counter the very limitations that existed: it was a deliberately rhetorical matter of aspiration, seeking to build up will, and not a measured description of the situation. This is true, for example, of the speech delivered by Josef Goebbels, Hitler's propaganda chief, in Berlin's *Sportpalast* on January 30, 1943. It was a call to action, rather than a description of already-existing means and results. Churchill's call, before a joint session of Congress in Washington on May 19, 1943, "to see this fearful quarrel through, at all costs, to the end," was a far more measured statement of the same theme.

The intensity of conflict on the Eastern Front was matched by a greater brutalization of non-combatants by both Germans and Soviets in Eastern Europe compared to the situation further west. This brutalization ranged from the harsh treatment of prisoners to the vicious slaughter of civilians judged unacceptable. About 3.3 million Soviet prisoners died in German captivity, and 1.1 million Germans in that of the Soviet Union. The slaughter of civilians focused on the Holocaust that the Germans inflicted on the Jews, but that was only a part of German brutality. The very process of occupation was made both cause of, and opportunity for, killing, enslaving imprisonment, disruption, and expropriation, as it also was when the Soviets gained control. Like the Germans, they believed in the enforced movement of people, and, in December 1939, Stalin considered the removal of Finns from Finland as a consequence of the Winter War.[48] Aside from enforced movements of peoples, the Soviet NKVD waged a rear-area campaign against those deemed questionable, categories that included Soviet POWs, the Polish resistance, and Polish Jews.

A recent study of the German divisions that, at different times between 1941 and 1943, operated in the Army Group Centre Rear Area, which covered much of present-day Belarus, indicates that a variety of factors played a role in German military brutality. The influences that conditioned German military thinking on anti-guerrilla warfare were brutalizing before the Nazis came to power, but Nazi ideas intensified these influences. In 1941, when there was little real partisan threat, the German use of indiscriminate brutality helped accentuate the problem. Subsequently, Soviet success on the front line that winter encouraged partisan resistance, and the Germans responded with increased mass killing. At the same time, efforts were made to cultivate support, contributing to the contradictions in policy that were so characteristic of the Nazi regime. The hearts-and-minds effort included public talks on Germany by Eastern workers home on leave from the Reich, in which positive accounts were offered of their treatment, and of the bountiful existence enjoyed by German workers. There were also films on German life and open letters enthusiastically recounting the happiness of Eastern workers in the Reich. Among the German officers were fanatics who could draw no distinction between partisans and the rest of the population, as well as moderates and self-styled pragmatists, and the last had the most decisive effect on troop conduct. Diversity did not, however, lead to any marked lessening of the institutional ruthlessness that was accentuated by Nazi ideology.[49]

As with Japanese attitudes and policies in China, those of the Nazis were self-defeating. Both the ruthlessness of the occupation policy and the lack of adequate resources for security made it difficult to conduct an effective occupation policy, whether peaceful or warlike, and particularly jeopardized the chances of economic benefit, while also throwing away the initial willingness of many to collaborate.[50] A lack of sufficient manpower for the extensive long-term occupation of areas susceptible to the partisans helped lead to a reliance on high-tempo brutality, a correlate of German operations at the front.

As the suppression of the Warsaw ghetto rising of 1943 and the Warsaw rising of 1944 indicated, however, the lack of troops was not the rationale for violence: German brutality and reprisals were also well in evidence when they had a clear advantage. The risings themselves indicated the role of politics, in terms of the equations of support and the role of goals. In 1944, Soviet forces were not willing to continue their offensive to relieve German pressure on Warsaw, mainly because Stalin did not wish to see Polish nationalists in control of their capital. This took precedence over the serious logistical problems arising from the advance. Equally, the 1944 rising was designed in order to further the goal for an independent Poland, and this political goal was pushed despite prudent military reasons for caution. Alongside German brutality came that of German allies, such as the Iron Cross fascist movement in Hungary and, from 1941, the Croat Ustashe regime. The last contributed to the totality of war in Yugoslavia, providing an instance of the way in which a global war interacted with long-standing local patterns.

A different type of war on civilians led to the bombing of cities in an attempt to break the opponent's will, or, at least, as a side effect of the bombing of industrial and communication targets when high-level planes dropping free-fall bombs could provide little by way of accuracy. A British strategic review of August 1941 noted the consequences of British forces being unable to compete with the Germans in continental Europe. The response of the operationally weaker power was to seek strategic advantage from indirect attack, in the shape of blockade, bombing, and subversion, each being designed to hit the German economy and German morale:

Bombing on a vast scale is the weapon upon which we principally depend for the destruction of German economic life and morale. To achieve its object the bombing offensive must be on the heaviest possible scale and we aim at a force limited in size only by operational difficulties in the UK. After meeting the needs of our own security we give to the heavy bomber first priority in production.

Our policy at present is concentrate upon targets which affect both the German transportation system and morale. As our forces increase we intend to pass to a planned attack on civilian morale with the intensity and continuity which are essential for success.

The emphasis was on scale, a clear instance of aspirations for total conflict, and also an indirect approach that at once comprehended and affected the entire German war effort, which reflected another aspect of this aspiration for total conflict: "we believe that by these methods applied on a vast scale the whole structure on which the German forces are based can be destroyed. As a result these forces will suffer such a decline in fighting power and mobility that direct [British] action will once more become possible." At the same time, there was a belief that this offensive might even make ground conflict redundant: "Although these methods may by themselves be enough to make Germany sue for peace we must be prepared to accelerate victory by landing on the Continent . . . and striking into Germany itself."[51]

The effectiveness of bombing has for long been a matter of debate,[52] but the morality of it, in the shape of numerous civilian casualties and a reliance on causing a collective psychic breakdown, has become even more so. Bombing campaigns have become more controversial, in part as Germans seek to lessen or shift blame from their conduct during the war.[53] This adds to the already strong contention over the use of the atom bomb against Japan.[54] In part, bombing arose from the presence of bombing forces, which owed their existence to the pre-war belief in the efficacy of this form of indirect warfare, which constituted a more directed and insistent instance of the habitual practice of maritime blockade in order to hinder economies and affect civil society. Wartime factors accentuated the use of bombing, not simply the determination to employ available forces, but also the need to show domestic and international audiences that efforts were being made. A desire to propitiate Soviet pressure for a "Second Front," combined with the need to convince public opinion that something was being done, lent political force to the British bombing of Germany. Furthermore, a belief that the war being waged was a total one was used to justify the policy of bombing, and, in turn, the latter was an instrumental demonstration that the war was indeed total.

Victory is rarely a simple process, but there is a strong desire about both victors and vanquished to construct a clear narrative and analysis. This leads to an underrating of the extent to which victory was an incremental process, and one to which a number of factors contributed, not least of all preparedness, planning, and the gaining of experience. Thus, for example, although the overlap in planning and personnel was limited, the experience of conducting amphibious operations, particularly, but not only, in the Mediterranean, was a useful preparation for the invasion of Normandy in 1944. In overall explanations, training and experience are less attractive than weaponry, but they must not be forgotten when considering Allied success in World War II. In addition, an emphasis on training and experience suggests a qualification of any emphasis on novelty or uniqueness for the war itself.

Training and experience have been highlighted in an instructive comparison of the motivation of American soldiers in the 1860s and 1940s, an approach that could profitably be repeated for other militaries. Drawing attention to major changes in American society, not least of which was a decline in "dense organic relationships," Thomas Rodgers has argued that its presence in the 1860s ensured that soldiers were able to perform courageously, despite little training, because of their identities as autonomous free men and proprietors of society, while, in the 1940s, the absence of such male identities ensured a need for basic training and the emotional bonding of unit cohesion if troops were to perform.[55] There are problems with all comparisons, not least, in this case, differences between fighting at home and abroad, as well as the extent to which the infantry got the worse of the pick of

American conscripts in World War II, because of a policy of directing better-grade recruits to the air force and the navy. The relationship between volunteering and conscription was also different in the two conflicts, with consequences that require probing. Furthermore, unit cohesion was important in the American Civil War.

Nevertheless, the suggestion that social change, at least in the United States, made it more difficult to inculcate morale and battle motivation, raises instructive questions about the extent to which the emphasis on "industrial war" reflected need as well as opportunity, specifically the need to address issues of morale by enhancing firepower, as well as the opportunities presented by technology. This, in turn, directs attention to the role of ideology and propaganda in maintaining morale. The relative absence of expressions of patriotism on the part of the troops of the Western Allies has been differently interpreted, with the argument about unexpressed patriotism being potent, vying with that of a lack of patriotic fervor and a reliance on comradeship.[56] In the case of German, Soviet, and Japanese forces, there are serious problems with the evidence, stemming from the impact of totalitarianism and defeat. If the emphasis, however, is on coercion as a means to ensure military service, with reference made to the execution of large numbers of German and Soviet soldiers as a penalty for supposed dereliction of duty—21,000 Germans and more Soviets—then again a limitation on the notion of total war is perceived. Such executions, which extended to generals accused of insufficient zeal, were extreme, but they also indicate that enthusiasm was more limited and conditional than sometimes argued. Large-scale executions were at once a sign of a total state directing a total war, and an indication that part of the military did not live up to this goal.

The determination of wartime populations to return to peacetime "normality"[57] was another qualification of total war. Despite the claims of some commentators, there was scant sense among the public that peace and war were simply aspects of conflict or different operational forms of a common strategy. This view was only possible in totalitarian societies, but, although it made them formidable threats in the short term, it helped distort their investment priorities so as to make them inefficient and unpopular in the long term, the eventual fate of the Soviet Union in the 1980s. The determination to return to normality was particularly important to post-war Western politics, and thus the tasking of the military. Just as, after World War I, a lack of support for another major conflict compromised Allied policy in the Russian Civil War and affected the response to a number of post-war crises including the Chanak and Ruhr ones, in the late 1940s, this attitude made it less likely that the Western Allies would respond forcibly to Communist advances, whether in Eastern Europe or in China, although there were other reasons as well for their reluctance. It was not until North Korea invaded the South in 1950 that this attitude changed.

In May 1945, considering the possibility of war between the Soviet Union and an Anglo-American alliance, the British Joint Planning Staff anticipated that Soviet resilience would prevent a speedy end, and that the conflict could only be waged as a total war, entailing a fully-mobilized American war economy, as well as German support.[58] This was to be the route fitfully pursued during the Cold War, but, even so, there was no full mobilization, no commitment to the rollback of Communist control, and, on the part of Britain and France until the early 1960s, a major continued military commitment, instead, to the maintenance of empire.

World War II had led to a considerable weakening of the opposition to Communism. This was the case directly in Eastern Europe and China, where, respectively, Soviet power advanced and the Kuomintang (Chinese nationalists) was gravely weakened by the war with Japan, and also in the formal and informal worlds of European empire, particularly the French and Dutch Empires, which had been badly compromised by defeat. Concern about these political aspects was very clear in Churchill's wartime attitude toward strategy, for example, his strong support for the reconquest of British colonies in Asia, such as Malaya, by British forces, and his support for an advance by Western forces into the Balkans. Despite popular hopes for peace and the aspirations that resulted in the establishment of the United Nations, the war led directly into a post-war world of fresh confrontation and conflict, although there was to be no other war comparable in scale to World War II.

# CHAPTER 8
# Postscript

Counter-intuitive approaches are instructive if they encourage thought. In forcing a focus on the definition and use of the phrase total war, it is profitable to consider the idea that, even if the concept is helpful, 1860–1945 is not the most appropriate period for discerning it. This indeed echoes the controversy over the early modern European military revolution, initially located in the century 1560–1660, when, in practice, aside from problems with the very concept, the preceding and subsequent centuries witnessed more change.[1] Furthermore, it is useful to probe the consequences of ending the link between definitions of total war and the notion that such conflict was an obvious stage in a clear practice and pattern of military modernization. Questioning the latter makes it possible to re-examine the earlier literature on military development, including the conceptual building blocks of the analysis. If the teleological character of the established definition of military modernization is challenged, and due weight is given to the variety of conflict in any one period, especially, but not only, outside the West, then it becomes easier to think of change as multilinear. Modernization, moreover, can be considered in terms of a response to circumstances, which led in many different directions, rather than as the definition and diffusion of a paradigm state of war. Total war, in short, however defined, was not the general solution, and this greatly diminishes the value of treating it as an ideal type of development.

Total war can also be separated from any developmental model of conflict, by decentering not only the West, but also Europe and the

United States, and offering, as a result, a more complex account of the West. For example, to compare Latin America's two bloodiest conflicts in this period, the War of the Triple Alliance (1864–70) and the Chaco War (1932–35), is to draw attention to two devastating conflicts, without discerning any clear trajectory toward a supposed totality of warfare. The War of the Triple Alliance opposed Argentina, Brazil, and the Uruguayan Colorados Party to an expansionist Paraguay. The campaigning was wide-ranging and large numbers died, many in frontal attacks, such as the unsuccessful Argentinean attack on entrenched Paraguayan forces at Curupaity in 1866. The inability to reach a negotiated end to the conflict was crucial to the character of the war: its longevity, the high casualty level, and the goals pursued. The removal of Francisco Solano López, the marshal president of Paraguay, was one of the conditions of the Allies, and he fought to the death; there was no equivalent to Lee's surrender at Appomattox, let alone the meeting there between Grant and Lee, which included Grant's offer of rations for Lee's army.[2] Instead, the Allies occupied Paraguay's capital, Ascunsion, in January 1869, but this did not lead to the end of the war. That did not occur until López's death brought hostilities to a close.

The Chaco War was also very bloody. Bolivia lost about 2 percent of its population and Paraguay about 3.5 percent, although the latter percentage was considerably lower than that in the War of the Triple Alliance. Aside from high casualty rates in both wars, there was also the mobilization of war economies. The Chaco War saw more sophisticated weaponry than the War of the Triple Alliance, including aircraft, tanks, machine guns, and automatic firearms, purchased at heavy cost, with Paraguay spending about 60 percent of its national income on arms in 1926–32.[3] Yet, it is not clear that compared to the 1860s, a different stage in warfare had been reached, whether in terms of goals, political context, intensity of fighting, mobilization of resources, or devastation. Logistics was key to both conflicts, while the difficult terrain and the weakness of transport systems created problems in each conflict. In the Chaco War, the defeated Bolivia was not conquered, as Paraguay had been in the 1860s, although a change in leadership was again crucial to ending the war: President Salamanca of Bolivia was overthrown in 1934.

Similarly, to take another narrative, although Chinese Communist writers differentiated the Civil War, through which Communism had prevailed in China, from earlier struggles, in terms of what they claimed was the limited proletarian consciousness of the peasantry prior to

Communism,[4] it is not clear that this account is satisfactory. Instead, important parallels can be drawn, particularly between the Taiping Rebellion of 1851–66 and the Chinese Civil War of 1946–49.

Yet, this does not undermine the extent to which the concept of revolutionary war employed for the Chinese Civil War offers an important narrative of total war, one that bridges the West/non-West divide, and is also not dependent on discussion about the supposed developmental consequences of technological capacity and change. Like the latter discussion, however, this narrative involves in many respects a belief system much of which is focused on an ideal type—in this case, of revolutionary warfare generally understood, from a left-wing perspective, as mass activism and a clear radical consciousness. Instead, revolutionary warfare, like industrial, seems perpetually to fade from grasp, with assertions of its existence, popularity, revolutionary credentials, and military and political potential proving problematic under analysis. Again, there is a teleology at work, with a line drawn from the French Revolution, via the liberal nationalist movements of the nineteenth and early twentieth centuries, such as the Italian *Risorgimento*, to the Russian Revolution, and then attention shifting to the Maoist theory and practice of revolutionary warfare, leading to interest in so-called wars of national liberation post-1945. As with military history in general, this also faces the question of how best to integrate other exemplars into the general narrative. In the case of revolutions, for example, it is understandable that, for the 1910s, the Russian Revolution should take precedence over those in China and Mexico, but that leaves it unclear how best the latter two should be considered.

The revolutionary war concept was more total than that of industrial warfare, in that it called for a more complete change in social structure, practice, and ethos, and also identified force as the necessary, indeed inevitable, means to achieve this. Furthermore, whereas industrial warfare required continual preparation in the shape of enhanced military-industrial potential, that was not the same as the constant conflict of class warfare. The extent to which these were modern forms is now less clear than it was a half-century ago, when the argument for each being a form of modern conflict was asserted in the light of contemporary perceptions that this was the case. By the 2000s, in contrast, the capacity, growth, and nature of industrial societies was such that modern warfare was possible without a high level of mobilization, as was seen in conflicts after the end of the Cold War. Furthermore, at the level of popular conflict, left-wing notions of class warfare no longer seemed so pertinent.

The supposed logic of class warfare was seen during the period of this book in the domestic policies of the Soviet Union. Terror and government-tolerated famine killed at least 11 million people in Stalin's "peacetime" years (1924–41, 1945–53), warped the lives of the remainder of the population, and made casualties of faith, hope, and truth. The secret police was the military of this war, a crucial prop to a government that routinely used violence. Aside from those killed, very large numbers were imprisoned in what effectively were concentration camps. The condition of prisoners in this domestic war was undoubtedly worse than that of soldiers captured in many conflicts.

Similarly, the Chinese Communist state was violent from the outset. The Agrarian Reform Law of 1950 was enforced at the cost (estimates vary) of two hundred thousand to two million landlords' lives, and, in other campaigns of the early 1950s, against alleged counter-revolutionaries, capitalists, and corrupt cadres, maybe five to eight hundred thousand were killed. In the Great Proletarian Cultural Revolution (1966–69), capitalism and bourgeois values were rejected, and, under the "Sixteen Points" adopted in 1966, a violent effort was made "to transform education, literature and art and all other parts of the superstructure not in correspondence with the socialist economic base." In furtherance of this policy, the revolutionary Red Guards brought disruption, not to say anarchy. A decade later, Pol Pot's attempt to transform Cambodian society between 1976 and 1979, again in the aftermath of a civil war, brought the mass slaughter of those who did not conform to his model. Such episodes, which were repeated, albeit not on this scale, are a reminder that the treatment of civilians, an issue returned to below from the perspective of total war, is not a separate question for proponents of revolutionary warfare, nor one restricted to formal periods of war. Phrased differently, for a revolutionary state, as for a terrorist, all time is a period of domestic and international conflict, and everyone is a combatant.

The tradition of revolutionary warfare may now seem dead from the perspective of left-wing radicalism, but this is only true if it is defined, in traditional Marxist or Maoist terms, as socially-conscious proletarian, mass violence. Furthermore, Maoist engagement with peasant-based guerrilla warfare is less credible as the peasantry became less important in an increasingly urbanized world. However, the proclamation of such a death may be premature, for three reasons. First, the weakness of theories and practice of guerrilla warfare, with their assumption of the creation of base areas that may in fact be vulnerable to counter-insurgency operations, led to an increased interest in terrorism from the late 1960s. This was true, for example, of the IRA in Northern Ireland and of Shining Path in Peru. Although unsuccessful in leading to any seizure of control, the disruptive character of terrorism certainly challenged social order, as well as counter-insurgency doctrine and practice.[5] Second, both popular mass violence and terrorism were taken up by movements that were not based on left-wing radicalism, the first most successfully with the Iranian Revolution of 1978–79. This suggested that the narrative of revolutionary warfare needs to be rewritten. In particular, it has to be removed from left-wing parameters and paradigms. At present, this is mostly an issue for how best to encompass radical Islam.

Third, however, looking to the future, it is very likely that the major strains of resource availability and allocation related to environmental pressures, population growth, popular expectations, and political pressure will impact on weak governmental structures, on systems of public politics that are not attuned to long-term crises of this nature, and on societies where support for modernization (or at least for many of its consequences) is limited, while opposition is often bitter. This will lead to a major extension of international and domestic violence. Some of the former may follow the path of terrorism, and much of the latter that of mass violence.[6]

This suggests the need to have an open-ended view on total war understood as revolutionary violence. It also offers one additional definition of total war, namely anarchy, a situation in which, in the absence of authority or social order, violence becomes endemic and indeed crucial to the social order. This was described as the natural state of man in Thomas Hobbes's *Leviathan* (1651), and is arguably more "total" in its social consequences than the highly-organized character of industrial warfare in which much of the population is necessarily involved in production, within a securely policed environment, in order to support the war machine. Anarchy has customarily been seen as a primitive stage of social development, but may become a key aspect of the future, indicating the problems with a linear approach to change.

To take a less drastic approach, if the relationship between total war and the mass state was a synergy, then the decline in social cohesion over the last four decades,[7] in both Western and authoritarian regimes, is a fundamental change. This can indeed be seen as altering the character of modern warfare, particularly with the ending of conscription in many states.

The conflicts of 1860–1945 can certainly be reconsidered in light of what has come since. Beginning with the American policy of massive retaliation, planning for large-scale war during the Cold War entailed considering an arithmetic of nuclear use, and, from the Soviet acquisition of nuclear weaponry in 1949 and, even more, from the subsequent American and Soviet development of intercontinental rockets, of nuclear exchange, in which millions died within minutes. Aside from the planned use of nuclear weapons for destroying civilian populations, they were also integrated into tactical and operational plans. As a result, any war between the Soviet Union and NATO would have been very different from the struggle between Germany and the Soviet Union in 1941–45. Yet, as a reminder of the subordination of conflict to politics, such a war did not occur. This indeed accounts for the habitual use of 1945 to mark the close of the age of total war. The close of World War II certainly brought peace to Europe. It involved foreign occupation and confrontation through deterrence, but with violence only in the form of low-level terrorism, occasional coups, and episodic military interventions to maintain the cohesion of the Communist bloc, most bloodily the suppression of Hungarian independence in 1956.

As a consequence, the Cold War capability for war at a level that would surely have justified the definition total—as any nuclear conflict, although probably short, would have been intense and wide-ranging, and would have involved the deliberate targeting of cities in order to cause very heavy civilian casualties—did not lead to such a conflict. This indeterminacy, specifically the failure to move from capability and doctrine to conflict, was, more generally, also a feature of the so-called age of total war. As already indicated, apparently inevitable ideological and/or geopolitical "slippage" toward war— most obviously, the German attack on the Soviet Union in 1941, and the Japanese counterpart for the United States—was not matched by a Japanese attack on the Soviet Union, nor an earlier Soviet attack on Germany, although both were considered, and the Soviet Union did not attack Japan until 1945. "Total war" might therefore be an ideal type,[8] and no situation with state players can preclude political constructions of reality in which prudential considerations of restraint play a role. Many, but by no means all, terrorists inhabit a different world in which showing that there is no restraint brings terror.

Change in military capability and practice was already apparent at the close of World War II. The war against Germany had ended in 1945 in a far-from-novel fashion, with the victors overrunning the country of the defeated and the leader of the latter dying in its capital. This could have been Tipu Sultan of Mysore dying unsuccessfully resisting the British at Seringapatam in 1799; not of course to suggest any moral equivalence, or to neglect Hitler's failure to die fighting. In Japan, in contrast, the planned Allied invasion never occurred. It would have been the last in a sequence of amphibious operations, one larger in scale than the invasion of Normandy in 1944. Instead, the war was brought to a rapid close when the dropping of two atomic bombs demonstrated that Japanese forces could not protect the homeland, a weakness underlined by the Soviet success in speedily overrunning the key colony of Manchuria. This removed any chance that the Soviets would act as mediators for a peace on more generous terms.[9]

The creation of the atomic bomb itself was indicative of the nature and scale of activity possible for an advanced industrial society. It was the product not only of the application of science, but also of the powerful industrial and technological capability of the United States, and the willingness to spend about $2 billion in rapidly creating a large nuclear industry. The electromagnets needed for isotope separation were particularly expensive, and required 13,500 tons of silver.[10]

In some respects, the use of atomic weaponry suggested the obsolescence and indeed limitations of recent military practices. More people were killed in the American conventional bombing of Japan earlier in 1945—the firebombing of Tokyo killing more than eighty-three thousand on one night—but that campaign required far more planes and raids.[11] Indeed, the use of atom bombs, like, at a far more modest level, that of jet aircraft by the Germans in the closing stages of the war in Europe, pointed the way toward a capability for war between regular forces in which far fewer units were able to wield far more power. This was related to the eventual shift away from conscription, such that the mass armies that fought the two world wars came, by the late 1970s, to appear very much part of a past military age, at the same time that veterans from them were still active.

Particular aspects of the conflicts of the age of total war made them seem limited, as well as dated. In place of the emphasis, derived largely from German newsreels, on the role of mechanized warfare in World War II, came an appreciation of its more restricted extent, particularly (but not only) for the Germans and Japanese. The continued reliance of the former on horse transport has been emphasized, as, more generally, has been the major battlefield role of infantry and artillery, rather than armor. The numbers of troops and quantities of supplies that had to be moved, combined with the nature of industrial and transport systems, and problems with the availability of oil, to ensure that World War II was the last of the large-scale railway wars, as much as the first of the petrol ones. Indeed, at one level, the period covered in this book can be presented as the age of railways and steamship warfare, although, like any description, this is a generalization that has only partial validity: Afghanistan, for example, has neither railways nor a coast.

At the same time, the new use of atomic weaponry in 1945 reflected not the limited capacity of pre-existing forms of warfare, but the extent to which they had created a military environment in which, in the event of determined conflict between major powers, success was almost too costly. In short, a total warfare existed, that would, it was hoped, be short-circuited by modern warfare in the shape of the atomic bomb, the latter a logical consequence of strategic bombing doctrine. The heavy Japanese and American losses on Iwo Jima, Okinawa, and Luzon earlier in 1945 suggested that an Allied invasion of Japan, in the face of a suicidal determination to fight on, would be very costly. The Japanese homeland army was poorly trained and equipped, and lacked mobility and air support, but, on the defensive, it would have the capacity to cause heavy casualties, particularly as it was unclear how to obtain the unconditional surrender that was an Allied war goal.[12] General Douglas MacArthur remarked in April 1945 that his troops had not yet met the Japanese army properly, and that when they did they were going to take heavy casualties.[13] President Harry Truman wrote, "My object is to save as many American lives as possible."[14]

At the Potsdam Conference, the Allied leaders had issued the Potsdam Declaration on July 26, demanding unconditional surrender, as well as the occupation of Japan, Japan's loss of its overseas possessions, and the establishment of democracy in the country. The threatened alternative was "prompt and utter destruction," but, on July 27, the Japanese government decided to ignore the declaration.

The delivery of such destruction in a concentrated fashion was a key element in tipping the balance against the need to fight a particularly difficult series of invasion and exploitation campaigns in the Japanese homeland. Compared to what was to come—in the form of hydrogen bombs (first tested by the United States in 1952), and accurately-aimed, nuclear-tipped, long-range, ballistic missiles, let alone such developments as multiple, independently targeted, reentry vehicles (MIRVs), which greatly enhanced the strike capacity of individual rockets, and were first tested by the United States in 1968—the small stock of free-fall atom bombs for dropping from a bomber that the United States possessed in 1945 was a very limited capability, but it was sufficient. The destruction was such that this seemed total war, and such was indeed the logic of subsequent planning for nuclear war, but, in 1945, the atomic bombs were in practice particularly destructive products of industrial warfare, used as a tool of limited war to achieve the total war goal of unconditional surrender without having to resort to the fight to the finish that would follow an Allied invasion. In the passage quoted above, Truman continued, "but I also have a human feeling for the women and children of Japan." Had the war continued, civilian casualties would indeed have been immense. Aside from the direct and indirect consequences of an invasion, the continuation of the conventional bombing campaign would have been very costly, both directly and indirectly. For example, had the war lasted to 1946, the destruction of the rail system would have led to famine, as it would have been impossible to move food supplies.

Atomic bombs as limited warfare may sound paradoxical, but it was possible in 1945. In part, this was a product of the one-sided nature of Allied and Axis capability. The Germans and Japanese had both been interested in developing an atomic bomb, but neither had made progress comparable to the Americans.[15] Had they possessed atomic bombs, the attitude of the German and Japanese governments suggests that they would have used them. This might well seem to suggest the prospect of total war in the shape of a nuclear exchange, although the likely level both of availability and of delivery systems for the bombs were such that they would not have been strategic, or even operational, tools, other than to instill fear and affect morale. In this, they would have been like the German VI and V2 rockets, although the latter were far more numerous.

The treatment of civilians is a key criterion held to characterize the age of total war. That owes much to the role of ideology in conflict in 1918–45, and culminates with the genocide of the Holocaust. Like many definitions advanced during the Cold War, this is an approach that now seems less secure. The Holocaust was a distinctive and horrifying conflation of the racial nationalism and anti-Semitism of the nineteenth and early-twentieth centuries, with the ideological division of the 1918–45 period, and the industrialized killing that was a characteristic of developments in economic capability and military thought and practice. However, the ethnic killing of the 1990s—particularly but not only in Rwanda, where possibly eight hundred thousand Tutsis were killed in 1994, and of the 2000s, especially in Sudan—indicated that large numbers of civilians could be killed without any relation to the ideological divisions of the early-twentieth century. Furthermore, the rate and nature of killing in Rwanda suggested that "industrial" processes were not a necessary condition for mass killing: many of those slaughtered were killed by the use of machetes and other handheld weapons. This was total war that was more contemporary than World War II, but not industrial. Furthermore, it was only possible to argue that this killing was not modern if Western teleological concepts of modernization were advanced.

The ethnic killings in Rwanda and Sudan were not isolated episodes. As with the aftermath of World War I in Eastern Europe and the Near East, decolonization led to greater volatility, as new entities struggled for independence (or independence on better terms), a process that led in the 1990s to chaos in what had been Yugoslavia, as well as in the Caucasus. Just as in the nineteenth century and after World War I, nation-building proved a painful process. The partition of British India in 1947 saw maybe one million killed in communal violence between Hindus and Moslems, with another fourteen million fleeing as refugees to the new states of India or Pakistan. In Nigeria, possibly thirty thousand Ibos were slaughtered after a coup in 1966. In the subsequent Nigerian Civil War of 1967–70, the successful blockade of secessionist Biafra by the Nigerian military was deliberately intended to sap the will, as well as the ability, of the Ibo people to maintain their separatism, and this helped lead to starvation. The Nigerian military was armed by both Britain and the Soviet Union.

Whereas, in 1945, no state had been capable of large-scale nuclear attack, the Cold War saw the deliberate targeting of civilians in nuclear planning by advanced industrialized states, both Western and non-Western. Furthermore, while both the Cold War and the post–Cold War age have seen large-scale killing in "small wars" as a key element of policy and/or as an expression of social breakdown, Cold War targeting was pushed by the United States in the 1950s. This was in response to Soviet conventional superiority on land, and to the extent that the Korean War had revealed that a conventional war, even if limited, would be very costly. In December 1955, the NATO Council authorized the employment of atomic weaponry against the Warsaw Pact, even if the latter did not use such weaponry. By the 1960s, however, the combination of a willingness to target civilians, massive American and Soviet nuclear stockpiles, and the appearance on both sides of a secure second-strike capability, ensuring that a surprise attack would not wipe out the opposition, were such that war was seen as likely to lead to mutually assured destruction (MAD). MAD was seen as a guarantee of deterrence that created a space for limited conflicts. The prospect of full-scale war was, indeed, truly cataclysmic, and this helped produce an uneasy stability that was the background in the 1970s to an attempt to lessen the possibility of nuclear war.

In contrast to the ethnic slaughter in Rwanda, for example, the total destruction of civilian populations was not generally or centrally the goal of regular forces during the age of total war. In World War II, it was accepted that large numbers of civilians would die as a result of bombing or rocket attacks, and the supposed impact on morale of such casualties was frequently welcomed or, in fact was the goal, but genocide was not the strategic objective of this policy. Furthermore, although the systematically murderous nature of German and Japanese military operations and occupation policies toward civilians is well established,[16] and much rested on ideological commitment to Nazi and Japanese racism,[17] the extent to which the mass killing amounted to a total genocide comparable to that directed toward the Jews is questionable. The Germans planned to colonize much of Eastern Europe and European Russia, and the Japanese sought to dominate China, but both wanted to leave a labor force of slaves in place,[18] although that is an indicator of totality. German brutality was mirrored in the conduct of some of their allies, for example, Croat forces.

The same dimension, of killing, albeit from a different perspective and at a lesser scale, was true of Soviet class-slaughter. However, prisoners captured by the Soviets were harshly treated, but not to the extent of those captured by the Germans and Japanese. Of the more than half a million Japanese troops and civilians captured by the Soviets in 1945 who were sent to camps in Eastern Siberia, more than sixty thousand died in the harsh Arctic conditions. The ratio would have been worse for those captured by the Axis. Furthermore, the driving of Germans from Eastern Europe was brutal, and involved some killing, but there was no mass slaughter.

Although there was interest among the Western Allies in annexing already-existing colonies, such as Churchill's wish to gain Libya for Britain, these were not seen as settlement colonies. With this exception, the Western Allies sought neither conquest nor permanent occupation, and thus had no interest in creating empty lands by slaughter or compulsory repatriation. France sought to regain territory annexed by Germany in 1940, not to gain new lands, although there was some interest in changes to the border with Italy. The United States gained a trusteeship over the former Japanese League of Nations mandated islands in the Western Pacific—the Mariana, Caroline, and Marshall Islands, and the Ryuku Islands were put under American administration, but there was no attempt to annex part of the Japanese home islands.

Large-scale killing, as policy and practice, has remained an important feature of conflict since the age of so-called total war came to a close, because of important shifts on the global scale. The most important shift was rapid decolonization after World War II, which ensured that much of the world, particularly in Africa, South Asia, and Oceania, ceased to be ruled by Western imperial powers, and, instead, gained independence, a process continued from 1989 within the Soviet-dominated part of Eurasia.

At one level, decolonization suggested the obsolescence of concepts of military proficiency based on weaponry. On land, the capability gap between imperial and insurrectionary forces was greater in 1945–75 than it had ever been before, in part because of the availability of air power to imperial forces, a flexibility that was extended by the use of helicopters. Yet, this was also the age in which imperial rule receded as never before. A number of factors were crucial, not least of which was shifting opinion in the metropoles about the desirability of such rule, and about the acceptability of the burdens it entailed. This helped underline the importance of the factor of will, by ensuring a gap in the willingness to fight, specifically a contrast between limited and total war mentalities represented by colonial powers and anti-imperial insurgencies, respectively. This gap made it difficult for imperial powers to prevail, and that helped to destabilize governments that sought to continue to do so, leading to the overthrow of that of Portugal in 1974.

It was difficult to prevail, but not impossible. There had been a contrast between limited commitment on the part of imperial powers and total resistance on the part of some of their opponents during the age of imperial expansion, but that had not prevented large-scale expansion. After 1945, indeed, a number of insurgencies were suppressed. This clearly underlined the degree to which the Cold War, far from being a readily-delimited period in military history, witnessed a considerable overlap in means and moods of warmaking; a conclusion that is also valid for other periods which historians are overly keen to discern and, having reified them, use as causative factors. For example, the retributive expeditions, forcible movement of suspect civilian populations, and use of native ancillaries, seen in counter-insurgency operations from 1945, had all been characteristic of earlier decades. Success, for example, by the French in Madagascar in 1947 and the British in Kenya and Malaya in the 1950s, did not suggest that this form of warfare was obsolescent.

The extent, however, to which such practice from 1945 should be defined as total warfare is far from clear. The resettlement of civilians was particularly disruptive, and captured the extent to which conflict was located in a broader pattern of social control and, if necessary, intimidation and coercion. Casualty figures, however, did not approach those of such earlier episodes as the German suppression of opposition in Southwest Africa and Tanganyika in the 1900s. The killing of large numbers of civilians by Western forces had been made unacceptable by the experience of World War II, and this aspect of "totality" largely awaited conflict between non-Western, mostly post-colonial, states. Although the United States certainly targeted civilians in "Free Fire" zones in Vietnam, the deliberate firing of missiles simply against civilian areas (military targets were not at issue) during the Iran-Iraq War of 1980–88 would not have been acceptable to post-1945 Western (and Japanese) publics. They had become sensitive to civilian casualties and collateral damage, just as the use of costly mass frontal attacks and gas would also have been unacceptable.

Imperial rule had also been accompanied by large-scale killing. This was a matter not only of the conquest stage, but also even more of the suppression of subsequent rebellions, such as by the Herero in German Southwest Africa. The initial rebellion stage can, however, be seen as part of the process of conquest, for example, in Syria in the early and mid-1920s, and resistance and internal violence diminished thereafter. To contrast Sudan in the 1870s–80s, 1920s–40s, and 1960s–2000s suggests that colonial rule there led to a lower level of such violence, and the same is true of many states. In part, indeed, this reflects the extent to which independent states themselves displayed features of imperial rule within their own territories. In independent Sudan, the Islamic, largely Arab, North continued the pre-colonial exploitation of the mostly non-Islamic Black South, as well as of Islamic, Black Darfur. In addition, conflict in the post-colonial world was partially fed by the rivalries of the major powers, not least of all by the supply of weaponry. As a result, it is possible to argue that wars during the Cold War and subsequently were far removed from the roots of indigenous conflict,[19] although this argument underrates the extent to which Great Power intervention was shaped and used by local forces. Recent conflict in Africa can be better understood if the extent to which pre-colonial warfare there was total, in terms of mobilization, and anti-societal is appreciated. This is important in the decentering of Western perspectives of total war.

An emphasis on the non-Western world calls the standard chronology and discussion of total warfare into question in a number of respects. First, it suggests that the groundwork for comparative studies is insufficient. If scale, mobilization, intensity, and brutality are to be used as criteria, then more work needs to be done on conflicts outside the West, such as the Chinese Civil War of 1946–49 and the Iran-Iraq War of 1980–88, possibly extending the chronological range of the age of total war. In contrast, the combination of global range with intensity of conflict seen in World War II was not matched during the Cold War, although the far-flung and disparate character of the latter was certainly prefigured in the first half of World War II, which included such distinct struggles as the Winter War between the Soviet Union and Finland in 1939–40, the British conquest of Iraq in 1941, and the conflict between Vichy French forces and Britain in Senegal, Syria, Lebanon, and Madagascar in 1940–42. Furthermore, to take a six-year period during the Cold War, 1966–72 saw conflicts related to its geopolitical and ideological axes in Vietnam, Laos, Cambodia, the Middle East, Portuguese Africa, and Southern Rhodesia. Although long-term local causes were also very important, the coup in Chile in 1973 can also be located in the Cold War, as can be the conflicts in Nicaragua and El Salvador in the 1980s.

The Vietnam War, which began in 1945 and lasted until 1975, with a short-lived reduction in intensity from 1954, adds a related qualification to the standard chronology and discussion of total warfare. It was a bitter conflict that contrasted markedly with the less-violent Japanese domination of Indochina in 1941–45, and that included the use of air power to an extent that South Vietnam became the most bombed country in history. The bulk of the world's population lives in East and South Asia, where 1945 did not bring a period of large-scale conflict to more than a very short-term close. If the Chinese Civil War, which flared up in 1946, the nationalist movement in Indonesia, against which the Dutch launched a large-scale but ultimately unsuccessful, "police action" in 1947, and the Korean War, which, in terms of conflict between regular forces, broke out in 1950, are included, then 1953, the armistice that brought the last to an end, seems a more pertinent date. There also appears to be little qualitative difference in terms of conflict in the region before and after 1945. In each period, there was civil warfare and conflict with non-mainland powers, although the goals of Japan, France in Indochina, and American and American-allied forces in Korea and, in 1963–72, Vietnam, were very different, and the last two, in particular, were wars waged by Western forces in an ostensibly and clearly limited fashion. In Korea, American forces operated with United Nations authorization. Although the provision of support for South Korea alone was substantially extended, with an Allied invasion of North Korea in 1950, there was no attack on China to counter the latter's powerful intervention against the UN forces.

Mention of East Asia draws attention to the extent to which the concept of "total war" and its use are very much located in the Western interpretation of military history. The genesis of the term is Western, as is the definition, chronology, and debate. It is far from clear that this is helpful for an account of global military history. The treatment of air power as a key component of total war is a good example of this problem. John Buckley has argued that World War II was total because of the nature of the fighting:

perhaps the single most important change was brought about by the coming of age of air power...striking at the heart of Western society both in a physical and psychological manner. Air power demanded mass mobilization of economies, industries and scientific establishments to a degree hitherto unknown.

Yet, Buckley continued by noting the extent to which few states could be major participants, other than as victims or as routes over which planes flew, "As a measure of a state's ability to wage total war, air power was by far the most useful yardstick, as only a few were able to meet the challenge of fusing technical know-how with mass production in this most demanding of fields."[20] Air power, indeed, contributed greatly to Allied victory, and was particularly important in the Pacific war against Japan. Nevertheless, eventual success in World War II rested on the ability to mount sustained pressure through successful sequential multi-front offensives, a strategic capability to wage operational warfare to strategic ends, a sphere in which the Allies prevailed over the Axis. Air power was important in the result, but did not lead to a key change in these offensives on land, although it did at sea. Indeed, by focusing on air power, Buckley adopted an approach that meant relatively little to most powers, not least of all China, during and even more after World War II: the Communists were successful in the Civil War of 1946–49, despite the nationalists' advantage in air power. This is an indication of the problem of adopting a single definition and, therefore, measure of capability.

In terms of the "non-West," 1860–1945 may, indeed, seem total in consequence because the period saw more of the area conquered and ruled as colonies than before and since. Yet, for China and India, the term is less appropriate. Although defeated and, in part, conquered by Japan in 1931–45, China did not experience the total conquest inflicted by the Mongols in the thirteenth century and the Manchus in the seventeenth century, the consequences of which each lasted for a considerable period. Both of these conquests were more devastating in character than the operations of the Western powers from the 1830s to the 1900s, and not notably less so than those of Japan. As far as civil warfare was concerned, the key transforming struggle, the Civil War of 1946–49, occurred after the period ended. As far as Chinese power projection was at issue, the successful expeditions against the Zunghars of Xinjiang in the 1750s were more impressive[21] than anything in the period 1860–1945, although, in the early 1870s, there was a vigorous and successful suppression of rebellion in Xinjiang. China did not launch fresh border campaigns of any scale until after the period closed, with Tibet overrun in 1950, India defeated in 1962, and Vietnam attacked in 1978—all limited wars.

As far as India was concerned, 1860–1945 was largely a period of limited conflict. After the "Mutiny" of 1857–59, the British became less eager for a major transformation of Indian society and, instead, settled far more for what has been described as the "night watchman state." There was also no war for independence. Conflicts continued on the borders, particularly with Afghanistan in 1878–80, but, thereafter, there was less thrust to British expansionism than there had been in the 1840s, and this became particularly the case in the early twentieth century. Instead, southern Asian frontiers became more stable. The Third Afghan War in 1919 was due to the assertiveness of the new emir of Afghanistan, Amanullah Khan, not to British expansionism, and it was only a brief conflict. India, however, continued to be a major basis for British expeditionary warfare, not only in World War I, but also thereafter. In World War II, this culminated with the recruitment of large numbers of volunteers—including eight hundred thousand troops from the Punjab.[22] They fought outside India, particularly in North and East Africa, Iraq, and Malaya, but also in defense of India. The Japanese were eventually outfought on the Indian frontier and in Burma. This was a serious conflict, but the roles involving Indian troops from 1860 to 1945 scarcely added up to a long-term period of total war. The absence of conscription was also important.

Looking to the future, Asia is again instructive, and it is the possibility of conflict between China and the United States that most suggests the limitation of any definition of pre-1945 conflict as total. Although China and Japan devoted much effort to conflict with each other between 1937 and 1945, and much harm was inflicted on the Chinese population, neither was in a position to wield the force both China and the United States can deploy today. When added to the volatility that may stem from North Korean nuclear ambitions, this suggests no room for complacency, but is also a reminder that total war always seems to lie in the future.

Victory and defeat appear to be absolutes, measured by such readily-apparent criteria as the defeat and capitulation of armies and the conquest of territory, all of which seem to be complete and unconditional, to use terms seen as the equivalent of total. Thus, in conventional accounts, war seems to be a matter of how best to ensure these goals, to give effect, in short, to a total result, and this is the basic narrative and analysis of military history and discussions. Indeed, the modern perception of conflict has been heavily shaped by the experience of World War II, by the Allies' insistence on the unconditional surrender of the Axis, and by the cataclysmic fate of the latter in 1945, in the shape of the fall of Berlin and the use of atomic weaponry against Japan. This emphasis has led to a neglect of how atypical such war endings are; and, indeed, in the case of Japan in 1945, it surrendered with the main home islands uninvaded, and with Japan still in control of far more territory than it had occupied prior to the attack on the Western Allies in 1941, including Malaya, Java and Sumatra. Most wars have ended with a far less complete victory, and this is certainly true of the situation since 1945, for example, the Korean, Indo-Pakistan, Arab-Israeli, and Iran-Iraq conflicts. Even the Israeli victory in the Six Day War of 1967, generally seen as a sweeping triumph, ended with the Israelis not in control of Cairo, Damascus, or Amman. The war also ended without the closure, in terms of Arab surrender, that Israel required, mainly because, with an army dependent on reservists, the country could not afford a sustained high level of confrontation. Furthermore, alongside Egyptian and Syrian refusal to accept Israel's gains and negotiate peace, the terrorist response by the Palestinian Liberation Organization became more intense.

Whatever the result in practice, however, the understanding of war in terms of campaigning—the operational approach to war—is far too narrow. Instead, it is more appropriate to understand war as a cultural process that focuses on the imposition of will. From this perspective, it is necessary to appreciate that people are beaten when they understand that they have lost, and that, in the absence of such an understanding, victory in battle can simply lead to the need for an onerous occupation, while much of the population continues to resist: for instance, the problem that faced Napoleonic forces in Spain in 1808–14, or their Nazi counterparts in Yugoslavia in 1941–45; or with the defeated preparing to fight on, as with the Egyptians and Syrians against Israel after 1967, which led in 1973 to the outbreak of another full-scale conflict. Mention of such examples is not intended to suggest any political or moral equivalence: the concern here is with the functional dimension of waging war, not the greatly contrasting contexts and intentions of very different governments. It is in the last, the sphere of goals, that war can most readily be total.

In many respects, success in war has become more difficult in recent decades, certainly from the perspective of imposing will, due to profound social changes across much of the world. These can be summarized as democratization, but the process is far more complex: as more of the world's population has become urban, literate, and engaged in industrial or service activities, so have political participation and expectations increased and deference declined. Linked to these social changes, which affect greatly the possibility of consent to defeat, and therefore the need to enforce victory by gaining consent and/or coercing the defeated, comes a transformation in the reporting, assessment, and commemoration of war. The central feature, in both democratic and authoritarian societies, is its public character, and governments in each are as one in trying to elicit support to a degree that would have surprised regimes in the eighteenth century; although, even then, careful attempts were made to ensure that war enhanced the *gloire* of rulers.

This modern drive for support during conflict, and for a public endorsement thereafter, ensures, however, a degree of controversy over reporting and commemoration. In Britain, for example, the nature and content of the public acts held after the Falklands War of 1982 and the Gulf War of 2003 led to controversy, not least over praying for Argentineans during the commemoration service in St. Paul's Cathedral after the Falklands War. In each case, this controversy was linked to differences over the morality of the conflicts or aspects of the conflicts, for example, the sinking in 1982 of the Argentinean warship the *General Belgrano* (a serious threat to the British task force but, arguably, not an immediate one when sunk), and in 2003 the decision to attack Iraq. Uneasiness over conflict or a particular conflict, which stems readily from the high rate of political awareness in democratized societies, is easily transferred into dissent over the assessment of victory as seen with the discussion of official histories of wars. This, in turn, ensures that regimes feel it more necessary to influence, if not control, the reporting of war, which is increasingly an important aspect of its commemoration.

The democratization in the reporting and commemoration of war has been taken a stage further with technology, ensuring that the immediate impact of war on civilian populations has become more insistent than in the age of so-called total war. The twentieth century brought radio, then the powerful visual medium of television, and then e-mail and the mobile phone with its camera capability. A more immediate impact (an aspect of modernity) interacted with the popular disquiet about aspects of what were seen as total war. The traumatic experience of World War I played a major role in the process by which public dissent over conflict developed, for what, at the time, was treated by Britain, France, and eventually the United States as a righteous struggle against German aggression, became a conflict with a far more ambivalent position in public memory. As a consequence, the victory, much applauded in and after 1918, a half century later appeared to be too hard won, if not an ironic counterpoint to the horrors of trench warfare: Thus, the very fact of war, and the process of conflict itself, appeared a defeat. The merits of the case were somewhat different—any attempt to resist German aggression against Belgium and France, and consequent German dominance of Europe, would have been very difficult—but the point at issue is that what became the dominant cultural trope of war in Western Europe was sufficiently anti-war to affect the understanding of victory. Far from mobilizing people for war, as had occurred during the conflict, the collective understanding of the war had made it harder to do so again. The impact varied by country. In the case of Britain, a long-term effect was to make it even more important to present war as an unfortunate necessity, made thus by confronting evil, which was how World War II was seen, particularly in hindsight as the nature and extent of the Holocaust were appreciated. This moralization ensured that, at the same time that major Western states had an unparalleled capability for causing destruction, attitudes toward war became more uncompromising: it was difficult to conceive of compromise, indeed of anything less than regime change in such a context. Possibly the unparalleled capability also led to the latter.

Conflict to secure regime change tends to be underrated, if not ignored, within the meta-narratives of military history, except insofar as the unconditional surrender demanded by the Allies in World War II (not World War I) is considered. More generally, regime change is involved in civil conflict, but that tends only to be considered when it took the form, at least in large part, of large-scale conventional warfare between the conventional forces of rival states, as in the English (1642–46), American (1861–65), and Spanish (1936–39) Civil Wars. While each was very important, these conflicts were in practice atypical as far as civil conflict is concerned. Instead, counter-insurgency warfare is more commonly on the pattern seen in Latin America over the last 150 years, with regular forces used against irregular opponents.

The dominant narrative and analysis of warfare devotes scant attention to such conflicts, but there is no inherent reason why, say, the Wars of German Unification (1864–71) should be seen as so much more important than the Latin American warfare of the late nineteenth century. Indeed, the German military trajectory led, in 1918 and 1945, to the military dead end of total failure, via a German general staff, with the lack of a strategic grasp to match its operational and, even more, tactical effectiveness. Much of the standard emphasis stems, indeed, from a belief that a certain type of conflict defines modern warfare, with the latter understood as total war, and that therefore its development needs to be the focus of attention. This teleological perspective appeared credible in the aftermath of World War II, and while a conflict between the United States and the Soviet Union seemed imminent, but appears less credible today. Instead rebellions and counter-insurgency warfare now appear more important.

This is linked to a geographical shift of attention from Europe to Asia, Africa and to a lesser extent, Latin America: the areas of greatest population growth will continue to be the most volatile, not least because resource pressures will be most acute, while there will be a high percentage of the population under age twenty-five, the male cohort that it is easiest to persuade to risk death. The last is an essential precondition for conflict: it is relatively easy to get people to kill others, but far less so to lead them while sober, and over a long period, to risk death. Furthermore, in many such societies, there is a political "impoverishment," in that the means to press for significant change peacefully within the political system are often absent. Again, this affects the perception of conflict, and thus of victory. The politics of grievances over resources make it easy to elicit popular support, providing a lightning rod for regional, ethnic, religious, and class tensions, and can make it very difficult to secure compromise. The resulting clashes are then remembered—in terms of victory or grievance—in the collective memories of these groups, as can be seen, for example, in the clashes between Hutu and Tutsi in Burundi and Rwanda.

Differences between cultures or states, in the causes and protocols of wars, and in the conditions of engagement, affect outcomes and aftermaths, and the understanding of them. The extent to which a focus on where wars are more common entails a re-examination of narratives, definitions, and norms of conflict, including the understanding of victory and its commemoration, has not yet been sufficiently appreciated; and this re-examination should extend to military history. As far as the wide sphere of modern and recent conflict from Israel to India is concerned, Western commentators appear readier to discuss this in terms of regular, rather than irregular, warfare. This preference creates problems in assessment, as well as reflecting the more genuine problems of the militaries involved, as their forces and doctrines respond to insurrections. This is readily apparent in the treatment of recent conflict in Palestine/Israel, Iraq, and Kashmir; let alone in the disorder that is Afghanistan. In recent decades, insurrectionary conflicts have often had a guerrilla dimension, and sometimes a terrorist one as well, insofar as the two can be distinguished. The legal definitions of warrior status are complex in this context. The 1977 Geneva protocol that recognized rights for guerrillas reflected hostility to foreign occupation, but notions of national sovereignty and therefore foreignness are problematic.[23]

The role and nature of insurrections and terrorism, again, is a reminder of the culturally specific character of warfare and therefore the need to be cautious in addressing the variety of circumstances simply in Western terms. The level of killing seen, for example, in Kashmir, and even more in Afghanistan, if repeated in Denmark, would lead to a sense of total breakdown, whereas, in contrast, attitudes are different in India. This argument has to be handled with care, as, in the United States, a highly armed population with a relatively high rate of person-to-person violence, especially in some communities, is nevertheless intolerant of political violence and apt to see it as a challenge to the community.

In the case of civil conflict, in the light of this emphasis on political-cultural variations, we therefore can reconsider the view that war, in the shape of large-scale organized violence, itself is a collapse of the system, akin, indeed, to the breakdown of international order seen with the outbreak of hostilities between states. Instead, it is possible to see such civil conflict as more in tune with established political practices. This was certainly the case for much of the world in the period covered in this book, most obviously for Latin America, but also for Spain, Arabia, Persia (Iran), and Afghanistan, although the politics of each was different. In societies where there was no acceptance of the legitimacy of opposition and the peaceful transfer of power, the use of force in order to gain control, and thus also to sustain dominance, was normative.

This is a long way from the standard definition and discussion of total war, but it underlines the need to consider the normative use of force for domestic reasons as a key criterion. Such a situation did not make the use of force by such regimes automatic in international relations, although there could be a correlation, nor did all such regimes necessarily use the rhetoric of war in order to try to ensure support. However, in such a situation, force played a key and direct role in the functioning of society. This was a situation that was apparent before the period in question, during it, and still today, for example, in modern Myanmar (Burma). In terms of the frequently discussed conflation of war and politics, such states should be a crucial subject, and more so than those, such as the United States, that waged modern war episodically and without either a fundamental reordering of their society or the use of force as a means of domestic control.

# Notes

**CHAPTER 1**

1. R.J. Overy, *The Rise and Fall of Total War* (London, 1994), p. 2.

2. The key works include S. Förster and J. Nagler (eds.), *On the Road to Total War: The American Civil War and the German Wars of Unification, 1861–1871* (Cambridge, 1997); M.F. Boemeke, R. Chickering, and S. Förster (eds.), *Anticipating Total War: The German and American Experiences, 1871–1914* (Cambridge, 1999); R. Chickering and S. Förster (eds.), *Great War, Total War: Combat and Mobilization on the Western Front, 1914–1918* (Cambridge, 2000) and *The Shadows of Total War: Europe, East Asia, and the United States, 1919–1938* (Cambridge, 2003).

3. A. Marwick, *Britain in the Century of Total War* (London, 1968), *War and Social Change in the Twentieth Century* (London, 1974); A. Marwick (ed.), *Total War and Social Change* (London, 1988), pp. x–xxi, and *The Deluge: British Society and the First World War*, 2d ed. (London, 1991), pp. 11–48. See also I.F.W. Beckett, "Total War," in *Warfare in the Twentieth Century: Theory and Practice* (London, 1988), pp. 1–23.

4. L. Keeley, *War before Civilization* (New York, 1996).

5. C. von Clausewitz, *On War*, ed. M. Howard and P. Paret (1832; Princeton, 1976), p. 702.

6. M.R. Smallman-Raynor and A.D. Cliff, *War Epidemics: An Historical Geography of Infectious Diseases in Military Conflict and Civil Strife, 1850–2000* (Oxford, 2004).

7. For a recent study, see M.R. Waters, *Lone Star Stalag: German Prisoners of War at Camp Hearne* (College Station, 2004).

8. W. Churchill, *The World Crisis, 1911–18*, 6 vols. (London, 1923), vol. I, pp. 10–11, quoted in I.F.W. Beckett, *The Great War 1914–1918* (Harlow, 2001), p. 158.

9. Overy, *Total War*, p. 4.

10. English translation, *The Nation at War* (London, 1936).

11. I.F. Clarke, *Voices Prophesying War 1763–1984* (Oxford, 1966); D. Pick, *War Machine: The Rationalisation of Slaughter in the Modern Age* (London, 1993); Overy, *Total War*, pp. 14–22.

12. A. Smith, *Wealth of Nations* (1776; Oxford, 1976), pp. 690–92.

13. Ibid., p. 708.

14. War Cabinet Minutes, 4, 12 Feb. 1941, NAA. A5954, 805/1, pp. 562, 572.

15. D. Hume, *The History of England*, 6 vols. (1762; Indianapolis, 1983), vol. III, p. 81.

16. M. van Creveld, *Supplying War: Logistics from Wallenstein to Patton*, 2d ed. (Cambridge, 2004), pp. 251–52.

17. R. Chickering and S. Förster, "Introduction," in Chickering and Foster, *Shadows of Total War*, p. 3.

18. H.P. Willmott, *When Men Lost Faith in Reason: Reflections on War and Society in the Twentieth Century* (Westport, 2000), p. 11.

19. I.F.W. Beckett, "Britain's Imperial War: A Question of Totality?" *Journal for Contemporary History* 25, no. 2 (Dec. 2000): 4, 7.

20. H. Strachan, "Total War in the Twentieth Century," in *Total War and Historical Change: Europe 1914–1955*, ed. A. Marwick, C. Emsley, and W. Simpson (Buckingham, 2001), esp. pp. 263, 271–75.

21. J.M. Black, *Kings, Nobles and Commoners: States and Societies in Early Modern Europe: A Revisionist History* (London, 2004).

22. M. Geyer and C. Bright, "Global Violence and Nationalizing Wars in Eurasia and America: The Geopolitics of War in the Mid-Nineteenth Century," *Comparative Studies in Society and History* 38 (1996): 619–37. An excellent global background is provided by C.A. Bayly, *The Birth of the Modern World, 1780–1914* (Oxford, 2004); see, e.g., for the contextualization of changing military capability, pp. 266–71.

## CHAPTER 2

1. D. Headrick, "The Tools of Imperialism and the Expansion of European Colonial Empires in the Nineteenth Century," *Journal of Modern History* 51 (1979): 231–63; R.W. Burns, *Communications: An International History of the Formative Years* (London, 2003).

2. S.C. Chu, "The Sino-Japanese War of 1894," *Bulletin of Academia Sinica, Institute of Modern History* 14 (1985): 355.

3. S. Soucek, *A History of Inner Asia* (Cambridge, 2000).

4. A.K. Hoagland, *Army Architecture in the West: Forts Laramie, Bridger, and D.A. Russell, 1849–1912* (Norman, 2004).

5. V.J. Cirillo, *Bullets and Bacilli: The Spanish-American War and Military Medicine* (New Brunswick, 2004).

6. Blamey to Curtin, Australian Prime Minister, 4 Dec. 1942, AWM. 3 DRL/6643, 2/11.

7. C. Newberry, *Patrons, Clients, and Empire: Chieftaincy and Over-rule in Asia, Africa, and the Pacific* (Oxford, 2003).

8. M. Lieven, " 'Butchering the Brutes All Over the Place': Total War and Massacre in Zululand, 1879," *History* 84 (1999): 614–32.

9. H. Bailes, "Technology and Imperialism: A Case Study of the Victorian Army in Africa," *Victorian Studies* 24 (1980–81): 82–104.

10. R.F. Bauman, "Subject Nationalities in the Military Service of Imperial Russia: The Case of the Bashkirs," *Slavic Review* 46 (1987): 489–502.

11. A. Fung, "Testing the Self-Strengthening: The Chinese Army in the Sino-Japanese War of 1894–95," *Modern Asian Studies* 30 (1996): 1007–31; S.C.M. Paine, *The Sino-Japanese War of 1894–1895: Perceptions, Power, and Primacy* (Cambridge, 2003).

12. J.M. Dorwart, *The Pigtail War: American Involvement in the Sino-Japanese War of 1894–1895* (Amherst, 1975).

13. D. O'Connor, "The Political Uses of Lawlessness: Kruger, Warren and the Bechuanaland Field Force, 1885," *RUSI* 150, no. 3 (June 2005): 71.

14. R.F. Weigley, *The American Way of War: A History of United States Military Strategy and Policy* (New York, 1973).

15. D. O'Connor, "Privateers, Cruisers and Colliers: The Limits of International Maritime Law in the Nineteenth Century," *RUSI* 150, no. 1 (Feb. 2005): 73.

16. N.B. Dukas, *A Military History of Sovereign Hawai'i* (Honolulu, 2004), pp. 147–64.

17. T. Moreman, "The British and Indian Armies and North-West Frontier Warfare, 1849–1914," *Journal of Imperial and Commonwealth History* 20 (1992): 35–64.

18. S.W. Baker, "Experience in Savage Warfare," *RUSI* 17 (1873–74): 904–21; H.C. Gawler, "British Troops and Savage Warfare," Ibid., 922–39; C. Callwell, "Notes on the Tactics of Our Small Wars," *Proceedings of the Royal Artillery Institution* 12 (1884): 531–52, and "Notes on the Strategy of Our Small Wars," Ibid., 13 (1885): 403–20; Callwell, "Lessons to Be Learnt from the Campaigns in which British Forces Have Been Employed since the Year 1865," *RUSI* 31 (1887–88): 357–411; A.C. Yate, "North West Frontier Warfare," Ibid., 42 (1898): 1171–93; H. Bailes, "Patterns of Thought in the Late Victorian Army," *Journal of Strategic Studies* 4 (1981): 29–45.

19. D. Porch, *The Conquest of Morocco* (New York, 1983).

20. C.H. Brown, *Agents of Manifest Destiny: The Lives and Times of the Filibusters* (Chapel Hill, 1980); R.E. May, *Manifest Destiny's Underworld: Filibustering in Antebellum America* (Chapel Hill, 2002).

**CHAPTER 3**

1. E. Hagerman, *The American Civil War and the Origins of Modern Warfare: Ideas, Organisation, and Field Command* (Bloomington, 1988); R.A. Doughty et al., *The American Civil War: The Emergence of Total Warfare* (Lexington, MA, 1996); D.E. Sutherland, *The Emergence of Total War* (Fort Worth, 1996); K. Hackemer, *The U.S. Navy and the Origins of the Military Industrial Complex, 1847–1883* (Annapolis, 2001); R.G. Angevine, *The Railroad and the State: War, Politics, and Technology in Nineteenth-Century America* (Stanford, 2004). The role of rail access was important to hospitals; see C.C. Green, *Chimborazo: The Confederacy's Largest Hospital* (Knoxville, 2004).

2. B. Catton, *U.S. Grant and the American Military Tradition* (Boston, 1954); T.H. Williams, *Americans at War: The Development of the American Military System* (Baton Rouge, 1960).

3. J.D. Smith (ed.), *Black Soldiers in Blue: African American Troops in the Civil War Era* (Chapel Hill, 2002).

4. G.J.W. Unwin (ed.), *Black Flag over Dixie: Racial Atrocities and Reprisals in the Civil War* (Carbondale, 2004).

5. J.M. McPherson, "No Peace without Victory, 1861–1865," *American Historical Review* (2004): 10.

6. G. McWhiney and P. Jamieson, *Attack and Die: Civil War Military Tactics and the Southern Heritage* (Tuscaloosa, 1982).

7. P. Griffith, *Battle Tactics of the Civil War* (New Haven, 1989).

8. For example, see P.L. Patterborze, "Crossroads of Destiny: Lew Wallace, the Battle of Monocacy, and the Outcome of Jubal Early's Drive on Washington, DC," *Army History* (spring 2005): 13.

9. S.E. Woodworth (ed.), *No Band of Brothers: Problems of the Rebel High Command* (Columbia, 1999).

10. For example, see D. Pfanz, *Richard S. Ewell* (Chapel Hill, 1998); L. Daniel, *Days of Glory: The Army of the Cumberland, 1861–1865* (Baton Rouge, 2004).

11. R.L. DiNardo, "Southern by the Grace of God but Prussian by Common Sense: James Longstreet and the Exercise of Command in the U.S. Civil War," *Journal of Military History* 66 (2002): 1011–32.

12. W.B. Feis, *Grant's Secret Service: The Intelligence War from Belmont to Appomattox* (Lincoln, 2002).

13. D.G. Surdam, *Northern Naval Superiority and the Economics of the American Civil War* (Columbia, SC, 2001).

14. L.S. Taylor, *"The Supply for Tomorrow Must Not Fail": The Civil War of Captain Simon Perkins Jr., a Union Quartermaster* (Kent, 2004), p. 93.

15. A. Bucholz, *Molke and the German Wars, 1864–1871* (New York, 2001); G. Wawro, *The Franco-Prussian War: The German Conquest of France in 1870–1871* (New York, 2003).

16. D.E. Sutherland, "Sideshow No Longer: A Historiographical Review of the Guerrilla War," *Civil War History* 46 (2000): 5–23.

17. P. Warner (ed.), *Letters Home from The Crimea* (Moreton-in-Marsh, 1999), p. 87.

18. F. Risley, *The Civil War: Primary Documents on Events from 1860 to 1865* (Westport, 2004), p. 249.

19. M. Grimsley, *The Hard Hand of War: Union Military Policy toward Southern Civilians* (New York, 1995).

20. J.B. Walters, "General William T. Sherman and Total War," *Journal of Southern History* 14 (1948): 447–48; L. Janda, "Shutting the Gates of Mercy: The American Origins of Total War, 1860–1880," *Journal of Military History* 59 (1995): 7–26.

21. Hôtel Carnavalet, Paris, inventory, p. 1628.

22. V.B. Reber, "The Demographics of Paraguay: A Reinterpretation of the Great War, 1864–70," *Hispanic American Historical Review* 68 (1988): 290–319; T.L. Whigham and B. Potthast-Jutkeit, "Some Strong Reservations: A Critique of Vera Blinn Reber's...," Ibid., 70 (1990): 667–78; H. Craay and Whigham (eds.), *I Die with My Country: Perspectives on the Paraguay War, 1864–1870* (Lincoln, 2005).

23. F.J. McLynn, "Consequences for Argentina of the War of Triple Alliance, 1865–1870," *The Americas* 41 (1984): 81–98; N.T. Strauss, "Brazil after the Paraguayan War: Six Years of Conflict, 1870–1876," *Journal of Latin American Studies* 10 (1978): 21–35.

24. H. Strachan, "On Total War and Modern War," *International History Review* 22 (2000): 341–70.

25. Wawro, *Franco-Prussian War*, pp. 264–65, 288–89.

26. R.R. Mackey, *The Uncivil War: Irregular Warfare in the Upper South, 1861–1865* (Norman, 2004).

## CHAPTER 4

1. P.W. Schroeder, "The Lost Intermediaries: The Impact of 1870 on the European System," *International History Review* 6 (1984): 1–27, and *The Transformation of European Politics 1763–1848* (Oxford, 1994).

2. For this approach to 1916, see R. Prior and T. Wilson, *The Somme* (New Haven, 2005).

3. J. Bushnell, "Miliutin and the Balkan War: Military Reform vs. Military Performance," in *Russia's Great Reforms, 1855–1881*, ed. B. Eklof, J. Bushnell, and L. Zakharova (Bloomington, 1994), pp. 139–58; F. Miller, *Dmitrii Miliutin and the Reform Era in Russia* (Nashville, 1968); D.S. van der Oye and B.W. Menning (eds.), *Reforming the Tsar's Army: Military Innovation in Imperial Russia from Peter the Great to the Revolution* (Cambridge, 2004).

4. W.F. Sater, *Chile and the War of the Pacific* (Lincoln, 1986); B. Farcau, *The Ten Cents War: Chile, Peru and Bolivia in the War of the Pacific* (New York, 2000).

5. For example, see J.A. Martini, *Fort Point* (San Francisco, 1991), pp. 22, 27.

6. A.W. Quiroz, "Loyalist Overkill: The Socioeconomic Costs of 'Repressing' the Separatist Insurrection in Cuba, 1868–1878," *Hispanic American Historical Review* 78 (1998): 261–305.

7. F.D. McCann, *Soldiers of the Pátria: A History of the Brazilian Army, 1889–1937* (Stanford, 2004).

8. D. Rock and F.L. Alves, "Statebuilding and Political Systems in Nineteenth-Century Argentina and Uruguay," *Past and Present* 167 (2002): 176–202; M.A. Centano, *Blood and Debt: War and the Nation-State in Latin America* (University Park, 2002).

9. C. Bergquist, *Coffee and Conflict in Colombia, 1886–1910* (Durham, NC, 1978).

10. A. Knight, *The Mexican Revolution*, 2 vols. (Cambridge, 1986).

11. R. Tombs, "Paris and the Rural Hordes: An Explanation of Myth and Reality in the French Civil War of 1871," *Historical Journal* 29 (1986): 795–808.

12. D.A. Shafer, *The Paris Commune* (Basingstoke, 2005), p. 89.

13. J. Bushnell, "The Revolution of 1905–06 in the Army: The Incidence and Impact of Mutiny," *Russian History* 12 (1985): 71–94.

14. G.E. Rothenberg, "The Habsburg Army and the Nationality Problem in the Nineteenth Century," *Austrian History Yearbook* 3 (1967): 70–87.

15. L.A. Perez, "Politics, Peasants, and People of Color: The 1912 'Race War' in Cuba Reconsidered," *Hispanic American Historical Review* 66 (1986): 509–39.

16. W.S. Dudley, "Professionalisation and Politisation as Motivational Factors in the Brazilian Army Coup of 15 November 1889," *Journal of Latin American Studies* 8 (1976): 101–25.

17. L. Ortega, "Nitrates, Chilean Entrepreneurs, and the Origins of the War of the Pacific," *Journal of Latin American Studies* 16 (1984): 337–80.

18. T. Travers, "Technology, Tactics and Morale: Jean de Bloch, the Boer War and British Military Theory, 1900–1914," *Journal of Modern History* 51 (1979): 264–86; I.F.W. Beckett, "Britain's Imperial War: A Question of Totality?" *Journal for Contemporary History* 25, no. 2 (Dec. 2000): 4–22.

19. See, in particular, B.M. Linn, *The U.S. Army and Counter-insurgency in the Philippine War, 1899–1902* (Chapel Hill, 1989). For a popular account of a particular episode, see B. Couttie, *Hang the Dogs: The True History of the Balangiga Massacre* (Quezon City, 2004).

20. R.K. Mazumder, *The Indian Army and the Making of Punjab* (Delhi, 2003), pp. 18–20.

21. P.S. Thompson, *The Natal Native Contingent in the Anglo-Zulu War*, 2d ed. (Scottsville, 2003).

22. W.F. Sater and H. Herwig, *The Grand Illusion: The Prussianisation of the Chilean Army* (Lincoln, 1999).

23. J.A. Grant, "The Arms Trade in Eastern Europe, 1870–1914," in *Girding for Battle: The Arms Trade in a Global Perspective, 1815–1940*, ed. D.J. Stoker and J.A. Grant (Westport, 2003), pp. 28–31.

24. J. Dunn, "Egypt's Nineteenth-Century Armaments Industry," in Stoker and Grant, *Girding for Battle*, p. 14.

25. E.J. Erickson, *Defeat in Detail: The Ottoman Army in the Balkans, 1912–1913* (Westport, 2003), p. 335.

26. M. Paris, "The First Air Wars in North Africa and the Balkans, 1911–1913," *Journal of Contemporary History* 26 (1991): 97–109.

27. N.A. Lambert, "Strategic Command and Control for Maneuver Warfare: Creation of the Royal Navy's 'War Room' System, 1905–1915," *Journal of Military History* 69 (2005): 361–410.

28. For example, see R.M. Ripperger, "The Development of French Artillery for the Offensive, 1890–1914," *Journal of Military History* 59 (1995): 599–618.

29. M.S. Seligmann, "A View from Berlin: Colonel Frederick Trench and the Development of British Perceptions of German Aggressive Intent, 1906–1910," *Journal of Strategic Studies* 23 (2000): 131.

30. M. Epkenhans, "Military-Industrial Relations in Imperial Germany, 1870–1914," *War in History* 10 (2003): 1–26.

31. D.N. Collins, "The Franco-Russian Alliance and Russia's Railways 1891–1914," *Historical Journal* 16 (1973): 777–88; D. Stevenson, "War by Timetable? The Railway Race before 1914," *Past and Present* 162 (1999): 163–94; A. Mitchell, *The Great Train Race: Railways and Franco-German Rivalry, 1815–1914* (New York, 2000).

32. I.F.W. Beckett, "The Nation in Arms, 1914–18," in *A Nation in Arms: A Social Study of the British Army in the First World War*, ed. I.F.W. Beckett and K. Simpson (Manchester, 1985), pp. 6–7.

33. M. Mayzel, "The Formation of the Russian General Staff, 1880–1917: A Social Study," *Cahiers du Monde Russe et Sovietique* 16 (1975): 297–321.

34. J. Bushnell, "Peasants in Uniform: The Tsarist Army as a Peasant Society," *Journal of Social History* 13 (1980): 565–75.

35. M. Howard, G.J. Andreopoulos, and M.R. Shulman (eds.), *The Laws of War: Constraints on Warfare in the Western World* (New Haven, 1994).

## CHAPTER 5

1. A. Rossos, *Russia and the Balkans: Inter-Balkan Rivalries and Russian Foreign Policy, 1908–1914* (Toronto, 1981).

2. Monash to wife, 29 Jan. 1915, AWM. 3 DRL/2316, 1/1, pp. 18–21.

3. H. Strachan, *The First World War in Africa* (Oxford, 2004).

4. D. Healey, *Drive to Hegemony: The United States in the Caribbean, 1898–1917* (Madison, 1988); M.A. Renda, *Taking Haiti: Military Occupation and the Culture of U.S. Imperialism, 1915–1940* (Chapel Hill, 2001).

5. E.S. Miller, *War Plan Orange: The U.S. Strategy to Defeat Japan, 1897–1945* (Annapolis, 1991), p. 82.

6. B. Albert, *South America and the First World War: The Impact of the War on Brazil, Argentina, Peru, and Chile* (Cambridge, 1988).

7. Birdwood to General Callwell, 15 May 1915, AWM. 3 DRL/3376, 11/4.

8. For example, R. Smith, *Jamaican Volunteers in the First World War: Race, Masculinity and the Development of National Consciousness* (Manchester, 2004) in part traces rising nationalism to the experience of wartime racism.

9. Birdwood to C. India in C. India, 3 Dec. 1915, AWM. 3 DRL 3376, 11/4.

10. P. Gatrell, *Russia's First World War: A Social and Economic History* (Harlow, 2005), pp. 189–91.

11. T. Travers, *Gallipoli* (Stroud, 2001), p. 310. See also J. MacLeod (ed.), *Reconsidering Gallipoli* (Manchester, 2004).

12. Godley to Birdwood, 27 Feb. 1917, AWM. 3 DRL/3376, 11/4; Travers, *Gallipoli*, p. 176.

13. L.C.F. Turner, "The Russian Mobilisation in 1914," *Journal of Contemporary History* 3 (1968): 65–88.

14. D. Stevenson, *Cataclysm: The First World War as Political Tragedy* (London, 2004).

15. C. Gray, *Modern Strategy* (Oxford, 1999), p. 189.

16. I.F.W. Beckett, *Ypres: The First Battle* (London, 2004).

17. G. Sheffield and J. Bourne (eds.), *Douglas Haig: War Diaries and Letters, 1914–1918* (London, 2005), p. 37.

18. H. Strachan, *The First World War, I: To Arms* (Oxford, 2001), p. 373.

19. W.A. Renzi, *In the Shadow of the Sword: Italy's Neutrality and Entrance into the Great War, 1914–1915* (New York, 1988).

20. P. von Wahlde, "A Pioneer of Russian Strategic Thought: G.A. Leer, 1829–1904," *Military Affairs* 35 (1971): 148–53.

21. P. Kenez, "The Russian Officer Corps before the Revolution: The Military Mind," *Russian Review* 31 (1972): 226–36.

22. P. Kenez, "Changes in the Social Composition of the Officer Corps during World War I," *Russian Review* 31 (1972): 369–75; D.R. Jones, "The Imperial Russian Life Guards Grenadier Regiment, 1906–1917: The Disintegration of an Elite Unit," *Military Affairs* 33 (1969): 289–302.

23. A. Wildman, "The February Revolution in the Russian Army," *Soviet Studies* 22 (1970): 3–23; M. Ferro, "The Russian Soldier in 1917: Undisciplined, Patriotic, and Revolutionary," *Slavic Review* 30 (1971): 483–512; G. Katkov, *Russia 1917, the Kornilov Affair, Kerensky and the Breakup of the Russian Army* (London, 1980).

24. R.A. Wade, *The Russian Revolution, 1917*, 2d ed. (Cambridge, 2005), pp. 264–65.

25. Helpful revisionist reviews of this literature can be found in B. Bond (ed.), *The First World War and British Military History* (Oxford, 1991) and G. Sheffield, "John Terraine as a Military Historian," *RUSI* 149, no. 2 (April 2004): 70–75. See also J.S.K. Watson, *Fighting Different Wars: Experience, Memory, and the First World War in Britain* (Cambridge, 2004). The conventional account, however, continues to appear, for example, J.E. Persico, *Eleventh Month, Eleventh Day, Eleventh Hour: Armistice Day, 1918; World War I and Its Violent Climax* (New York, 2004).

26. Birdwood to Maxwell, 8 June 1915, AWM. 3 DRL 3376, 11/4.

27. For an effective popular account emphasizing improvement, see R. Holmes, *Tommy: The British Soldier on the Western Front, 1914–1918* (London, 2004).

28. Birdwood to C. India in C. India, 3 Dec. 1915, AWM. 3 DRL 3376, 11/4.

29. I have benefited from the assistance of Anthony Saunders.

30. P. Hart, *The Somme* (London, 2005), pp. 487–88; G. Sheffield, *The Somme* (London, 2004).

31. R.S. Feldman, "The Russian General Staff and the June 1917 Offensive," *Soviet Studies* 19 (1968): 526–43.

32. R. Prior and T. Wilson, *The Somme* (New Haven, 2005), pp. 306–7.

33. R. Foley, *German Strategy and the Path to Verdun: Erich von Falkenhayn and the Development of Attrition, 1870–1916* (Cambridge, 2005).

34. J. Mosier, *The Myth of the Great War: A New Military History of World War One* (New York, 2002).

35. R.H. Ferrell, *Collapse at Meuse-Argonne: The Failure of the Missouri-Kansas Division* (Columbia, MO, 2004).

36. Callwell to Birdwood, 31 Mar. 1915, AWM. 3 DRL 3376, 11/4.

37. L. Kennett, *The First Air War, 1914–1918* (New York, 1991).

38. Monash to wife, 18 July 1916, AWM. 3 DRL/2316, 1/1, pp. 201–2.

39. D. Juniper, "Gothas Over London," *RUSI* 148, no. 4 (2003): 74–80.

40. G.E. Rothenberg, *The Army of Francis Joseph* (West Lafayette, 1998), pp. 213–15.

41. I.V. Hull, *Absolute Destruction: Military Culture and the Practices of War in Imperial Germany* (Ithaca, 2004).

42. D. Moran and A. Waldron (eds.), *The People in Arms: Military Myth and National Mobilization since the French Revolution* (New York, 2003).

43. Intelligence report by Lieu. H. Pirie-Gordon, 13 Nov. 1915, AWM. 3 DRL/3376, 11/4.

44. J. Horne and A. Kramer, *German Atrocities, 1914: A History of Denial* (New Haven, 2001).

45. R. Prior and T. Wilson, "15 September 1916: The Dawn of the Tank," *RUSI* 136, no. 4 (autumn 1991): 61–65.

46. "Characteristics and Tactics of the Mark V, Mark V One Star and Medium 'A' Tanks," 27 June 1918, AWM. 3 DRL 6643, 5/27, pp. 1–3.

47. B.W. Harvey and C. Fitzgerald (eds.), *Edward Heron-Allen's Journal: The Great War: From Sussex Shore to Flanders Fields* (Lewes, 2002), p. 244.

48. D.J. Childs, *A Peripheral Weapon? The Production and Employment of British Tanks in the First World War* (Westport, 1999).

49. J. Sheldon, *The German Army on the Somme, 1914–1916* (Barnsley, 2005), p. 398.

50. S.E. Rolls, *Steel Chariots in the Desert* (London, 1937).

51. S. Biddle, *Military Power: Explaining Victory and Defeat in Modern Battle* (Princeton, 2004).

52. S.B. Schreiber, *Shock Army of the British Empire: The Canadian Corps in the Last 100 Days of the Great War* (Westport, 1997); P. Dennis and J. Grey (eds.), *1918: Defining Victory* (Canberra, 1999).

53. A. Clayton, *Paths of Glory: The French Army, 1914–18* (London, 2003).

54. Report on operations, AWM. 3 DRL/6643 5/27, pp. 4–27.

55. Monash to wife, 16 May 1915, AWM. 3 DRL/2316, 1/1, p. 64.

56. Monash to wife, 20 June 1916, AWM. 3 DRL/2316, 1/1, p. 195.

57. Monash to wife, 30 May 1915, AWM. 3 DRL/2316, 1/I, p. 72.

58. For a perceptive review, see B. Schwarz, "Was the Great War Necessary?" *Atlantic Monthly* (May 1999): 118–28.

59. R. Aron, *The Century of Total War* (London, 1954), p. 21.

60. L. Sondhaus, *Franz Conrad von Hötzendorf: Architect of the Apocalypse* (Boston, 2000), p. 92.

61. E. Rosenberg, "Anglo-American Economic Rivalry in Brazil during World War I," *Diplomatic History* 2 (1978): 131–52.

62. R.M. Browning, *From Cape Charles to Cape Fear: The North Atlantic Blockading Squadron during the Civil War* (Tuscaloosa, 1993).

63. J. Kocka, *Facing Total War: German Society, 1914–1918* (Leamington Spa, 1984); C.P. Vincent, *The Politics of Hunger: The Allied Blockade of Germany, 1915–1919* (Athens, GA, 1985).

64. H.H. Herwig, "Total Rhetoric, Limited War: Germany's U-Boat Campaign, 1917–1918," in *Great War, Total War*, ed. R. Chickering and S. Förster (New York, 2000), pp. 189–206.

65. P.G. Halpern, *A Naval History of World War I* (Annapolis, 1994).

66. Harvey and Fitzgerald, *Edward Heron-Allen's Journal of the Great War*, pp. 253–55.

67. J. McWilliams and R.J. Steel, *Amiens, 1918* (Stroud, 2004), p. 281.

68. G. Oram, *Military Executions during World War I* (London, 2003).

69. B. Shephard, *A War of Nerves: Soldiers and Psychiatrists 1914–1994* (London, 2000).

70. For example, see J. Jackson, *Private 12768: Memoir of a Tommy* (Stroud, 2004).

71. C. Barnett, "The Western Front Experience as Interpreted through Literature," *RUSI* 148, no. 6 (Dec. 2003): 50–55.

72. M. Hughes, "The French Army at Gallipoli," *RUSI* 150, no. 3 (June 2005): 65.

73. J.F. Vance, *Death So Noble: Memory, Meaning, and the First World War* (Vancouver, 1997).

74. J. McQuilton, *Rural Australia and the Great War: From Tarrawingee to Tangrambalanga* (Melbourne, 2001).

75. W.W. Haddad and W. Ochsenwald (eds.), *Nationalism in a Non-National State: The Dissolution of the Ottoman Empire* (Columbus, 1977); D. Quataert, *The Ottoman Empire, 1700–1922*, 2d ed. (Cambridge, 2005), pp. 191–92.

76. M. MacMillan, *Peacemakers: The Paris Conference of 1919 and Its Attempt to End War* (London, 2003).

## CHAPTER 6

1. J. Corum, "The Spanish Civil War: Lessons Learned and Not Learned by the Great Powers," *Journal of Military History* 62 (1998): 313–34; M. Alpert, "The Clash of Spanish Armies: Contrasting Ways of War in Spain,

1936–39," *War in History* 6 (1999): 331–51; M. Hughes and E. Garrido, "The 'European Aldershot' for the Second World War? The Battle of the Ebro, 1938," *RUSI* 147, no. 6 (Dec. 2002): 76–81.

2. See, for example, among a massive literature, J.S.K. Watson, *Fighting Different Wars: Experience, Memory, and the First World War in Britain* (Cambridge, 2004) and J.F. Vance, "Remembering Armageddon," in *Canada and the First World War*, ed. D. Mackenzie (Toronto, 2005), pp. 409–33.

3. E.A. Huelfer, *The "Casualty Issue" in American Military Practice: The Impact of World War I* (Westport, 2003).

4. E.A. McCord, "Civil War and the Emergence of Warlordism in Early Twentieth Century China," *War and Society* 102 (1992): 35–56.

5. F. Ribeiro de Meneses, *Portugal 1914–1926: From the First World War to Military Dictatorship* (Bristol, 2004).

6. A. Waldron, *From War to Nationalism: China's Turning Point, 1924–1925* (Cambridge, 1995), p. 71.

7. H.H. Nolte, "Stalinism as Total Social War," in *The Shadows of Total War: Europe, East Asia, and the United States, 1919–1939*, ed. R. Chickering and S. Förster (Cambridge, 2003), pp. 295–311.

8. D.J. Raleigh, *Experiencing Russia's Civil War: Politics, Society, and Revolutionary Culture in Saratov, 1917–1922* (Princeton, 2002), p. 410.

9. M. Butler, *Popular Piety and Political Identity in Mexico's Cristero Rebellion: Michoacán, 1927–1929* (Oxford, 2004).

10. R.D. Burns, "Regulating Submarine Warfare, 1921–41: A Case Study in Arms Control and Limited War," *Military Affairs* 35 (1971): 56–63.

11. S.G. Payne, *A History of Fascism, 1914–45* (London, 1995), p. 355.

12. H. van de Ven, *Warfare and Nationalism in China, 1925–1945* (London, 2003).

13. M. Jacobsen, "Only by the Sword: British Counter-insurgency in Iraq, 1920," *Small Wars and Insurgencies* 2 (1991): 323–63.

14. B.C. Denning, "Modern Problems of Guerilla Warfare," *Army Quarterly* 13 (1927): 347–54.

15. D. Killingray, "A Swift Agent of Government: Air Power in British Colonial Africa, 1916–39," *Journal of African History* 25 (1984): 429–44; J.L. Cox, "A Splendid Training Ground: The Importance to the RAF of Iraq, 1913–32," *Journal of Imperial and Commonwealth History* 13 (1985): 157–84.

16. W. Ryan, "The Influence of the Imperial Frontier on British Doctrines of Mechanised Warfare," *Albion* 15 (1983): 123–42; E. Spiers, "Gas and the North West Frontier," *Journal of Strategic Studies* 6 (1983): 94–112.

17. Z. Steiner, *The Lights That Failed: European International History, 1919–1933* (Oxford, 2005).

18. J.M. Young, *The Brazilian Revolution of 1930 and the Aftermath* (New Brunswick, 1967); R.M. Levine, *The Vargas Regime: The Critical Years, 1934–1938* (New York, 1970).

19. F. Dorn, *The Sino-Japanese War, 1937–41: From Marco Polo Bridge to Pearl Harbor* (New York, 1974).

20. G. Benton, *Mountain Fires: The Red Army's Three Year War in South China, 1934–1938* (Berkeley, 1992).

21. Mao Tse-tung, *On Guerilla Warfare*, trans. S.B. Griffith (Urbana, 2000), pp. 41–42, 80.

22. Ibid., p. 46.

23. Ibid., pp. 47–48.

24. Ibid., p. 47.

25. R.A. Wade, *Red Guards and Workers' Militias in the Russian Revolution* (Stanford, 1984); J.J. Schneider, *The Structure of Strategic Revolution: Total War and the Roots of the Soviet Warfare State* (Novato, 1994).

26. C. Townshend, "The Defence of Palestine: Insurrection and Public Security, 1936–39," *English Historical Review* 103 (1988): 917–49.

27. Hughes and Garrido, "'European Aldershot.'"

28. S.T. Ross (ed.), *Plans for Global War: Rainbow-5 and the Victory Program, 1941* (New York, 1992), p. x.

29. G. Franklin, *Britain's Anti-Submarine Capability, 1919–1939* (London, 2003).

30. A.R. Millett and W. Murray (eds.), *Military Effectiveness II: The Inter-war Period* (Boston, 1988) and *Military Innovation in the Inter-war Period* (Cambridge, 1996).

31. M. Smith, "'A Matter of Faith': British Strategic Air Doctrine Between the Wars," *Journal of Contemporary History* 15 (1980): 423–42; P.S. Meilinger, "Trenchard and 'Morale Bombing': The Evolution of Royal Air Force Doctrine before World War II," *Journal of Military History* 60 (1996): 243–70.

32. B. Bond, *British Military Policy between the Two World Wars* (Oxford, 1980); H. Winton, *To Change an Army: General Sir John Burnett-Stuart and British Armored Doctrine, 1927–1938* (Lawrence, 1988); J.P. Harris, *Men, Ideas, and Tanks: British Military Thought and Armoured Forces, 1903–1939* (Manchester, 1995).

33. T. Travers, *How the War Was Won: Command and Technology in the British Army on the Western Front, 1917–1918* (London, 1992), pp. 179–82.

34. I.M. Philpott, *The Royal Air Force . . . the Inter-war Years, I: The Trenchard Years, 1918 to 1929* (Barnsley, 2005), pp. 194–208.

35. D.E. Showalter, "German Grand Strategy: A Contradiction in Terms?" *Militärgeschichtliche Mitteilungen* 48 (1990): 65–102.

36. M.S. Alexander, "The Fall of France, 1940," *Journal of Strategic Studies* 13 (1990).

37. I. Lukes, "The Tukhachevsky Affair and President Edvard Benes: Solutions and Open Questions," *Diplomacy and Statecraft* 7 (1996): 505–29.

38. R.W. Harrison, *The Russian Way of War: Operational Art, 1904–1940* (Lawrence, 2001).

39. D.M. Glantz, *Stumbling Colossus: The Red Army on the Eve of World War II* (Lawrence, 1998).

## CHAPTER 7

1. R. Overy, "Mobilization for Total War in Germany, 1939–41," *English Historical Review* 103 (1988).

2. A.J. Prazmowska, *Civil War in Poland, 1942–1948* (Basingstoke, 2004), pp. 143–67.

3. Strategic review for regional commanders, 16 Aug. 1941, AWM. 3 DRL/6643, 1/27.

4. D.M. Glantz, *Barbarossa: Hitler's Invasion of Russia, 1941* (Stroud, 2001).

5. R.A. Doughty, "Myth of the *Blitzkrieg*," in *Challenging the United States Symmetrically and Asymmetrically: Can America Be Defeated*, ed. L.J. Matthews (Carlisle Barracks, 1998), pp. 57–79.

6. N. Jordan, "Strategy and Scapegoatism: Reflections on the French National Catastrophe, 1940," in *The French Defeat of 1940: Reassessments*, ed. J. Blatt (Oxford, 1998), pp. 13–38.

7. J.A. Gunsburg, "The Battle of Gembloux, 14–15 May: The 'Blitzkrieg' Checked," *Journal of Military History* 64 (2000): 97–140.

8. P. Fritzsche, "Machine Dreams and the Reinvention of Germany," *American Historical Review* 98 (1993): 685–709.

9. J.S. Corum, "Myths of *Blitzkrieg*—The Enduring Mythology of the German Campaign," *Historically Speaking* 6, no. 4 (Mar.–Apr. 2005), p. 11, citing Raborg, *Mechanized Might: The Story of Mechanized Warfare* (1942), p. 255.

10. Wilson to Blamey, 19 April 1941, AWM. 3 DRL/6643, 1/3.

11. Menzies to Blamey, 21 June 1941, AWM. 3 DRL/6643, 1/1.

12. A.B. Rossino, *Hitler Strikes Poland: Blitzkrieg, Ideology, and Atrocity* (Lawrence, 2003); R. Scheck, " 'They Are Just Savages': German Massacres of Black Soldiers from the French Army in 1940," *Journal of Modern History* 77 (2005): 325–44.

13. A. Sella, "Khalkhin-Gol: The Forgotten War," *Journal of Contemporary History* 18 (1983): 658–67.

14. Report from GHQ Middle East Forces, 15 July 1941, AWM. 3 DRL/6643, 1/27.

15. Auchinleck, memorandum, 18 Oct. 1941, AWM. 3 DRL/6643, 1/27.

16. A.F. Chew, *The White Death: The Epic of the Soviet-Finnish Winter War* (East Lansing, 1971); C. Van Dyke, *The Soviet Invasion of Finland, 1939–40* (London, 1997); H. Shukman (ed.), *Stalin and the Soviet-Finnish War, 1939–1940* (London, 2001).

17. S. Biddle, *Military Power: Explaining Victory and Defeat in Modern Battle* (Princeton, 2004).

18. D.M. Glantz, *The Soviet Strategic Offensive in Manchuria, 1945: "August Storm"* (London, 2003) and *Soviet Operational and Tactical Combat in Manchuria, 1945: "August Storm"* (London, 2003).

19. K.E. Bonn, *When the Odds Were Even: The Vosges Mountains Campaign, October 1944–January 1945* (Novato, 1994); C. Whiting, *The Battle of Huertgen Forest: The Untold Story of a Disastrous Campaign* (London, 1989); E.G. Miller, *A Dark and Bloody Ground: The Huertgen Forest and the Roer River Dams, 1944–1945* (College Station, 1995); P.R. Mansoor, *The GI Offensive In Europe: The Triumph of American Infantry Divisions, 1941–1945* (Lawrence, 1999); R.S. Rush, *Hell in the Hürtgen Forest: The Ordeal and Triumph of an American Infantry Regiment* (Lawrence, 2001); M.D. Dobler, *Closing with the Enemy: How GIs Fought the War in Europe, 1944–1945* (Lawrence, 1994) is more positive than M. Van Creveld, *Fighting Power: German and U.S. Army Performance, 1939–1945* (Westport, 1982).

20. D.P. Marston, *Phoenix from the Ashes: The Indian Army in the Burma Campaign* (Westport, 2004).

21. R. Lyman, *Slim, Master of War* (London, 2004).

22. AWM. 3 DRL/6643, 3/10.

23. AWM. 3 DRL/6643, 3/12.

24. D. Ford, "British Intelligence on Japanese Army Morale during the Pacific War: Logical Analysis or Racial Stereotyping?" *Journal of Military History* 69 (2005): 469.

25. M. Harrison, *Medicine and Victory: British Military Medicine in the Second World War* (Oxford, 2004).

26. C.H. Waddington, *O.R. in World War 2: Operational Research against the U-Boat* (London, 1973).

27. H.H. Herwig, "Germany and the Battle of the Atlantic," in Chickering, Förster, and Greiner, *World at Total War*, pp. 81–85.

28. Blamey to Minister for Army, 1 Sept. 1941, AWM. 3 DRL/6643, 1/2.

29. Blamey to Minister for Army, 15 Aug. 1941, AWM. 3 DRL/6643, 1/2, cf. 2 Aug. 1941.

30. B.M. Bechthold, "'The Development of an Unbeatable Combination': U.S. Close Air Support in Normandy," *Canadian Military History* 8 (1999): 7–20; D.I. Hall, "From Khaki and Light Blue to Purple: The Long and

Troubled Development of Army/Air Co-operation in Britain, 1914–1945,"
*RUSI* 147, no. 5 (2002): 78–83.

31. Blamey to Curtin, Australian Prime Minister, 27 Sept. 1941, AWM. 3 DRL/6643, 1/2.

32. N.J.W. Goda, *Tomorrow the World: Hitler, Northwest Africa, and the Path toward America* (College Station, 1998); J.P. Duffy, *Target: America. Hitler's Plan to Attack the United States* (Westport, 2004).

33. K. Ungváry, *Battle for Budapest: One Hundred Days in World War II* (London, 2005), p. 315.

34. D. Porch, *Hitler's Mediterranean Gamble: The North African and the Mediterranean Campaigns in World War II* (London, 2004), p. 24.

35. K.C. Berkhoff, *Harvest of Despair: Life and Death in Ukraine under Nazi Rule* (Cambridge, MA, 2004).

36. M. Hauner, *India in Axis Strategy: Germany, Japan and Indian Nationalists in the Second World War* (Stuttgart, 1981).

37. N. Smith, *American Empire: Roosevelt's Geographer and the Prelude to Globalization* (Berkeley, 2003), p. 360; W.R. Louis, *Imperialism at Bay: The United States and the Decolonisation of the British Empire, 1941–1945* (New York, 1978); A.J. Whitfield, *Hong Kong, Empire, and the Anglo-American Alliance at War, 1941–45* (Basingstoke, 2001).

38. B.J.C. McKercher, *Transition of Power: Britain's Loss of Global Pre-eminence to the United States, 1930–1945* (Cambridge, 1999); P. Orders, *Britain, Australia, New Zealand and the Expansion of American Power in the South-West Pacific, 1941–46* (Basingstoke, 2002).

39. M. Hastings, *Armageddon: The Battle for Germany, 1944–45* (London, 2004), pp. xiii.

40. Ibid., p. 588.

41. Ibid., p. 105. See also, D. French, "'You Cannot Hate the Bastard Who Is Trying to Kill You . . .': Combat and Ideology in the British Army in the War against Germany, 1939–45," *Twentieth Century British History* 11 (2000).

42. J. Penrose (ed.), *The D-Day Companion* (London, 2004).

43. Blamey to Curtin, 4 Dec. 1942, AWM. 3 DRL/6643, 2/11.

44. Ford, "Intelligence," pp. 439–74.

45. H.T. Cook, "Turning Women into Weapons: Japan's Women, the Battle of Saipan, and the 'Nature of the Pacific War,'" in *Women and War in the Twentieth Century: Enlisted With or Without Consent*, ed. N.A. Dombrowski (London, 2004), p. 254.

46. H. Johnston, *A Bridge Not Attacked: Chemical Warfare Civilian Research during World War II* (River Edge, NJ, 2003).

47. R. Bassett, *Hitler's Spy Chief: The Wilhelm Canaris Mystery* (London, 2005).

48. O. Manninen, "The Winter War in Global Perspective," *RUSI* 148, no. 2 (Apr. 2003): 80–81.

49. B. Shepherd, *War in the Wild East: The German Army and Soviet Partisans* (Cambridge, MA, 2004); T. Anderson, "Incident at Baranivka: German Reprisals and the Soviet Partisan Movement in Ukraine, October–December 1941," *Journal of Modern History* 71 (1999): 589–623.

50. J. Steinberg, "The Third Reich Reflected: German Civil Administration in the Occupied Soviet Union, 1941–44," *English Historical Review* 110 (1995): 620–51.

51. Strategic review for regional commanders, 16 Aug. 1941, AWM. 3 DRL/6643, 1/27.

52. B.J. Bernstein, "Compelling Japan's Surrender without the A-bomb, Soviet Entry, or Invasion: Reconsidering the U.S. Bombing Survey's Early-Surrender Conclusions," *Journal of Strategic Studies* 18 (1995): 101–48; G. Gentile, "Advocacy or Assessment: The United States Strategic Bombing Survey of Germany and Japan," *Pacific Historical Review* 66 (1997): 53–79, and "Shaping the Past Battlefield, 'For the Future': The United States Strategic Bombing Survey's Evaluation of the American Air War against Japan," *Journal of Military History* 64 (2000): 1085–112.

53. H. Knell, *To Destroy a City: Strategic Bombing and Its Human Consequences in World War II* (London, 2003); N. Stargadt, "Victims of Bombing and Retaliation," *German Historical Institute London Bulletin* 26, no. 2 (2004): 57–70.

54. B.J. Bernstein, "Truman and the A-Bomb," *Journal of Military History* 62 (1998): 547–70.

55. T.E. Rodgers, "Billy Yank and G.I. Joe: An Exploratory Essay on the Socio-political Dimensions of Soldier Motivation," *Journal of Military History* 69 (2005): 93–121.

56. Ibid., pp. 116–17. For high American morale and purposefulness, see D.E. Showalter, "Global Yet Not Total: The U.S. War Effort and Its Consequences," in Chickering, Förster, and Greiner, *World at Total War*, pp. 119–20.

57. N. Barr, "Societies in Total War, 1914–45," in *100 Years of Conflict 1900–2000*, ed. S. Trew and G. Sheffield (Stroud, 2000), p. 254.

58. J. Lewis, *Changing Direction: British Military Planning for Post-War Strategic Defence, 1942–47*, 2d ed. (London, 2003).

## CHAPTER 8

1. M. Roberts, *The Military Revolution* (Belfast, 1956); J.M. Black, *European Warfare 1494–1660* (London, 2002).

2. R.F. Weigley, *A Great Civil War: A Military and Political History, 1861–1865* (Bloomington, 2000), p. 441.

3. M. Hughes, "Logistics and the Chaco War: Bolivia versus Paraguay, 1932–1935," *Journal of Military History* 69 (2005): 411–37.

4. For example, see History Departments of Futan University and Shanghai Teachers' University, *The Taiping Revolution* (Beijing, 1976), pp. 172–73, 178.

5. I.F.W. Beckett, *Modern Insurgencies and Counter-Insurgencies* (London, 2001).

6. J.M. Black, *War and the New Disorder in the 21st Century* (New York, 2004).

7. H.P. Willmott, *When Men Lost Faith in Reason: Reflections on War and Society in the Twentieth Century* (Westport, 2002), pp. 14–16.

8. Chickering, "Use and Abuse of a Concept," in Boemeke, Chickering, and Förster, *Anticipating Total War*, p. 24.

9. H. Feis, *The Atomic Bomb and the End of World War II* (Princeton, 1966); R.B. Frank, *Downfall: The End of the Imperial Japanese Empire* (New York, 1999).

10. G. DeGroot, *The Bomb, A Life* (London, 2004).

11. K.P. Werrell, *Blankets of Fire: U.S. Bombers over Japan during World War II* (Washington, 1996).

12. G. Feifer, *Tennozan: The Battle of Okinawa and the Atomic Bomb* (New York, 1992); J.R. Skates, *The Invasion of Japan: Alternative to the Bomb* (Columbia, SC, 1994), esp. pp. 254–57.

13. Major-General William Penney, director of intelligence, HQ, supreme allied commander, S.E. Asia 1944–45, to Major-General John Sinclair, director of military intelligence, British War Office, 2 May 1945, London, King's College, Liddell Hart Centre for Military History, Penney papers 5/1.

14. D. McCullough, *Truman* (New York, 1992), p. 458.

15. M. Walker, *German National Socialism and the Quest for Nuclear Power, 1939–1945* (New York, 1989); P. Henshall, *The Nuclear Axis: Germany, Japan, and the Atomic Bomb Race, 1939–1945* (Phoenix Hall, 2001).

16. O. Bartov, *The Eastern Front, 1941–1945: German Troops and the Barbarisation of Warfare* (Basingstoke, 1985); H. Heer, "The Difficulty of Ending a War: Reactions to the Exhibition War of Extermination: Crimes of the Wehrmacht, 1941 to 1944," *History Workshop Journal* 46 (1988): 187–203.

17. E.B. Westermann, "'Ordinary Men' or 'Ideological Soldiers'? Police Battalion 310 in Russia, 1942," *German Studies Review* 21 (1998).

18. T.P. Mulligan, *The Politics of Illusion and Empire: German Occupation Policy in the Soviet Union, 1942–1943* (London, 1988); T. Schulte, *The German Army and Nazi Policies in Occupied Russia* (Oxford, 1989).

19. M. Huband, *The Skull Beneath the Skin: Africa after the Cold War* (Boulder, 2001), e.g., p. 43.

20. J. Buckley, *Air Power in the Age of Total War* (London, 1999), p. 168.

21. P.C. Perdue, *China Marches West: The Qing Conquest of Central Asia* (Cambridge, MA, 2005).

22. T. T. Yong, *The Garrison State: The Military Government and Society in Colonial Punjab, 1949–1947* (London, 2005), p. 301.

23. G. Best, *War and Law since 1945* (Oxford, 1994); G.J. Andreopoulos, "The Age of National Liberation Movements," in *The Laws of War: Constraints on Warfare in the Western World*, ed. M. Howard, G.J. Andreopoulos, and M.R. Shulman (New Haven, 1994), p. 191.

# Selected Further Reading

Adams, R.J.Q. *Arms and the Wizard: Lloyd George and the Ministry of Munitions, 1915–1916* (London, 1978).

Aron, R. *The Century of Total War* (London, 1954).

Barnhart, M.A. *Japan Prepares for Total War: The Search for Economic Security, 1919–1941* (Ithaca, 1987).

Bartov, O. *Hitler's Army: Soldiers, Nazis, and War in the Third Reich* (Oxford, 1991).

Black, J.M. *Warfare in the Western World, 1882–1975* (Chesham, 2002).

———. *Rethinking Military History* (London, 2004).

———. *Introduction to Global Military History* (London, 2005).

Black, J.M. (ed.). *War in the Modern World since 1815* (London, 2003).

Boemeke, M.F., R. Chickering, and S. Förster (eds.). *Anticipating Total War: The German and American Experiences, 1871–1914* (New York, 1999).

Bond, B. *War and Society in Europe, 1870–1970* (London, 1984).

Bourke, J. *An Intimate History of Killing: Face-to-Face Killing in Twentieth-Century Warfare* (London, 1999).

Buckley, J. *Air Power in the Age of Total War* (London, 1999).

Burnham, J. *Total War: The Economic Theory of a War Economy* (Boston, 1943).

Calvocoressi, P., and G. Wint. *Total War* (New York, 1972).

Cecil, H., and P. Liddle (eds.). *Facing Armageddon: The First World War Experienced* (Barnsley, 1996).

Chickering, R., and S. Förster (eds.). *Great War, Total War: Combat and Mobilization on the Western Front, 1914–1918* (New York, 2000).

———. *The Shadows of Total War: Europe, East Asia, and the United States, 1919–1939* (New York, 2003).

Chickering, R., S. Förster, and B. Greiner (eds.). *A World at Total War: Global Conflict and the Politics of Destruction, 1937–1945* (New York, 2005).

Corum, J.S. *The Roots of Blitzkrieg: Hans von Seeckt and German Military Reform* (Lawrence, 1992).

Farrell, T., and T. Terriff (eds.). *The Sources of Military Change: Culture, Politics, Technology* (Boulder, 2002).

Feldman, G.D. *Army, Industry, and Labor in Germany, 1914–1918* (Princeton, 1966).

Förster, S., and J. Nagler (eds.). *On the Road to Total War: The American Civil War and the German Wars of Unification, 1861–1871* (New York, 1997).

Glantz, D.M., and J. House. *When Titans Clashed: How the Red Army Stopped Hitler* (Lawrence, 1995).

Hagerman, E. *The American Civil War and the Origins of Modern Warfare: Ideas, Organization, and Field Command* (Bloomington, 1988).

Harris, J.P. *Men, Ideas, and Tanks: British Military Thought and Armoured Forces, 1903–1939* (Manchester, 1996).

Harrison, M. (ed.). *The Economics of World War II: Six Great Powers in International Comparison* (Cambridge, 1998).

Herrmann, D. *The Arming of Europe and the Making of the First World War* (Princeton, 1996).

Jablonsky, D. *Churchill, the Great Game, and Total War* (London, 1991).

Kenedy, P. (ed.). *The War Plans of the Great Powers, 1880–1914* (London, 1979).

Kiesling, E. *Arming against Hitler: France and the Limits of Military Planning* (Lawrence, 1996).

Knox, M. *Common Destiny: Dictatorship, Foreign Policy, and War in Fascist Italy and Nazi Germany* (Cambridge, 2000).

Markusen, E., and D. Kopf. *The Holocaust and Strategic Bombing: Genocide and Total War in the Twentieth Century* (Boulder, 1995).

Menning, B.W. *Bayonets before Bullets: The Imperial Russian Army, 1861–1914* (Bloomington, 1992).

Murray, W., and A.R. Millett (eds.). *Military Innovation in the Inter-war Period* (Cambridge, 1996).

Offer, A. *The First World War: An Agrarian Interpretation* (Oxford, 1989).

Overy, R.J. *The Rise and Fall of Total War* (London, 1994).

———. *Why the Allies Won* (New York, 1995).

Pick, D. *War Machine: The Rationalisation of Slaughter in the Modern Age* (New Haven, 1993).

Powers, T., and R. Tremain. *Total War: What It Is, How It Got That Way* (New York, 1988).

Reese, R.R. *The Soviet Military Experience* (London, 2000).

Shaw, M. *Dialectics of War: An Essay in the Social Theory of Total War and Peace* (London, 1988).

Showalter, D.E. *Railroads, Rifles, and the Unification of Germany* (Hamden, 1975).

Sondhaus, L. *Naval Warfare, 1915–1914* (London, 2000).

Speier, H. "Ludendorff: The German Concept of Total War," in *Makers of Modern Strategy: Military Thought from Machiavelli to Hitler*, ed. E.M. Earle (New York, 1966).

Stevenson, D. *Armaments and the Coming of War: Europe, 1904–1914* (Oxford, 1996).

Stone, N. *The Eastern Front, 1914–1917* (London, 1978).

Strachan, H. "On Total War and Modern War," *International History Review* 22 (2000).

———. *The First World War, I: To Arms* (Oxford, 2001).

Vandervort, B. *Wars of Imperial Conquest in Africa, 1830–1914* (London, 1998).

Wawro, G. *The Austro-Prussian War* (Cambridge, 1996).

Weigley, R.F. *The American Way of War: A History of United States Military Strategy and Policy* (Bloomington, 1973).

Weinberg, G. *A World at Arms: A Global History of World War II* (Cambridge, 1994).

Willmott, H.P. *When Men Lost Faith in Reason: Reflections on War and Society in the Twentieth Century* (Westport, 2002).

Winter, J., G. Parker, and M.R. Habeck (eds.). *The Great War and the Twentieth Century* (New Haven, 2000).

Wright, G. *The Ordeal of Total War, 1939–1945* (New York, 1968).

# Index

## About the Author

JEREMY BLACK, author of more than forty books on military history and international affairs, is Professor of History at Exeter University in the United Kingdom.

**Recent Titles in**
**Studies in Military History and International Affairs**
*Jeremy Black, Series Editor*